Atonement: A Guide for the Perplexed

BLOOMSBURY GUIDES FOR THE PERPLEXED

Bloomsbury's Guides for the Perplexed are clear, concise and accessible introductions to thinkers, writers and subjects that students and readers can find especially challenging. Concentrating specifically on what it is that makes the subject difficult to grasp, these books explain and explore key themes and ideas, guiding the reader towards a thorough understanding of demanding material.

Guides for the Perplexed available from Bloomsbury include:

Balthasar: A Guide for the Perplexed, Rodney Howsare

Benedict XVI: A Guide for the Perplexed, Tracey Rowland

Bonhoeffer: A Guide for the Perplexed, Joel Lawrence

Calvin: A Guide for the Perplexed, Paul Helm

De Lubac: A Guide for the Perplexed, David Grummett

Luther: A Guide for the Perplexed, David M. Whitford

Pannenberg: A Guide for the Perplexed, Timothy Bradshaw

Pneumatology: A Guide for the Perplexed, Daniel Castelo

Political Theology: A Guide for the Perplexed, Elizabeth Philips

Postliberal Theology: A Guide for the Perplexed, Ronald T. Michener

Schleiermacher: A Guide for the Perplexed, Theodore Vial

Scripture: A Guide for the Perplexed, William Lamb

Tillich: A Guide for the Perplexed, Andrew O' Neil

Wesley: A Guide for the Perplexed, Jason A. Vickers

Žižek: A Guide for the Perplexed, Sean Sheehan

Forthcoming Guides for the Perplexed available from Bloomsbury include:

Barth: A Guide for the Perplexed, Paul T. Nimmo

Catholic Social Teaching: A Guide for the Perplexed, Anna Rowlands

Ecumenism: A Guide for the Perplexed, R. David Nelson

God-Talk: A Guide for the Perplexed, Aaron B. James and Ryan S. Peterson

Prayer: A Guide for the Perplexed, Ashley Cocksworth

Resurrection: A Guide for the Perplexed, Lidija Novakovic

Salvation: A Guide for the Perplexed, Ivor J. Davidson

Schillebeeckx: A Guide for the Perplexed, Stephan van Erp

Atonement: A Guide for the Perplexed

Adam J. Johnson

Bloomsbury T&T Clark
An imprint of Bloomsbury Publishing Plc

B L O O M S B U R Y
LONDON · NEW DELHI · NEW YORK · SYDNEY

Bloomsbury T&T Clark

An imprint of Bloomsbury Publishing Plc

Imprint previously known as T&T Clark

50 Bedford Square	1385 Broadway
London	New York
WC1B 3DP	NY 10018
UK	USA

www.bloomsbury.com

**BLOOMSBURY, T&T CLARK and the Diana logo are trademarks of
Bloomsbury Publishing Plc**

First published 2015

British Library Cataloguing-in-Publication Data
A catalogue record for this book is available from the British Library.

ISBN: HB: 978-0-567-42468-6
PB: 978-0-567-25402-3
ePDF: 978-0-567-44085-3
ePub: 978-0-567-47741-5

Library of Congress Cataloging-in-Publication Data
Johnson, Adam J.
Atonement: a guide for the perplexed / Adam J. Johnson.
pages cm.
ISBN 978-0-567-42468-6 (hardback) – ISBN 978-0-567-25402-3 (pbk) –
ISBN 978-0-567-47741-5 (epub) 1. Atonement. I. Title.
BT265.3.J63 2015
232'.3–dc23
2014037718

Series: Guides for the Perplexed

Typeset by Deanta Global Publishing Services, Chennai, India
Printed and bound in India

CONTENTS

ACKNOWLEDGEMENTS

Writing this book has been energizing, delightful and worshipful. But as energy, delight and worship are some of the many gifts of God, more often than not I have experienced these blessings through the involvement of God's people in my life and writing.

Tom Kraft and Anna Turton at T&T Clark trusted me with this opportunity in the first place. Unbeknownst to them, the contract for this book came the day prior to my doctoral graduation from TEDS, making for quite a celebration! Biola University and the Torrey Honors Institute have generously supported my research, and my students proved an eager trying-ground for much of this material. Some of the following material is the direct result of our joint in-class exploration of theological classics and the Bible.

A host of friends, colleagues and students helped me to edit and revise this book. My wife, Katrina, used scarce time away from the boys to edit the manuscript. Rachael Smith's work as my research assistant was a great help. Tentative about my ability to communicate to a broad audience, I sought the assistance of some of my current and former students. I give my sincere thanks to Daniel Chrosniak, Susanna Downer, Evan McGee, Josh Steele and Phil Worrall, among others, for their valuable feedback. A number of friends and colleagues played a significant role in this book, including Michael Allen, Uche Anizor, David Clough, Scott Harrower, Joe Henderson, Aaron James, Matt Jenson, Matthew Levering, David Moffitt, Paul Molnar, Ryan Peterson, Gabriel Renfro, Fred Sanders, Ben Sutton, Jeremy Treat and Kevin Vanhoozer. I am particularly grateful for my theological and philosophical colleagues during my 2 years at Cedarville University, who read and critiqued the first few chapters of this book. Unfortunately I was unable to benefit from the promised help of my dear friend and colleague Chris Mitchell, due to his untimely death this summer.

The lion's share of my thanks goes to those who made the biggest contribution and sacrifice, particularly during the summers. Though we have had our share of camping, swimming and outdoor fun, I thank my wife and our three boys, Reuben, Nathan and Simeon, for those valuable summer hours of writing. My hope is that my boys will someday be able to appreciate this book in its own right, and in the meantime enjoy it by means of the ways it has shaped me.

I dedicate this book to my parents, Glen and Susie Johnson. They are in large part responsible for cultivating in me the joy, curiosity, creativity and love which I hope exude from this book.

LIST OF ABBREVIATIONS

AH   *Against Heresies*, Irenaeus of Lyons

CD   *Church Dogmatics*, Karl Barth

CDH   *Cur Deus Homo*, Anselm

DCF   *Defence of the Catholic Faith*, Hugo Grotius

De inc *On the Incarnation*, Athanasius

Inst   *Institutes of the Christian Religion*, John Calvin

LW   *Luther's Works*, Martin Luther

MP   *Mysterium Paschale*, Hans Urs von Balthasar

ST   *Summa Theologica*, Thomas Aquinas

TD   *Theo-Drama IV: Action*, Hans Urs von Balthasar

1

Mining the Riches

As I told my veteran pastor of my plans to do graduate studies in the doctrine of the atonement, a wry smile creased his face as he asked: 'So . . . which theory of the atonement do you believe in?' I responded: 'All of them!' The purpose of this book is to offer a more expansive answer to this question, sharing a vision for a fuller understanding of the atonement which is eager to explore, embrace and apply new aspects of God's work in Christ to reconcile all things to himself.

But by way of preparation, it behoves us to inquire: Why did my pastor ask this particular question? The questions we ask, and the order in which we ask them, are of great importance. They influence which premises we draw upon and which ones we neglect, direct the ensuing line of thought in terms of what will and will not be considered, and determine to a great extent which (re)sources we might turn to for support. 'Where we begin shapes where we will end up.'[1] Through the centuries, theologians, schools and branches of the Church began their accounts of the atonement with certain key questions, which were themselves built upon certain assumptions and premises. This led to well-worn paths of theological discussion and privileged passages of Scripture.[2]

My pastor asked this question because, until recently, it was a commonplace assumption in theological education, largely due to

---

[1] Scot McKnight, *A Community Called Atonement* (Nashville, TN: Abingdon Press, 2007), 15.

[2] Note, for instance, the way that John McLeod Campbell follows the trajectory of questions asked by the Reformed theologians. John McLeod Campbell, *The Nature of the Atonement and Its Relation to Remission of Sins and Eternal Life* (London: Macmillan, 1869), 35.

the influential work of Gustaf Aulén, that throughout the history of the Church there have been roughly three main theories of the atonement.[3] This thesis suggests that the early Church held to *Christus victor*, the medieval Church to satisfaction and the modern Church to exemplarist accounts of the doctrine. *Christus victor*, a theory affirmed by such theologians as Athanasius, Gregory of Nyssa, Thomas and Calvin, holds that the purpose of Christ's death and resurrection was to overcome the power of Satan – a work prophesied in Genesis 3:15, and expounded in more depth in Ephesians and Colossians. Satisfaction theories, developed by the likes of Athanasius, Anselm, Thomas and Calvin, diversely explore ways in which the work of Christ satisfies the goodness (Athanasius), honour (Anselm) or justice/righteousness (Calvin) of God in face of our sin, drawing upon such passages as Romans 3:21-26, 2 Corinthians 5:21 and 1 Peter 3:18 for support. Exemplarist theories – affirmed by Athanasius, Peter Abelard, Thomas, Luther and Calvin, and touted by modern theologians such as Ritschl and Harnack – hold that Christ lived, died and rose again in order to be an absolutely unique example for us, that through this example we might be reformed and restored to fellowship with the Father.

Familiar with this debate, my pastor asked his question because such categorization of atonement theories into three main types is the precursor for questions that seek to establish which of the

---

[3] Gustaf Aulén, *Christus Victor: An Historical Study of the Three Main Types of the Idea of Atonement*, trans. A. G. Hebert (New York: Macmillan, 1951). Towards the end of the previous century, the tide began to turn against Aulén, in favour of holding to multiple accounts of the atonement simultaneously. Cf. John McIntyre, *The Shape of Soteriology: Studies in the Doctrine of the Death of Christ* (Edinburgh: T & T Clark, 1992); Colin E. Gunton, *The Actuality of Atonement: A Study of Metaphor, Rationality, and the Christian Tradition* (Grand Rapids, MI: Eerdmans, 1989). My work contributes to this movement, providing a distinctly theological emphasis (that is, an emphasis building upon the key features of the doctrine of the Trinity and the divine attributes) as the basis for both the unity and diversity of the work of Christ.

Locating my argument within the trajectory of the last 150 years, one could say that mine is an emphasis on 'the cross as an event in God's being', employed towards a '"unified" atonement', combining the fifth and seventh trajectories noted in: Kevin J. Vanhoozer, 'Atonement', in *Mapping Modern Theology: A Thematic and Historical Introduction*, ed. Kelly M. Kapic and Bruce L. McCormack (Grand Rapids, MI: Baker Academic, 2012), 191–6, 199–201.

theories one adheres to, why, and whether this theory incorporates aspects of the others or simply stands over and against them. Adherents of *Christus victor*, for example, might say that Christ offered satisfaction to God (or Satan) in order to rescue us from Satan. This loving work of rescue provides us with a governing paradigm or example for the Christian life (exemplarism), thus accounting for each of the main theories of the atonement within a single overarching theory.[4] However, one might emphasize a satisfaction theory, in which Christ's primary work was to satisfy God's righteousness. This also resulted in both our release from captivity to Satan and our debt of obedience to live out lives of righteousness within our communities on the basis of Christ's example.

More telling than the question itself, however, was my pastor's wry smile – for he knew that his question was a trap. Jesus' death and resurrection accomplished all three of these things: he defeated Satan, satisfied the goodness, honour and justice of God, and taught us to love God and neighbour by means of his absolutely unique and unprecedented example. Choosing any one of the traditional theories as an answer to his question would have received an immediate rejoinder in favour of the other two theories, accompanied by a list of great theologians touting the theory, and Bible verses supporting it. Not only is each of these theories biblical, it is also quite difficult (if not impossible) to discern which among them is pre-eminent. Did Jesus offer satisfaction in order to free us from Satan (emphasizing *Christus victor*), or was freeing us from Satan a mere accident of offering satisfaction to God (emphasizing satisfaction)? And was his example a by-product of these, or was it the focus (emphasizing exemplarism), as Christ sought to restore in us the divine image?

While there may be in fact answers to these and other common questions, there are better ways to engage the doctrine, better questions to ask at the beginning of our exploration of the nature and benefits of Christ's death and resurrection, which encourage us to have a balanced and proportioned interaction with the doctrine as a whole. To do otherwise is to risk delving into culturally significant but ultimately short-sighted questions of less ultimate consequence,

---

[4] Graham A. Cole, *God the Peacemaker* (Downers Grove, IL: InterVarsity Press, 2009), 233–43.

dooming such efforts to unnecessary inadequacy and shallowness. Different questions will lead us to new or less-trodden paths at dogmatic, historical and biblical levels, ultimately offering the possibility of significant new insights into and appreciation of the work of Christ. And they will entail significant changes for works building their inquiry upon supposedly competing or antithetical theories – a premise which sidesteps many of the fundamental issues within the doctrine, resulting in highly distorted and parochial accounts of Christ's work.

Before considering how else we might begin our approach to the doctrine of the atonement, we will take a moment to explore some of the reasons that the above approach is inadequate. I listed Athanasius, Thomas and Calvin as supporting each of the aforementioned theories. What makes this so interesting is that if this is true, we have theologians from the early, medieval and Reformation periods of the Church, each holding to a range of explanations, undermining both the theological and historical plausibility of Aulén's thesis. In a sample passage, Thomas writes that many things besides deliverance from sin concurred for man's salvation through Christ's passion:

> In the first place, man knows thereby how much God loves him, and is thereby stirred to love him in return. . . . Secondly, because thereby He set us an example of obedience, humility, constancy, justice, and the other virtues displayed in the Passion, which are requisite for man's salvation. . . . Thirdly, because Christ by His Passion not only delivered man from sin, but also merited justifying grace for him and the glory of bliss, as shall be shown later. . . . Fourthly, because by this man is all the more bound to refrain from sin. . . . Fifthly, because it redounded to man's greater dignity, that as man was overcome and deceived by the devil, so also it should be a man that should overthrow the devil; and as man deserved death, so a man by dying should vanquish death. (*ST*, 3.46.3)

The first, second and fourth points refer to exemplarism, the third to Thomas' development of Anselm's satisfaction theory, and the fifth to *Christus victor*. But if Thomas, perhaps the paradigmatic systematizer of the Church, holds these elements of Christ's passion in harmony with each other, something must be amiss with assuming from the outset that these views are somehow in competition with each other. Perhaps atonement theories, rather than being seen as competing to offer a comprehensive and sufficient account of the work of Christ, are best understood as mutually complementary accounts of different aspects of the work of Christ, which together work to fill out the substance of the doctrine (more of this in Chapter 2).

The task of the Church, I suggest, is not to determine which is the theory of the atonement, or which theory of the atonement has pride of place among others. Rather, following Thomas (who stands clearly in line with the majority position of the history of theology), we ought to witness to the fittingness of the atonement: to demonstrate how the death and resurrection of Jesus Christ brings together a wide array of benefits for the sake of the reconciliation of all things to God, that we might have as full an understanding as possible of the work God accomplished in Christ.[5] Accordingly, one of the governing images behind this book is one of exceeding riches, of a treasure trove.[6] That is to say, it attempts 'to articulate a theory that explains the saving significance of Jesus' death without betraying the rich testimonies to the event of his death'.[7] We reject the pursuit of the one theory of the atonement that is at the heart of the biblical witness and allows us to account for

exceeding riches of a treasure trove

[5] Adam Johnson, 'A Fuller Account: The Role of "Fittingness" in Thomas Aquinas' Development of the Doctrine of the Atonement', *International Journal of Systematic Theology* 12, no. 3 (2010): 304–7. In support of my use of reconciliation as the broadest term for exploring the work of Christ, cf. I. Howard Marshall, *Aspects of the Atonement: Cross and Resurrection in the Reconciling of God and Humanity* (Colorado Springs: Paternoster, 2007), 98ff. Note, however, Baker and Green's caution regarding biblical vocabulary and biblical concepts, pertaining to the atonement. Mark D. Baker and Joel B. Green, *Recovering the Scandal of the Cross: Atonement in New Testament and Contemporary Contexts* (Downers Grove, IL: InterVarsity Press, 2003), 36.

[6] This is opposed to the image of heart, foundation or centre that one often finds in the literature. My thesis works well with other similar arguments, though as we will see I have a distinctive approach rooted in theology proper. For a project working along similar lines, see: McKnight, *Community*, 114. The danger with the images of treasure is that it is static, whereas a more perfect image would be living, moving towards life in Christ. The image of treasure is merely to communicate the riches, abundance and variety of blessings we have in Christ through his saving work.

[7] Kevin J. Vanhoozer, 'Atonement in Postmodernity: Guilt, Goats and Gifts', in *The Glory of the Atonement: Biblical, Historical and Practical Perspectives*, ed. Charles E. Hill and Frank A. James (Downers Grove, IL: InterVarsity Press, 2004), 369.

and systematize the others, and the ensuing temptation to fight skirmishes with other competing theories.[8] Rather, the goal of this book is to explore, understand, cherish and employ the abundant riches we have in Christ – the host of necessary, fitting and mutually complementary theories of Christ's saving work which are founded in Scripture and developed throughout the history of the Church. For 'it is impossible to designate this dramatic climax in the relations between God and man with a single, isolated concept. . . . There can only be a dénouement when all the dimensions of the mystery are before us' (*TD*, 229).

In keeping with the complexity inherent in the doctrine of the atonement, this book aims to delight in and employ the exceedingly abundant riches with which we have been 'overwhelmed [by the] divine largess' in Christ.[9] For in Christ, the ever-rich God took upon himself a human nature, fully entering our fallen condition and its circumstances, sharing those riches with us in the form of a multidimensional work of atonement, yielding a manifold salvation and reconciliation of all things. As Barth says:

> Although theology is certainly confronted with the one God, he is One in the fullness of his existence, action, and revelation. In the school of the witness theology can in no way become monolithic, monomanic, monotonous, and infallibly boring. In no way can it bind or limit itself to one special subject or another. . . . The eternally rich God is the content of the knowledge of evangelical theology. His unique mystery is known only in the overflowing fullness of his counsels, ways and judgments.[10]

---

[8]That is to say, I resist 'the search for a controlling category', for these run 'the risk of restricting the other categories'. Charles B. Cousar, *A Theology of the Cross: The Death of Jesus in the Pauline Letters* (Minneapolis: Fortress Press, 1990), 54. Jeremy Treat offers a helpful list of terms denoting controlling categories, as used by defendants of penal substitution: Jeremy R. Treat, *The Crucified King: Atonement and Kingdom in Biblical and Systematic Theology* (Grand Rapids, MI: Zondervan, 2014), 222.

[9]Ivor J. Davidson, 'Introduction: God of Salvation', in *God of Salvation*, ed. Ivor J. Davidson and Murray A. Rae (Burlington, VT: Ashgate, 2011), 4. This work, we might say, is a 'saturated phenomenon': one 'so overflowing in meaning as to be in excess of any intention'. Vanhoozer, 'Atonement in Postmodernity', 394.

[10]Karl Barth, *Evangelical Theology: An Introduction*, trans. Grover Foley (London: Weidenfeld and Nicolson, 1963), 33–4.

And nowhere is this more the case than in the doctrine of the atonement – for here we have the fullness of God reconciling all things to himself in the fullness of time, in the face of the fullness of our sinful opposition to him and its consequences.[11] Our theme is superabundant fullness of riches grounded in the eternally rich God and employed in the saving work of Christ.[12] For 'salvation comes from God, is wrought by God, and is for God', and it is by dwelling on the riches of this God wrought upon and for us that we properly understand his saving work.[13]

How does this approach differ from other standard approaches? In the way that it works with the given data of different images and theories throughout the Bible and the history of theology. Rather than focusing on these theories and their relationships as the primary task of the doctrine, our approach is to explore the underlying reason for the complexity of Christ's saving work – by rooting this diversity in the underlying diversity proper to the eternal life of the triune God, thereby following Barth in allowing 'the eternally rich God' to be 'the content of the knowledge of [an] evangelical' doctrine of the atonement.[14] By means of this approach, we will sample the breadth of answers we should give to the question of why Christ died and rose again. For while the answer is not simple, there is an answer nonetheless – an exceptionally rich, varied and multifaceted answer, rooted in the diversity proper to the God whose act this is, which sheds light upon every area of Christian doctrine and practice.

rich, varied, multifaceted answer

[11] Throughout the book, I define atonement in a comprehensive manner to encompass the meaning and significance of Christ's saving work. As such, it builds on the origins of the word, 'at-one-ment', including both that which we are saved from, and that which we are saved for. In contrast, some works limit atonement to that which Christ saved us from by means of his death alone. The flexibility has to do with the fact that 'atonement' is a word unique to the English language, and as such is not constrained by the meaning of any particular term in Scripture.

[12] In fact, one could develop a riches theory of the atonement, in which the ever-rich God, in the face of our sin, became poor in Jesus Christ, that in him we might be made rich once more. As a subtext, one could weave in the themes of debt and repayment, recontextualizing what are typically interpreted as judicial themes within a framework of God's riches and abundance, rather than God's justice. This would make for interesting dialogue with the work of liberation theologians, as well as those who proclaim a prosperity gospel.

[13] Davidson, 'Introduction: God of Salvation', 14.

[14] Barth, *Evangelical Theology*, 33–4.

A glimpse of the 'Riches'

My talk of dazzling riches may suggest a beautiful and inspiring picture, but I would not be the first theologian accused of overzealously painting on clouds, failing to deliver on the substance of the matter (cf. *CDH*, I.4), were I to fail in my task. A brief overview of certain key figures in the history of the doctrine will offer a down payment on this promise of riches, to be followed by further disbursements in the ensuing chapters.

Why did Christ die and rise again? Athanasius, as one part of a manifold answer to this question, writes:

> For what profit would there be for those who were made, if they did not know their own Maker? Or how would they be rational, not knowing the Word of the Father, in whom they came to be? . . . And why would God have made those by whom he did not wish to be known? (*De inc*, §11)

The dilemma, for Athanasius, is that it is monstrously unfitting for the Creator that his creature fail to attain its end. Specifically, it is abhorrent to consider that humankind fail to fulfil its purpose as a reasonable creature – to know, love and worship its Creator. We were helpless in our self-inflicted condition of collapse into culpable deceit and irrationality, so what was God to do? Athanasius' answer: 'What should be done, except to renew again the "in the image," so that through it human beings would be able once again to know him? But how could this have occurred except by the coming of the very image of God, our Savior Jesus Christ?' (*De inc*, §13). Through his death, Christ did away with our corruption (particularly that of our minds), and through both his life and resurrection, renewed us after his own image by revealing himself to us 'as the Word of the Father, the ruler and king of the universe' (*De inc*, §16). The atonement, in other words, is the re-establishment and culmination of God's creative purpose of self-communicating, that we might know and worship him thereby. It is a matter of changing the creature's condition, focused primarily on knowledge and worship of the Creator through our restoration as rational creatures.[15]

---

[15]As Ivor Davidson puts it, God wills 'that contingent creation should know its creator still, should yet find its intended *telos* of peace and fulfillment in communion

why would God make those whom he did not wish to know?

Again we ask: Why did Christ die and rise again? Returning to Athanasius, as a reminder of just how wide-ranging so many doctors of the Church are in their account of Christ's work, we find him exploring the poetic fittingness of Christ's crucified position. Prior to canvassing Christ's elevation in the air as appropriate to one who is thereby defeating Satan and clearing the air that we might ascend to heaven (a strong affirmation of *Christus victor*), he considers the outstretched arms of Christ:

> Therefore it was fitting for the Lord to endure this, and to stretch out his hands, that with the one he might draw the ancient people and with the other those from the Gentiles, and join both together in Himself. This he himself said when he indicated by what manner of his death he was going to redeem all, 'When I am lifted up, I shall draw all to myself.' (Jn 12.32; *De inc*, §25)

While the poetic nature of Athanasius' argument may seem questionable to the modern reader, the underlying insight is a profound one, echoed throughout the New Testament: that Christ died so as to reconcile all peoples with God and with each other.[16] While this may seem like a mere implication of the Gospel, I would argue, to the contrary, that it is the message of the Gospel itself. God, who lives in an everlasting triune fellowship, shared this reality with his creatures in the form of a twofold fellowship: fellowship between God and the creature, and fellowship between creatures.[17] We, in our sin, pursue distorted and fragmented relationships, which exude animosity and harm towards others, one aspect of which is ethnic conflict. Christ bore this sin and its consequences of violent exclusion, exile and persecution in himself, shunned by Jew and Roman alike, that he might restore all peoples to fellowship by means of their restoration to fellowship with God.

---

with him. In the unfathomable love that God is, God does not give up on his world, but moves in mercy to bring it back to himself.' Davidson, 'Introduction: God of Salvation', 1.

[16]For an entry into this discussion, see: Darrin W. Snyder Belousek, *Atonement, Justice, and Peace: The Message of the Cross and the Mission of the Church* (Grand Rapids, MI: William B. Eerdmans, 2012), 573–86. While the biblical focus is on the reconciliation of Jews and Gentiles, this provides the seeds for ethnic and racial reconciliation generally. Cf. Timothy G. Gombis, 'Racial Reconciliation and the Christian Gospel', *ACT 3 Review* 15, no. 3 (2006): 117–28.

[17]Think here of Jesus' two-part summary of the law.

Why did Christ die? With Athanasius, we affirm that he died to draw the Jews and Gentiles to each other in himself; and with Paul we affirm that Christ's 'purpose was to make the two groups of people become one new people' through his blood (Eph. 2:13-15; cf. Gal. 3:13-14).

A third time, we ask: why did Christ die and rise again? John Calvin, as part of his multifaceted answer to this question,[18] writes:

> But that these things may take root firmly and deeply in our hearts, let us keep sacrifice and cleansing constantly in mind. For we could not believe with assurance that Christ is our redemption, ransom, and propitiation unless he had been a sacrificial victim. Blood is accordingly mentioned wherever Scripture discusses the mode of redemption. Yet Christ's shed blood served, not only as a satisfaction, but also as a laver [cf. Eph 5:26; Titus 3:5; Rev. 1:5] to wash away our corruption. (*Inst*, II.xvi.6)

While in the vicinity of this passage Calvin affirms his well-known doctrine of penal substitution, it is worth stopping to consider the significance of the above claim. God is most certainly loving and just, but he is just as much loving and holy – accordingly, he seeks to deal with our sin comprehensively in both its guilt and uncleanness. Jesus came as our sacrifice, then, not merely to pay a penalty (for sacrifices and penalties are distinct though related realities), but to make us clean, to 'wash away our corruption' that we might once more rejoice in being fit to enter the presence of our holy God. Christ died and rose again to make us clean and holy, that we might be holy as he is holy (Lev. 20:26; 1 Pet. 1:16).

Once more we ask: Why did Christ die and rise again? Jonathan Edwards, in a series of sermons on the wisdom of God, writes:

> So hath the wisdom of God contrived this affair, that the benefit of what he has done therein should be so extensive, as to reach the elect angels. . . . The angels cannot partake in [redemption], having never fallen; yet they have great indirect benefit by it. – God hath

---

[18] For a helpful treatment of Calvin's view(s) of the atonement, cf. Robert A. Peterson, *Calvin and the Atonement* (Fearne, Scotland: Christian Focus Publications, 2008).

so wisely ordered, that what has been done in this directly and especially for men, should redound to the exceeding benefit of all intelligent creatures who are in favour with God. The benefit of it is so diffusive as to reach heaven itself.[19]

We will explore how the work of Christ benefited the angels in a later chapter. The point to be made here is that Christ died not only for fallen humankind, not only to defeat Satan and his forces, but also for the sake and benefit of the angels in heaven! Scripture provides strong warrant for this incredibly broad understanding of Christ's work: 'Through [Christ God sought] to reconcile to himself all things, whether on earth or in heaven' (Col. 1:20). Why did Christ die and rise again? To accomplish a cosmic reconciliation – a work that would impact every aspect of God's vast creation, ranging from the earth groaning beneath our feet (Rom. 8:22) to the angels in the highest heavens.

In this brief section we have seen how three theologians from diverse eras of the Church construed the work of Christ in four different ways. To sum up, Christ died that he might (1) restore the image of God in us, (2) accomplish ethnic reconciliation of all peoples in Christ, (3) cleanse us from our filth of sin and (4) effect a cosmic reconciliation, including that of the un-fallen angels to himself. But in touching on these four aspects of the saving work of Christ, we have only begun to develop the many insights that Athanasius, Calvin and Edwards have into the work of Christ – not to mention Irenaeus, Gregory of Nazianzus, John of Damascus, Bernard of Clairvaux and so many other great theologians and pastors in the history of the Church – a treasure trove indeed!

But why, one might ask, am I drawing so heavily from the theologians of the Church, rather than Moses, Isaiah, John and Paul?[20] My answer is that this is a false dichotomy: as the biblical

---

[19]Jonathan Edwards, 'The Wisdom of God Displayed in the Way of Salvation', in *The Works of Jonathan Edwards*, ed. Henry Rogers, Sereno Edwards Dwight and Edward Hickman (Peabody, MA: Hendrickson, 1998), 147.

[20]In other words, why not seek to follow in the footsteps of someone like Leon Morris, whose kaleidoscopic approach has strong affinities with my own thesis? Leon Morris, *The Cross in the New Testament* (Grand Rapids, MI: Eerdmans, 1965), 395.

references above indicate, I am committed to doing theology on the basis, and after the pattern of Holy Scripture. While the bulk of my argument is theological in nature, theological and biblical studies should be fully integrated: they are (or ought to be) two modes of faith seeking to understand the Gospel of Jesus Christ and the triune God of which it speaks. Both in theology and biblical interpretation, we fall into ruts and patterns of thought which limit our awareness of the whole of the Gospel in all its riches. These ruts and patterns run the risk of over-prioritizing certain passages, themes or books of the Bible, culturally induced misunderstandings of sources, or theological biases misinforming our reading of Scripture.[21] My theological focus is an attempt to glean from the insight of biblical scholars throughout the history of the Church, so as to equip the Church today with the vision and resources to strive for an ever-greater understanding of the Gospel and its God, and an ever better reading of Scripture.

And this task is vital, for Scripture's witness to Christ's saving work is exceptionally varied. For example, Christ is our ransom (Mk 10:45), propitiation/expiation (Rom. 3:25), Passover lamb (1 Cor. 5:7) and saviour (Phil. 3:20). He is the lamb slain before the foundation of the world (Rev. 13:8), the only Mediator between God and man (1 Tim. 2:5), who accomplished the defeat of Satan (Jn 12:31, 14:30), sought that which was lost (Lk. 15:3-7) and gives us the victory (1 Cor. 15:56). He accomplished our redemption (Gal. 4:5), made purification for sins (Heb. 1:3), paid our debt (Col. 2:14), abolished death and brought life and immortality (2 Tim. 1:10), brought about the reconciliation of all things (Col. 1:20) and asked God to forgive us (Lk. 23:34). He was delivered over for us (Rom. 8:32), became a curse for us (Gal. 3:13) and summed up all things in himself (Eph. 1:10). And to offer such a list is but to scratch the surface.

---

[21]As Kevin Vanhoozer has made amply clear throughout many of his works, the reading of Scripture is itself a thoroughly theological movement. Kevin J. Vanhoozer, *The Drama of Doctrine: A Canonical-Linguistic Approach to Christian Theology* (Louisville, KY: WJK, 2005); *First Theology: God, Scripture and Hermeneutics* (Downers Grove, IL: InterVarsity Press, 2002); *Is There a Meaning in This Text? The Bible, the Reader, and the Morality of Literary Knowledge* (Grand Rapids, MI: Zondervan, 1998). Cf. John Webster, *Holy Scripture: A Dogmatic Sketch* (New York: Cambridge University Press, 2003).

I emphasize the theological task on the basis of, in dialogue with and for the sake of the Church's and my own careful reading of Holy Scripture. The present work is an exercise in theological interpretation of Scripture, intended to equip and motivate the Church to further and better study of the Bible by means of a systematic account of the doctrine of the atonement rooted in both the witness of Scripture and its interpretation by theologians over the centuries.[22]

Aren't we rich enough?
A revised exemplarism

But is this vision too ambitious? Am I the overzealous neighbour who, when asked for a saw, replies: 'Well . . . do you want a table-saw, jig-saw, band-saw, chop saw, coping saw, radial-arm saw . . . ?' Don't we just need a normal handsaw most of the time – the kind you move up and down against a board to cut it in half? Why can't doctrine be more like that – why can't we just have one theory of the atonement which can be the basis for our preaching, missions work, statements of faith, etc.? This seems rather like the story of the astronomer who, after Barth's sermon, said: 'I'm an astronomer, you know, and as far as I am concerned, the whole of Christianity can be summed up by saying: "Do unto others as you would have others do unto you."' Barth's retort: 'I am just a humble theologian, and as far as I am concerned the whole of astronomy can be summed up by saying "Twinkle, twinkle little star, how I wonder what you are."'[23] There is something powerful in our longing for simplicity, yet unsatisfying as well, for those who have explored the depth of these realities. 'An account of the gospel which neglected theological metaphysics,' the depth and complexity of the realities

---

[22]My commitment to biblical studies is evident in my article on the Temple, which I plan to expand into a book-length treatment on the Old Testament foundation for a proper understanding of Christ's saving work. Adam Johnson, 'A Temple Framework of the Atonement', *JETS* 54, no. 2 (2011): 225–37. I intend to follow up this work with similar explorations, continuing to develop the role of the Old Testament in our understanding of the work of Christ.

[23]John D. Godsey, 'Reminiscences of Karl Barth', *The Princeton Seminary Bulletin* (2002): 321.

at play in the atonement, 'would soon falter in its attempts to speak of the God of the gospel'.[24]

We could answer the question of whether this vision is overwhelming in a number of different ways, but for our purposes two will suffice: (1) the traditional concept of 'faith seeking understanding' and (2) a variation of the exemplarist theory of the atonement. Augustine writes in his *Confessions:* 'You stir man to take pleasure in praising you, because you have made us for yourself, and our heart is restless until it rests in you.' Immediately following this petition, he prays: 'Grant me Lord to know and understand.' The ensuing few pages are filled with an impassioned plea for knowledge of God, culminating in: 'What a wretch I am! In your mercies, Lord God, tell me what you are to me. "Say to my soul, I am your salvation" (Ps. 34:3). . . . Do not hide your face from me (cf. Ps. 26:9). Lest I die, let me die so that I may see it.'[25] Why does Augustine implore the God in whom he already believes that he might know and understand him? What is the role of understanding within faith? According to Augustine, faith is by nature a relationship involving motion towards its object through understanding or 'full vision': 'When a mind is filled with the beginning of that faith which works through love, it progresses by a good life even toward vision, in which holy and perfect hearts know that unspeakable beauty, the full vision of which is the highest happiness.'[26] Faith is the kind of thing that moves towards a goal – in this case, movement towards God, through knowledge and understanding. Faith embraces understanding because that is its end, its goal.

---

[24]John Webster, '"It Was the Will of the Lord to Bruise Him": Soteriology and the Doctrine of God', in *God of Salvation*, ed. Ivor J. Davidson and Murray A. Rae (Burlington, VT: Ashgate, 2011), 25. It was commonplace in the nineteenth and early twentieth century to argue for embracing the fact of the atonement, without the need to speculate about its meaning or necessity. Cf. many of the essays in: Frédéric Louis Godet, *The Atonement in Modern Religious Thought, a Theological Symposium* (New York: Thomas Whittaker, 1901). To this, Luther would respond: 'It is not enough to know and accept the fact' – something the papists do all too well. Rather, 'one must also accept the function and power of the fact. If we have this, we stand unconquered on the royal road, and the Holy Spirit is present in the face of all sects and deceptions.' *LW*17, 223.

[25]Augustine, *Confessions*, trans. Henry Chadwick (Oxford: Oxford University Press, 1991), 3–5.

[26]*The Augustine Catechism: The Enchiridion on Faith, Hope, and Love*, ed. Boniface Ramsey, trans. Bruce Harbert (Hyde Park: New City Press, 1999), 34.

Faith & Inquiry – Inseparable

Further developed by Anselm and others, we find in Daniel Migliore a delightful summary of this line of thought: 'Faith and inquiry are inseparable. . . . The work of theology [is] a continuing search for the fullness of the truth of God made known in Jesus Christ.'[27] Applying this insight to the concern of this book, the work of the doctrine of the atonement is a continuing search on the part of faith for the fullness of the truth of God made known in Jesus Christ, a search for understanding of the fullness of the work of Christ, and the rest, life and salvation which are bound up with it. The alternative, to rest content with what little knowledge of God we have, would be to violate the very nature of the faith we have been given – to disdain the complex simplicity, which we are offered to delight in both now and in eternity.

A vision of Christian faith inherently and delightedly seeking an understanding of the riches of the Gospel and its God is an ample answer to our question. However, it is fitting for us to turn our attention back to the doctrine of the atonement, for in its richness and diversity, it has its own unique and provocative answer to our question. Recall Thomas' first two reasons for the death of Christ: 'In the first place, man knows thereby how much God loves him, and is thereby stirred to love him in return. . . . Secondly, because thereby He set us an example of obedience, humility, constancy, justice, and the other virtues displayed in the Passion, which are requisite for man's salvation' (*ST*, 3.46.3).[28] These are two different angles to the exemplarist (or the 'moral' or 'subjective') theory of the atonement. The first angle is more objective in nature, and explores the way in which Christ makes the Father known to us (that God loves us and that he is love), while the second angle is more subjective in nature, teaching us certain virtues through the example provided by Christ. The second view is popularly attributed to Peter Abelard, who wrote that 'his Son has taken upon himself our nature and persevered therein in teaching us by word and example even unto death . . . with the result that our hearts should be enkindled by such a gift of divine grace, and true charity should not now shrink from

---

[27]Daniel L. Migliore, *Faith Seeking Understanding: An Introduction to Christian Theology* (Grand Rapids, MI: Eerdmans, 2004), 1.

[28]The virtues are a necessary aspect of our salvation – not a necessary step towards our salvation (salvation by works).

enduring anything from him'.[29] In this case, however, we will focus on the first of Thomas' points: that we know thereby how much God loves us.

How important is it that we know that the life, death and resurrection of Christ was an event in the life of the triune God, an event in which God decisively revealed his love for us?[30] We noted earlier that Athanasius explained that the Son fulfilled his work that we might once again know and worship the Father. Is a full and relational knowledge (and the worship flowing from it) really that central to the atonement? Barth would suggest that it is:

> We can and must ask about the being of God because as the Subject of His works God is so decisively characteristic for their nature and understanding that without this Subject they would be something quite different from what they are in accordance with God's Word, and on the basis of the Word of God we can necessarily recognize and understand them only together with this their subject (*CD* II/1, 260).

---

[29]Peter Abelard is supposedly the father of exemplarist theories of the atonement, which were then greatly developed in the Enlightenment and beyond. Recent scholarship argues that Abelard was not in fact an exemplarist, in that he did not explain the work of Christ exclusively as one that provides us with an example. Cf. Thomas Williams, 'Sin, Grace, and Redemption', in *The Cambridge Companion to Abelard*, ed. Jeffrey E. Brower and Kevin Guilfoy (New York: Cambridge University Press, 2004); Richard E. Weingart, *The Logic of Divine Love: A Critical Analysis of the Soteriology of Peter Abailard* (London: Clarendon, 1970); Gregory Anderson Love, 'In Search of a Non-Violent Atonement Theory: Are Abelard and Girard a Help or a Problem?', in *Theology as Conversation: The Significance of Dialogue in Historical and Contemporary Theology*, ed. Bruce L. McCormack and Kimlyn J. Bender (Grand Rapids, MI: Eerdmans, 2009).

The implication is that exemplarism is not one of the historic theories of the atonement, and was a relatively late innovation developed during the Enlightenment and modern period. Alister E. McGrath, 'The Moral Theory of the Atonement: An Historical and Theological Critique', *Scottish Journal of Theology* 38, no. 2 (1985): 205–20.

[30]'God has carried out the central events of this economy with the definite intention of making himself known in them.' Fred Sanders, *The Deep Things of God: How the Trinity Changes Everything* (Wheaton: Crossway, 2010), 130. As Julian puts it, 'God wants to be known', Julian of Norwich, *Showings*, trans. Edmund Colledge and James Walsh (New York: Paulist Press, 1978), 161. It is this theological perspective which affords us the alternative to a merely anthropological view – an ontological perspective from which to view the work of Christ. Marit Trelstad, 'Lavish Love: A Covenantal Ontology', in *Cross Examinations: Readings on the Meaning of the Cross Today*, ed. Marit Trelstad (Minneapolis: Fortress, 2006), 117.

That is, the mere event of the death and resurrection of Jesus is not particularly significant apart from the fact that this was an event in the life of God, by the will of God, and a self-revelation of the character of God.[31] Without this, it stands as simply another incomprehensible and therefore apparently insignificant event among a host of others (such as the experiences of Enoch, Elisha and Lazarus). Without this knowledge of 'a divine happening, a divine deed, an absolutely divine action',[32] we have no sense whatsoever of the meaning and significance of this event; our knowledge and understanding is key to God's purposes for the work of Christ.[33] But we must go further still.

The Gospel of John would suggest that we can, and in fact must, emphasize the role of knowledge within the atonement – not merely as the means by which we become aware of this reality, but in the very substance of atonement itself! Christ's goal is that we hear his word and believe in the one who sent him, that we might have eternal life (5:24); that we labour for that which the Son gives us and which leads to eternal life (6:27); and that we hear his voice, follow him and thereby receive eternal life (12:27-28). This much is clear from these verses: hearing the words of Jesus Christ, knowing the Father through him and receiving eternal life are all intimately connected. But in the high-priestly prayer, Jesus weaves these themes together, specifying that 'this is eternal life, that they know you the only true God, and Jesus Christ whom you have sent' (17:3). Continuing, he says: 'I glorified you on earth, having accomplished the work that you gave me to do' (17:4), namely, 'I have manifested your name to the people whom you gave me' (17:6). Concluding, Jesus says: 'I made known to them your name, and I will continue to make it known, that the love with which you have loved me may be in them, and I in them' (17:26).

---

[31] As Hengel notes, 'What we have here is God's communication of himself, the free action through which he establishes the effective basis of our salvation. . . . To assert that God himself accepted death in the form of a crucified Jewish manual worker from Galilee in order to break the power of death and bring salvation to all men could only seem [and still seems] folly and madness.' Martin Hengel, *Crucifixion in the Ancient World and the Folly of the Message of the Cross*, trans. John Bowden (Philadelphia: Fortress, 1977), 89.

[32] G. W. F. Hegel, *Lectures on the Philosophy of Religion: The Lectures of 1827*, trans. Peter Crafts Hodgson and Robert F. Brown (New York: Clarendon Press, 2006), 147.

[33] Cf. Hans Boersma, *Violence, Hospitality, and the Cross: Reappropriating the Atonement Tradition* (Grand Rapids, MI: Baker Academic, 2004), 115–32.

What are we to make of this? The purpose of the work of Christ was that we might know his Father – and this knowledge of the Father, a knowledge which occurs in Christ, is itself our salvation, eternal life.[34] In this sense, we must affirm that knowledge is salvation, and vice versa. Why did the Son of God become man? That we might know, and in this knowledge partake of salvation. Christ came that we, creatures of the darkness who hate light (3:19), might see (9:39) and know (17:3). The atonement of Jesus Christ was for the sake of enlightenment, or better yet, revelation. Just as significant as overcoming our guilt, shame and sloth was Christ's mission to overcome our ignorance and blindness – not with knowledge generally, but with knowledge of the Father. And in order to do away with this darkness Christ took upon himself this reality, experiencing the darkness of death, a darkness that is utterly abolished in the resurrection light and ascension to the Father (20:17). John thus leads us to an understanding of the work of Christ as saving by means of revelation, for salvation is the knowledge of the Father in and through Christ.[35]

To return once more to Thomas:

> A stain is properly ascribed to corporeal things, when a comely body loses its comeliness through contact with another body. . . . Now man's soul has a two-fold comeliness; one from the refulgence of the natural light of reason, whereby he is directed in his actions; the other, from the refulgence of the Divine light. . . . Now, when a soul cleaves to things by love, there is a kind of contact in the soul: and when man sins, he cleaves to certain things, against the light of reason and of the Divine law. . . . Wherefore the loss of comeliness occasioned by this contact, is metaphorically called a stain on the soul. (*ST*, II.86.1)

---

[34]As Hegel puts it, knowledge is more than a 'simple connection of myself with my object', for it is deeply relational and transformative, 'an *elevation to God*'. Hegel, *Lectures on the Philosophy of Religion: The Lectures of 1827*, 162.

[35]Such an account demonstrates the significant limitation of categorizing theories of the atonement as either subjective or objective. Robert Sherman, *King, Priest and Prophet: A Trinitarian Theology of Atonement* (Edinburgh: T & T Clark, 2004), 19; James K. Beilby and Paul R. Eddy, eds, *The Nature of the Atonement: Four Views* (Downers Grove, IL: IVP Academic, 2006), 14–20.

Thus far, Thomas has accounted for the nature of sin within epistemic/psychological categories – sinning, or cleaving to certain lesser goods, results in a stain of the soul, by which our use of natural reason and our knowledge of God is dimmed and distorted, such that we become creatures of darkness (Jn 3:19). But 'as soon as, moved by grace, [the sinner] returns to the Divine light and to the light of reason, the stain is removed' (*ST*, II.86.1). This movement of grace, we should add, is rooted in the incarnation of the eternal Son, the divine light himself, who makes the soul comely once more, through his refulgence in the soul. And it is precisely in this movement of grace, the work of Jesus Christ, that the stain is removed and we are brought to knowledge of the Father and the eternal life this knowledge entails. In short, the atonement is revelation for the sake of knowledge of the Father, in which the divine light enlightens us. Jesus lived, died and rose again that we might know God – a revelation theory of the atonement, if you will.[36]

How does this line of thought relate to the riches of the atonement we seek? Salvation is knowledge of the Father. But our knowledge of the Father is mediated through the person and work of Jesus Christ and his Spirit – which is to say that our knowledge of the Father comes through the death and resurrection of Jesus Christ, which is at the centre of his earthly mission. Accordingly Christ's atonement is our salvation because it reveals the Father to us, a revelation which is itself salvation and not merely a by-product of it. The reason we should be hungry to explore, develop and embrace a manifold witness to the work of Christ, to develop an abundance of theories of the atonement, is that each of these theories explores the self-revelation of the Father through the Son from a specific vantage point, which is to say that it explores the reality of our salvation. The riches we have in the manifold nature of Christ's atoning work are themselves the heavenly riches of the Father, revealed and enacted for us and for our salvation in Christ. To turn away from the riches of the atonement for the

---

[36]This account of revelation is thoroughly (though not exclusively) indebted to Barth. Cf. Adam Johnson, *God's Being in Reconciliation: The Theological Basis of the Unity and Diversity of the Atonement in the Theology of Karl Barth* (New York: T & T Clark, 2012), 85–91. For a similar line of thought, cf. Benedict XVI, *Jesus of Nazareth: Holy Week* (San Francisco: Ignatius, 2011), 76–102.

Self revelation = Salvation
Knowledge of God = ↑

sake of expedience or lethargy[37] is to squander knowledge of the Father, to turn away from salvation itself; for the riches of the atonement, knowledge of the Father and salvation itself are one and the same thing.

The goal: Gleaning the treasure

Because the faith we have is inherently a faith seeking understanding, and because the atoning work of Christ is a work of self-revelation in which salvation is knowledge and vice versa, we should be eager to collect and employ the treasures we have in Christ. But we should do so with systematic rigour, laying out a vision that equips and sustains the Church for this ongoing work.[38] The distinctive feature of this approach is the way I emphasize theological tools for equipping the Church – a move relying upon a specific understanding of the nature of systematic theology. Briefly, I hold that systematic theology makes explicit in its own language and categories the implicit content, premises and patterns of thought found in the Bible and employed by its

---

[37]This is precisely what we find in a host of typologies of the doctrine that break the doctrine up into three major types. While Gustaf Aulén's typology is simplistic, this is compounded disastrously by those who repeat his basic thesis devoid of his research into the history of theology.

[38]Examples of works which favour concrete development of different theories of the atonement from historical perspectives, in contrast to my methodological emphasis, include: Aulén, *Christus Victor*; Laurence W. Grensted, *A Short History of the Doctrine of the Atonement* (London: Longmans, Green & co., 1920); Donald Macleod, 'The Atonement of the Death of Christ: In Faith, Revelation, and History', *Scottish Journal of Theology* 41, no. 4 (1988): 535; Henry Nutcombe Oxenham, *The Catholic Doctrine of the Atonement*(London: W.H. Allen, 1881); Auguste Sabatier, *The Doctrine of the Atonement and Its Historical Evolution; and, Religion and Modern Culture* (London: Williams & Norgate, 1904); Ferdinand Christian Baur, *Die Christliche Lehre Von Der Versöhnung in Ihrer Geschichtlichen Entwicklung Von Der Ältesten Zeit Bis Auf Die Neueste* (Tübingen: C.F. Osiander, 1838); Henry Ernest William Turner, *The Patristic Doctrine of Redemption: A Study of the Development of Doctrine During the First Five Centuries* (New York: Mowbray, 1952). More recent volumes seeking to capture the diversity inherent to Christ's saving work include: Peter Schmiechen, *Saving Power: Theories of Atonement and Forms of the Church* (Grand Rapids, MI: Eerdmans, 2005); McKnight, *Community*; Baker and Green, *Recovering*.

authors. For instance, the Trinitarian doctrine of appropriations (cf. Chapter 3) is nowhere stated as such in Scripture. Rather, it is a hard-won theological insight making explicit the logic implicit within the biblical authors' writings about the distinct works of Father, Son and Holy Spirit. But this doctrine, far from a mere summary or abstraction of the biblical material, is a tool for further study of Scripture, allowing us to better read Scripture in conformity with its implicit Trinitarian logic. This book works at precisely this intersection, drawing on theological doctrines as tools for the study of Scripture, within the particular confines of the doctrine of the atonement.

A secondary objective of this book is to develop a number of the different aspects and theories of Christ's saving work, which can serve as enticements and examples for further work. But what sets this book apart from other introductions to the doctrine is not the development of *more* theories of the atonement. A volume such as this simply cannot compete with the comprehensive nature of histories of the doctrine. Rather, in a theological environment increasingly sensitive to diversity at every level, the contribution of this book lies in its exploration of the logic, or more specifically, the theo-logic, underlying the riches of Christ's saving work. Appreciating this logic equips the Church to appropriate the work of theologians throughout the history of the Church, but also (and more importantly) to venture forth into new or underutilized accounts of Christ's atonement through careful and reinvigorated reading of Scripture, history of doctrine and culture.

But why must explanations of a man's death and resurrection be such a complicated affair? First, events are often far richer in character than we initially perceive. For instance, when Jesse Owens crossed the finish line in the 1936 Olympics in Berlin, one could explain that Owens won a race. While true, such an account would fail to honour the complexity of the event, which could and should be explained at various levels, including chemistry, physics, sport, race, politics, economics, nationalism and religion to name but a few. Events, and particularly key historical events, are complex in nature, and we are wise to honour them as such. Like any other significant historical happening, Christ's passion was a complex, multidimensional event, calling for rich exposition at a number of levels, including but not limited to: Jewish religion, Roman politics and law, interpersonal dynamics, Jesus' self-understanding,

Roman execution practices, biological processes relevant to death by crucifixion and social norms involving mockery and shaming.[39]

A second layer adding complexity and richness to events in general and the atonement in particular involves the complexities inherent in our speech about these events, with particular attention paid to the role of metaphor. While early in the twentieth century metaphor was regarded as an unnecessary husk surrounding a kernel of truth in the atonement,[40] it is now commonplace to embrace atonement language as necessarily and constructively metaphorical, based in part on the influence of Colin Gunton (and his employment of Janet Soskice's work).[41] The scholarship on this topic is wide-ranging and complex, and its implications for the doctrine of the atonement are quite significant. In keeping with the constructive focus of this book, however, it suffices to make two points. First, the approach taken in this book is compatible with a range of positions regarding the nature and function of metaphorical language. Second, while discussions concerning the role of metaphor are significant, my goal is to move the discussion to a line of thought which will (1) de-emphasize the debate over the role of metaphor within the atonement, while (2) speaking to many of the same concerns those discussions seek to address.[42]

---

[39]For some of this material, see: Raymond Edward Brown, *The Death of the Messiah: From Gethsemane to the Grave* (New York: Doubleday, 1994); N. T. Wright, *Jesus and the Victory of God* (Minneapolis: Fortress, 1996); Hengel, *Crucifixion*.

[40]Cf. Adolf von Harnack, *What Is Christianity?* (New York: Harper, 1957), 55.

[41]Gunton, *Actuality*, 27–52; Janet Martin Soskice, *Metaphor and Religious Language* (Oxford: Oxford, 1985). Just how commonplace this is can be seen in the near ubiquity of chapters or sections on 'metaphor' in books on the atonement. E.g. McKnight, *Community*, 35ff; Boersma, *Violence*, 99–114. For a helpful essay on the topic, cf. Henri Blocher, 'Biblical Metaphors and the Doctrine of the Atonement', *Journal of the Evangelical Theological Society* 47, no. 4 (2004): 629–45. It is worth noting that though metaphor may be an essential and salutary feature of our speech, it is not always good or helpful. Metaphorical language, as Linda Radzik notes, can take on a life of its own, eventually losing its power by its distance and isolation from that which it originally sought to address. Linda Radzik, *Making Amends: Atonement in Morality, Law, and Politics* (New York: Oxford University Press, 2009), 54.

[42]The primary purpose of discussions concerning metaphors within the atonement is to explain the diversity in the biblical and theological witness to the meaning of Christ's death and resurrection (cf. Baker and Green, *Recovering*, 98–9; Gunton, *Actuality*, 25). As I understand it, there are better and more properly theological explanations for this phenomenon than appeals to the nature of language and

Unlike other historical events, however, the death and resurrection of Jesus Christ was uniquely significant and rich, for it was an event in the life of God himself, willed and experienced by Father, Son and Holy Spirit.[43] Beyond the complexity proper to any significant historical act mentioned above, and the further complexity of our metaphorical speech about this event, there is an additional and unique diversity proper to this act – the diversity proper to the triune God whose act this was, in the fullness of his divine attributes.[44] 'God was in Christ,' accomplishing the work of reconciling 'all things' (1 Cor. 5:19). God; Father, Son and Holy Spirit; the God of Abraham, Isaac and Jacob; the God who is merciful, gracious, patient, loving, good, kind, righteous, faithful, constant, wrathful, holy, omniscient . . . . This God, in the fullness of his character, was in Christ, reconciling all things to himself. And by means of this work 'all things' are taken up and reconciled to God by means of God himself, by means of the diversity and richness proper to God's own being and life. This threefold diversity (proper to events generally, intrinsic to the metaphorical nature of speech and founded in the diversity proper to the God whose act this is) provides the explanation for the diversity and complexity inherent to this event, calling forth our multifaceted witness.

Outline of the book

In keeping with the vision detailed above, this book unfolds in two primary movements. Chapter 2 sets the stage for our inquiry, exploring the question of orthodoxy and the parameters for working out the doctrine of the atonement. Chapters 3 and 4 constitute

---

culture. Shifting the ground of the discussion will free linguistic and cultural discussion to play their proper role, rather than burdening them (and the doctrine of the atonement) with a weight that they were not meant to carry. McIntyre is likewise uneasy about the prominence of metaphor within soteriological discussions, for distinct though related reasons. Cf. McIntyre, *Soteriology*, 73–5.

[43] With regard to 'mode', 'way', or 'manner' of being, I am drawing on Barth's understanding of that term, as found in *CD* I/1, pp. 413ff. Cf. Johnson, *God's Being*, 70n. 33.

[44] In this book I use divine 'perfections' and 'attributes' interchangeably. Barth preferred the former term inasmuch as it speaks of something uniquely God's, rather than something that he has in common with the being of others. *CD* II/1, 322.

the first movement, delving into the ways in which the diversity proper to the being and life of God give shape to the doctrine of the atonement. Specifically, Chapter 3 explores the Trinitarian nature and shape of the doctrine of the atonement, while Chapter 4 explores the vital role of a proper understanding of the divine attributes for this doctrine. The second movement takes place in Chapters 5 and 6, which explore the diversity proper to the event at a more generic level. Chapter 5 considers the diversity inherent in the 'all things' which are reconciled to Christ, ranging from the earth itself to the angels in the highest heavens, and everything in between. Chapter 6 unfolds the diversity of the atonement as a 3-day event (Good Friday, Holy Saturday and Easter Sunday), considering how the life, death and resurrection of Christ are all essential to his work. Chapter 7 concludes by laying out a vision for further work in exploring the riches we have in Christ and how we might employ those riches by integrating them into other areas of our lives.

Throughout the book we will develop the work of theologians from the history of the Church.[45] For two reasons I choose to incorporate my use of the history of doctrine into my systematic account, rather than offering a discrete chapter on the subject. First, in acknowledgement of my limitations, the primary purpose of this book is to offer a systematic thesis, by means of which I hope to equip the readers to re-enter the old discussions through their own historical and biblical studies. A chapter (or set of chapters) on the history of doctrine would eschew the systematic focus of the book, undermining its vision for the integration of biblical, historical and systematic work in the theological task. My goal is to 'avoid fetishistic repetition of old sacred formulas . . . and seek to understand these formulas, try to capture the reality that they attempt to convey',[46] and to do so by means of a theological approach. Second, the

---

[45]Please note that my use of these theologians does not imply I agree with all or even most of their theology. The purpose of this work is to be an irenic and reconciling vision-casting exercise. While I do incorporate some critique in the pages which follow, for the most part I avoid polemic interaction. The overall theological systems of many of the figures included here could not come together into a coherent whole without a great deal of change, but I hope that my use of their works, to which I owe a great debt of gratitude, is nonetheless both faithful and coherent.

[46]Leonardo Boff, *Passion of Christ, Passion of the World: The Facts, Their Interpretation, and Their Meaning Yesterday and Today* (Maryknoll, NY: Orbis, 1987), 87.

history of the doctrine is so complex and varied that even were I to devote the whole of the present book to the topic, it would be a perverse oversimplification of little benefit to the reader. Other theologians, upon whose work I draw throughout this book, offer valuable surveys of the relevant biblical and historical material. My hope is that the present work will provide a valuable perspective from which the reader will be able to fruitfully re-engage those same materials, furthering our understanding of the doctrine, its foundation and its history. My hope is that this perspective will better enable us to heed Anselm's exhortation:

> Consider where and what is the strength of thy salvation, occupy thyself in meditating thereon, delight thyself in the contemplation thereof; put away thy daintiness, force thyself, give thy mind thereto; taste of the goodness of thy Redeemer, kindle within thyself the love of the Saviour.[47]

---

[47]Anselm, 'The Devotions of Saint Anselm', ed. Clement C. J. Webb (London: Methuen & Co, 1903), 105.

2

On Aspects,
Theories and Orthodoxy

The first chapter cast a vision of the abundant riches within the doctrine of the atonement – riches funded by the diversity proper to the triune God in the fullness of his attributes. In subsequent chapters we will delve into this diversity, but for the time being we will attend to the nature and purpose of atonement theories, and the underlying question of orthodoxy. Together, these two lines of inquiry will bring a sense of order to what might otherwise be an overwhelming emphasis on diversity.[1] Properly developed theories of the atonement, I suggest, are non-competitive and mutually reinforcing explanations of how Christ's death and resurrection are saving by means of distinct elaborations of five key elements. Orthodoxy is therefore an abundant affair involving multiple theories rather than a singular reality in which various theories compete for legitimacy.

When we think about a theologian's view of the atonement, we tend to think in terms of her 'theory' of the atonement, asking such questions as whether or not she has an exemplarist theory. But why do we do this? It is not as though theologians have provable hypotheses that we could replicate in a laboratory setting; nor do they have lists of suspects, with competing and mutually exclusive explanations as to who might have committed the crime. Some, perhaps, use the word

---

[1] As Vanhoozer notes, '[A] non-reductive orthodoxy will be expansive, but not to the point of dissolution. The danger of including too many voices is that the message becomes garbled, drowned out in an unholy cacophony.' Vanhoozer, *Drama*, 30. This chapter provides some of the framework and order necessary to keep us from becoming garbled.

loosely as a device for labelling the thought of another ('Ah yes – that is a variant of a governmental theory of the atonement . . .'). For many, it has to do with a theologian's (or theological tradition's) unique explanation of the causal efficacy of the passion, the precise way in which the death and resurrection of Jesus Christ was effective for our salvation. But why use the word 'theory' at all? Is its use of significant benefit to discussions of the atonement?

Many contemporary works on the atonement take 'theory' language for granted, referring to different historical theories without accounting for their understanding of the term. But few theologians prior to the nineteenth century used this term of their own work; we would do well to give an account for the way(s) in which we use it. McKnight writes that a metaphor or theory 'of the atonement is a set of lenses through which we describe *God's acts of resolving sin and of bringing humans back home in their relationship with God, with self, with others, and with the world'.*[2] Vanhoozer notes that theories must 'ultimately explain why our experience of God's love and forgiveness depends on or requires just this cruciform climax to the divine action'.[3] Von Balthasar, upon whom Vanhoozer draws, suggests that there are five main components to the biblical witness to Christ's atonement, which must be incorporated into any successful theory of the atonement: that (1) the atonement is the eternal Son giving himself for us by (2) changing places with us, in such a way as both to (3) do away with evil and its consequences, and (4) restore us to freedom through drawing us into the divine life, all of which must be understood primarily as (5) a work of God's gracious love.[4]

In preliminary fashion, we might say that theories of atonement explain the efficacy of Christ's death and resurrection, so as to explain how it is God's way of saving us, others and the world *from* sin and its consequences, and *for* life in and with God.[5] These elements cohere by means of their conceptually unified role, and

---

[2]McKnight, *Community*, 36. Though McKnight speaks here of metaphor, he clearly sees this as bound up with theory, as evident from the context.

[3]Vanhoozer, *Drama*, 383.

[4]Hans Urs von Balthasar, *Theo-Drama: Theological Dramatic Theory*, trans. Graham Harrison, vol. 4: The Action (San Francisco: Ignatius, 1988), 241–3.

[5]Cf. Sykes' account of theories, particularly regarding his emphasis on explanatory value and the distinction between reason and rationalism. Stephen Sykes, *The Story of Atonement* (London: Darton, Longman and Todd, 1997), 10–12.

are animated and further characterized by a set or constellation of metaphors appropriate to that model or theory.[6]

Subsequent to clarifying a theologian's theory, one naturally enquires into its orthodoxy: namely, whether it comports with the Bible, and the established teaching of the Church on this doctrine. The question of orthodoxy is complicated by the lack of the creedal specificity provided by the early Church to such doctrines as the Trinity and Christology.[7] Beyond that, the diversity of the biblical and historical material makes specific criteria for orthodoxy difficult to discern.[8] What, precisely, makes a theory of the atonement (un)orthodox, and is this even a helpful way of thinking?

We begin this chapter by taking a brief look at a handful of theologians significant to the history of the doctrine, paying particular attention to how they approach the diversity of the work of Christ. This will pave the way for our reflection on the nature and role of theories of the atonement in the second half of the chapter, as we develop (1) our own account of theories and aspects of the atonement and (2) the place these have within discussions of the orthodoxy of the same. This framework will provide a significant source of conceptual unity to the project as a whole, which otherwise might suffer from an overwhelming and chaotic diversity. The task, after all, is an awesome one: to explain how God, in Christ's death and resurrection, was reconciling all things to himself (2 Cor. 5:19). No simple explanation will suffice for those wholly giving themselves over to this task.

Snapshots of the history of the doctrine

Irenaeus' description of the work of Christ relies upon a hermeneutic of recapitulation, in which he notes the different ways in

---

[6]McIntyre, *Soteriology*, 53–67, 75–8. McIntyre offers an advanced account of theories and models in this work which is quite helpful. While he argues for dimensionality, I tend to favour an account of complementarity rooted in what we might call the complementarity of the divine attributes.

[7]*Soteriology*, 1–25.

[8]McIntyre suggests that orthodoxy is determined by the biblical criterion on the one hand and coherence with previously developed models which themselves cohere with the biblical norm on the other. We will return to this later in the chapter.

which events and actions in the life of Christ sum up, or repeat and consummate key events in humankind's sinful history with God.[9] For instance:

> For by summing up in Himself the whole human race from the beginning to the end, He has also summed up its death. From this it is clear that the Lord suffered death, in obedience to His Father, upon that day on which Adam died while he disobeyed God. Now He died on the same day in which He did eat. For God said, 'In that day on which ye shall eat of it, ye shall die by death.' The Lord, therefore, recapitulating in Himself this day, underwent His sufferings upon the day preceding the Sabbath, that is, the sixth day of the creation, on which day man was created; thus granting him a second creation by means of His passion, which is that [creation out of death].[10]

In this particular passage, Irenaeus demonstrates that Jesus was obedient where we were disobedient, and in such a way as to create us 'out of death' on the same day of the week in which we were created out of nothing. That is, he explores different details of Christ's life (particularly his passion), noting how these details repeat and either reverse or fulfil the details of our fall into sin. The result is an incredibly broad understanding of Christ's work, which can be explained in any number of ways. For instance, Irenaeus writes: 'The Son of God . . . to recapitulate all things, became a man

---

[9]Irenaeus' thought is receiving significant attention in popular accounts of the atonement. Cf. McKnight, *Community*, 101–6; Boersma, *Violence*, 126–9; Andrew P. Klager, 'Retaining and Reclaiming the Divine: Identification and the Recapitulation of Peace in St. Irenaeus of Lyons' Atonement Narrative', in *Stricken by God? Nonviolent Identification and the Victory of Christ*, ed. Brad Jersak and Michael Hardin (Grand Rapids, MI: Eerdmans, 2007); Adam Kotsko, *The Politics of Redemption: The Social Logic of Salvation* (New York: T&T Clark, 2010), 74–9. Some of these authors refer to Irenaeus' account of recapitulation as a theory, but many of them appropriately refer to it more modestly as an idea or concept. The most insightful analysis of Irenaeus that I have found is: Trevor A. Hart, 'Irenaeus, Recapitulation and Physical Redemption', in *Christ in Our Place: The Humanity of God in Christ for the Reconciliation of the World*, ed. Trevor A. Hart and Daniel P. Thimell (Allison Park, PA: Pickwick Publications, 1989).

It is worth noting that Irenaeus' contribution is not limited to recapitulation. Cf. McIntyre, *Soteriology*, 4.

[10]Irenaeus, 'Against Heresies', in *The Ante-Nicene Fathers*, ed. Alexander Roberts and James Donaldson (Peabody, MA: Hendrickson Publishers, 2004), 551; V.xxiii.552.

amongst men . . . in order to abolish death, to demonstrate life, and
to effect communion between God and man.'[11] Later he offers a far
more sustained account of how Christ effects this communion:

> We, being unable to have any participation in incorruptibility
> if it were not for His coming to us. . . . He became visible, that
> we might, in all ways, obtain a participation in incorruptibility.
> And because all are implicated in the first-formation of Adam,
> we were bound to death through the disobedience, it was fitting,
> [therefore], by means of the obedience of the One, who on our
> account became man, to be loosed from death. Since death
> reigned over the flesh, it was necessary that, abolished through
> flesh, it release man from its oppression.[12]

Whereas the previous quote focused on death, life and communion,
Irenaeus now turns his attention to disobedience, obedience, the
flesh and incorruptibility. Of course these themes can be connected –
but as they stand, they are discrete accounts of the work of Christ.

We might ask: what is Irenaeus' 'theory' of the atonement? But
our efforts would be wasted in seeking the answer to this question,
for what we find is a hermeneutic, a way of reading the events of
the passion of Christ, which sees his saving work as summing up
or bringing to fulfilment the whole of God's creative purpose, while
reversing the whole of the effects of our sin. But this itself is no
theory – for within this account are embedded multiple unique yet
interdependent accounts of Christ's saving work which in more or
less detail develop what we might call 'theories' of the atonement.
Looking at the most recent quote from Irenaeus, we see how he
works with the concepts of incorruptibility and death to explain
the efficacy of Christ's work. But we may hardly say that in this
we have found the key to his thoughts on the work of Christ, for
elsewhere he employs the hermeneutic of recapitulation in an entirely
different direction, focusing on transgression and bondage:

> For as in the beginning [Satan] enticed man to transgress his
> Maker's law, and thereby got him into his power . . . so again,
> on the other hand, it was necessary that through man himself he

---

[11] *On the Apostolic Preaching*, trans. John Behr (Crestwood: St. Vladimir's Seminary
Press, 1997), 43–4.
[12] Ibid., 60.

should, when conquered, be bound with the same chains with which he had bound man, in order that man, being set free, might return to his Lord, leaving to him (Satan) those bonds by which he himself had been fettered, that is, sin.[13]

In sum, we find in Irenaeus a concept or hermeneutic of recapitulation, enabling him to offer a unified reading of the Old and New Testaments in light of the work of Christ. This reading is complex and varied, pulling together a whole range of explanations of Christ's death and resurrection. While Irenaeus rarely develops these at length, it would be fair to say that through his concept or hermeneutic of recapitulation, he develops *in nuce* an array of theories of the atonement. To elevate or prioritize any one of these as Irenaeus' theory would be a grievous reductionism, reducing a feast to a single dish.

Jumping ahead many centuries, John of Damascus writes that 'the death of Christ . . . clothed us with the enhypostatic wisdom and power of God',[14] and later explains that Christ 'gave us . . . a second birth in order that, just as we who are born of Adam are in his image and are the heirs of the curse and corruption, so also being born of Him we may be in His likeness and heirs of His incorruption and blessing and glory'.[15] In the same chapter, he explains that we partake of the Eucharist that 'we may be inflamed and deified by the participation in the divine fire' – a participation he elaborates in terms of an adoption which means nothing less than sharing in Christ's likeness in the form of the divine incorruption, blessing and glory. Should we say that John has an atonement theory of deification, of salvation through participation in the life of God?

Perhaps – but we do well to keep our eyes open, for John, like Irenaeus, has a rich account of Christ's work. Dwelling on the cross of Christ, he writes:

For no other thing has subdued death, expiated the sin of the first parent, despoiled Hades, bestowed the resurrection, granted

---

[13]'Against Heresies', 550; V.xxi.553.
[14]John of Damascus, *Exposition of the Orthodox Faith*, trans. S. D. F. Salmond (Grand Rapids, MI: Eerdmans, 1983), 80; IV.xi.
[15]Ibid., 82; IV.xiii.

the power to us of contemning the present and even death itself, prepared the return to our former blessedness, opened the gates of Paradise, given our nature a seat at the right hand of God, and made us the children and heirs of God, save the Cross of our Lord Jesus Christ.[16]

Summing up this line of thought, he concludes: '[F]or by the Cross all things have been made right' – a statement echoing the thought of Irenaeus.[17] Elsewhere, John adds to this list, writing:

He dies, therefore, because He took on Himself death on our behalf, and He makes Himself an offering to the Father for our sakes. For we had sinned against Him, and it was meet that He should receive the ransom for us, and that we should thus be delivered from the condemnation. God forbid that the blood of the Lord should have been offered to the tyrant. Wherefore death approaches, and swallowing up the body as a bait is transfixed on the hook of divinity, and after tasting of a sinless and life-giving body, perishes, and brings up again all whom of old he swallowed up.[18]

Sacrificial offering, *Christus victor*, ransom, deliverance from condemnation, expiation of sin, restoration to an Edenic state, adoption . . . while John of Damascus clearly develops an account of divinization in keeping with many of the Eastern fathers,[19] his account of the cross of Christ resounds with a manifold witness.

In Anselm we come across something unique – though I do not refer to his theory of satisfaction.[20] While there are many unique features to Anselm's answer to why God became man, perhaps the

---

[16]*Orthodox Faith*, 80; IV.xi.

[17]Irenaeus' hermeneutic was of great significance to the history of thought, and is found in many Patristic and medieval theologians.

[18]Damascus, *Orthodox Faith*, 72; III.xxvii. Cf. John's affirmation of Christus victor in: *Orthodox Faith*, 75; IV.iv.

[19]Cf. Part III in Michael J. Christensen and Jeffery A. Wittung, *Partakers of the Divine Nature: The History and Development of Deificiation in the Christian Traditions* (Grand Rapids, MI: Baker Academic, 2007).

[20]In multiple ways, Athanasius anticipates Anselm's argument, though in terms of satisfying God's creative goodness rather than his honour. Of course Anselm's argument is far more developed – but critics of Anselm would do well to study Athanasius to better appreciate Anselm.

most striking fact is the one-dimensionality of his account.[21] Like John of Damascus, Anselm eschews a ransom to Satan (*CDH*, I.7), focusing his account on the question of God's honour (*CDH*, I.11-15). He ultimately proposes that Christ's freely offered and unnecessary death was a satisfaction of God's honour in place of the punishment of humankind that would otherwise be requisite, given the way we had dishonoured God. The most striking feature of this account, when viewed in light of his predecessors, is its one-dimensionality – one might even go so far as to say that Anselm is the father of one-dimensional accounts of the atonement, departing from centuries of Church tradition. Yet even that would be to say too much, for while his satisfaction theory is the mainstay of his account, it incorporates the defeat of Satan (*CDH*, II. 21) and Christ's example to us (*CDH*, II.18-19).[22]

When we turn to Anselm's *Meditation on Human Redemption*, written just after *Cur Deus Homo*,[23] we find a very different tone:

> O Christian soul, soul raised up from a grievous death, soul redeemed and delivered from a miserable slavery by the blood of God, arouse thy mind from sleep, bethink thee of thy resurrection, remember thy redemption and deliverance. . . . He, the good Samaritan, hath healed thee; He, thy good Friend, with His own life hath redeemed and delivered thee.'[24]

Anselm's one-dimensionality was unique for his time. Cf. Bernard of Clairvaux's view, summarized in: Tony Lane, 'Bernard of Clairvaux: Theologian of the Cross', in *The Atonement Debate: Papers from the London Symposium on the Theology of Atonement*, ed. Derek Tidball, David Hilborn and Justin Thacker (Grand Rapids, MI: Zondervan, 2008).

[21]This is not to suggest that from that point on, theologians became one-dimensional in their accounts of the atonement. That remained the exception for many centuries to come.

[22]Note that Kerr has gone so far as to argue that Anselm holds to a *theosis* view of atonement: Nathan R. Kerr, 'St. Anselm: *Theoria* and the Doctrinal Logic of Perfection', in *Partakers of the Divine Nature: The History and Development of Deificiation in the Christian Traditions*, ed. Michael J. Christensen and Jeffery Wittung (Madison: Fairleigh Dickinson University Press, 2007).

[23]Southern tell us that the '*Meditation on Human Redemption* was certainly composed in 1099 as a devotional summary of the *Cur Deus Homo*'. R. W. Southern, *Saint Anselm: A Portrait in a Landscape* (Cambridge: Cambridge University Press, 1990), 36.

[24]Anselm, 'The Devotions of Saint Anselm', 105.

What ensues is a rich, poetic meditation upon the theme of recapitulation and an abundance of biblical images. While the meditation admittedly focuses largely upon material covered in more depth in *Cur Deus Homo*, it has two noteworthy features. First, Anselm briefly develops an account of Christ's saving work revolving around the divine freedom and obedience (rather than divine honour) which frees us from debt which we owed to God, doing so in such a way as to call for our obedience-in-freedom. Essentially, this is a complementary version of his satisfaction theory rooted in freedom rather than honour. Second, in his conclusion Anselm returns to the abundance of themes characterizing the beginning of the meditation, indicating that while his focus on satisfaction is indeed important to him, there is more to the work of Christ than he has explained – and he is eager to remind us to continue in our search.[25]

Moving on to Francis Turretin, we find a truly one-dimensional account of the atonement. Turretin affirms the absolute necessity of the atonement in the following manner: 'God not only has not willed to remit our sins without a satisfaction, but could not do so on account of his justice.'[26] Our sin, in this system, is a 'debt which we are bound to pay to divine justice' and 'a crime by which, before God, the supreme Ruler and Judge of the world, we become worthy of everlasting death and malediction'.[27] From the very beginning, judicial terminology and distinctions dominate the scene. Given that God is the just ruler of the universe and that we have sinned, a solution is sought which will guarantee that God remains the just ruler of the universe, through destroying the sin, guilt and debt of humanity. Every other consideration falls under this fundamental rubric. In this line of thought, mercy and love are optional for God and must fit within the system of God's necessary justice.[28] Christ, as our penal substitute, bears our sin and guilt, suffering the punishment and wrath of the Father, thereby freeing us *from* the penalty, and *for* life with God.

---

[25]Ibid., 113–19.
[26]François Turrettini, *Institutes of Elenctic Theology*, vol. 2 (Phillipsburg: P & R Publishing, 1992), 418.
[27]Ibid.
[28]Ibid., 422–3.

It is interesting to note that while Jonathan Edwards wholly follows Turretin in his essay 'Concerning the Necessity and Reasonableness of the Christian Doctrine of Satisfaction for Sin', he offers an incredibly rich and multi-aspectual account of the work of Christ in his collection of sermons The Wisdom of God Displayed in the Way of Salvation. We return to Edwards in Chapter 4, but for the time being it suffices to note that one-dimensional and multidimensional accounts of the atonement continue to coexist throughout the history of the Church, sometimes even within the works of individual theologians (Anselm and Edwards, for instance). By the beginning of the nineteenth century, however, a new development was afoot: more and more, theologians referred to and categorized the accounts of the atonement by their predecessors as 'theories', in which they sought to draw out the unique point(s) characterizing the view of each theologian (or theological tradition), while simultaneously offering their own increasingly one-dimensional accounts of the work of Christ. Though this point must be employed judiciously, it is worth noting that there is a strong tendency for Enlightenment theologians to offer manifold explanations of the work of Christ, whereas those coming after them were much more likely to offer one-dimensional accounts, both in their historical analysis of their predecessors, and their constructive work.[29]

Atonement: Aspect and theories

Touching on some of the key figures in the history of the doctrine of the atonement, we have seen how rich and varied accounts of the work of Christ were the rule, with occasional exceptions, until after the Reformation, and particularly after the Enlightenment, during which time Christ's work tended to be treated one-dimensionally, and talk of 'theories' of the atonement became commonplace. What

---

[29]Sonderegger charges Adolf Harnack with 'set[ting] the tone and [giving] the language for modern opposition to Anselm's doctrine', largely through the move of interpreting theologians (and Anselm in particular) in terms of 'models' or 'theories'. Katherine Sonderegger, 'Anselm, Defensor Fidei', International Journal of Systematic Theology 9, no. 3 (2007): 342. While model and theory language pertaining to the atonement preceded Harnack, his influence for the modern period is undisputed.

are we to make of this development, and how should we respond to it? In this section we consider how we might approach the doctrine of the atonement in light of aspects and theories.

The doctrine of the atonement is a conceptually unified account of how the life, death and resurrection of Jesus Christ are effective for the reconciliation of all things to God (Col. 1:20). A fundamental distinction attends this definition. First, there is the event itself, 'the life, death and resurrection of Jesus Christ', and its manifold consequences, the 'reconciliation of all things to God'. The emphasis here is upon the real and effective event of Christ's death and resurrection and its consequences, irrespective of our awareness and comprehension of its reality and meaning. Constitutive of the event is the complex divine intent motivating the action, such that the event includes the divine motive or interpretation.[30] Second, there is the present work of the Church: the vocation to give a conceptually unified account of this event and its consequences, including an account of the divine interpretation of this event – what God himself intends, thinks and communicates about Christ's work in Scripture. The emphasis here is upon seeking to understand and meaningfully convey to others the nature of this event and its consequences and implications.

Throughout this book I differentiate the reality of the atonement, and the theories that seek to understand and explain it. Because this act of witnessing is a creaturely act, 'no doctrine of this central mystery can exhaustively and precisely grasp and express the extent to which God has intervened for us here. Do not confuse [the] theory of the reconciliation with the thing itself. All theories of reconciliation can be but pointers.'[31] And as we saw in Chapter 1, because diversity attends both of these realities, I distinguish the atonement into multiple 'aspects' and the Church's witness into diverse 'theories'. Aspects in this case refer to discrete though

---

[30]I am sympathetic with McIntyre's concerns regarding a distinction between 'data' and 'interpretation', and sought to offer my version of his account by means of the notion of 'divine interpretation'. McIntyre, *Soteriology*, 80–4. Cf. Susan Nelson's distinction between the cross and ways we construe it. Susan L. Nelson, 'Imagining the Cross: Through the Eyes of Marian Kolodziej', in *Cross Examinations: Readings on the Meaning of the Cross Today*, ed. Marit Trelstad (Minneapolis: Fortress, 2006), 167.

[31]Karl Barth, *Dogmatics in Outline*, trans. G. T. Thompson (New York: Harper, 1959), 89. Cf. McKnight, *Community*, 89.

mutually dependent dimensions or elements of the atoning event.[32] For instance, there are the political and religious aspects of Christ's death and resurrection. Theories, on the other hand, are the Church's witness to these various aspects by means of offering conceptually unified accounts of these various aspects, as we seek to understand them by distinguishing their various elements.

Building on this material, in the next section I delve into the constitutive elements of theories of the atonement, exploring the five main features present (implicitly or explicitly) in any fully developed account of the work of Christ.

The five elements of theories of the atonement

Theories of the atonement are synthetic in nature, in that they necessarily bring together and depend upon a number of other doctrines.[33] While all Christian doctrine stands in relation to the triune God, doctrines such as creation, anthropology and hamartiology (doctrine of sin) can be (and have been) developed without sustained reference to other doctrines.[34] The atonement is relatively unique in this regard, for without the doctrine of sin, there is no need for it; without a doctrine of salvation (or eschatology), there is no reason for it; without anthropology (and demonology, etc.), there are no agents for whom it would be relevant; above all, without the triune God acting in and through this event, there would be no ultimate meaning, significance and purpose to this action which transcended the history of fallen creaturely existence. In short, the atonement is a uniquely synthetic doctrine, for it is the point at which all Christian theology comes together.

While one could go on to develop the natural and necessary relationships between the atonement and every Christian doctrine,

---

[32]Cf. the McIntyre, *Soteriology*, 63ff.

[33]Webster writes: '[S]oteriology pervades the entire corpus of Christian teaching, and its exposition necessarily entails sustained attention to trinitarian and incarnational dogma, as well as to the theology of creatures and their ends.' In other words, to properly study soteriology is to study the whole of Christian doctrine. Webster, 'It Was the Will', 15–16.

[34]Whether this ought to be the case is an altogether different question.

for the purposes of our present task, we highlight five main elements essential to every theory of the atonement, which cohere as an image or metaphor. Together, they set the cast and plot for the drama unfolding in the work of Jesus Christ.[35] Together, these five features allow us to explore the logic of the atonement, the specific ways in which Christ's death and resurrection was the triune God's chosen way of overcoming sin and reconciling all things to himself. For while the whole of Christian doctrine is bound up with the atonement, these five elements prove to be essential ingredients in explaining the necessity, efficacy and meaning of the cross and empty tomb, providing a helpful framework within which the rest of Christian doctrine can be brought to bear. To be clear, my intent in this section is not descriptive, but prescriptive: these are necessary criteria for a full and sufficient theory of the atonement, serving as standards for analysing and critiquing any given theory of the atonement.[36]

The first element to consider is *the cast*, for without a cast there is no drama, no action. The triune God, Father, Son and Holy Spirit, maker of heaven and earth takes centre stage, with special attention to Jesus Christ, the incarnate Son of God. The drama revolves around this one person, Jesus Christ, as the one who unites in himself the life, purpose and character of God on the one hand, and the plight of creation on the other. In addition, we must add humankind, for as the Nicene Creed states, it was 'for us and for our salvation' that God became man. Beyond that, however, there are a whole host of characters playing a role: Satan and the fallen angels on the one hand, and the angelic hierarchies on the other play a (more or less prominent) part, as does the created order generally, both in the form of animals and the earth itself. At present, we will direct our attention to the first two members of our cast (the triune God and humankind), returning to the others in Chapter 6.

The second element we consider is the doctrine of God upon which the theory is built, and in particular *the divine attribute or*

---

[35]For other delineations of the elements constitutive of theories of the atonement, cf. *TD*, 240–43.

[36]Barth and von Balthasar offer particularly helpful alternative ways of parsing out the constitutive elements of a theory. Cf. *CD* IV/1, 275–83 and *TD*, 240–43. We will not develop the point at present, but I would argue that these formulations are compatible with (and in significant ways the inspiration for) my own construal.

set of divine attributes which it emphasizes – for it is this attribute (or set thereof) which provides the primary means of describing the relations between these two members of our cast. While God has many attributes, and we should resist limiting these arbitrarily, we naturally do so when speaking of the atonement for the sake of developing something concrete to say. An attempt to incorporate all the attributes of God into a statement about the work of Christ would either be impossible or impracticable – one needs to start somewhere. Accordingly, the selection of one or two divine attributes is necessary for coherent speech about the work of Christ, and, as we will see in Chapter 4, such a selection is of decisive significance for the shape of the ensuing account of the work of Christ.

Think back to the theologians we have surveyed thus far: Irenaeus' emphasis on God's incorruptibility, Athanasius' commitment to the goodness of God, Anselm's use of God's honour, Calvin's development of God's righteousness and justice, which is brought to the point of overemphasis in Turretin. None of these theologians would deny the attributes chosen by the others (even if they might develop them somewhat differently); yet each emphasized one attribute in particular by means of which to explain the necessity or governing impetus behind the work of God in Christ, even while mentioning and occasionally drawing upon other attributes. And this selection, a necessary reality given the time-bound constraints of human thought and speech patterns, plays an immense role in shaping our understanding of Christ's work.

The third element is derivative of the second, for it is that which denies and perverts the will and ultimately the character or attributes of God, by bending in on itself.[37] It is that which Christ overcomes – for without that which opposes God and his will, there would be no need for the death of Jesus Christ. The atonement, as we know it, confronts our sin and its consequences, and our development of sin within the doctrine explains the nature of our plight and opposition to God. But because (per Augustine) sin is not a creature of God, but rather a perversion of God's character and will, there is a precise connection between the second (divine attributes) and third (character of sin) elements, rooted in the parasitical nature of sin as

---

[37] Cf. Matt Jenson, *Gravity of Sin: Augustine, Luther and Barth on 'Homo Incurvatus in Se'* (New York: T & T Clark, 2006).

a perverse imitation or distortion of God's character. Accordingly, where Irenaeus dwells on God's incorruptibility, sin is corruption leading to death; where Anselm notes God's honour, our sin is dishonour; and where Calvin attends to God's righteous justice, we stand guilty. Sin ultimately consists in all of these dimensions simultaneously, but we necessarily emphasize certain aspects of this complex reality both in regard to the atonement and as a matter of course in everyday life.

Just as the second and third elements are intrinsically related (the latter being a creaturely corruption of the former), the fourth and fifth are likewise connected, consisting of *that which Christ came to save us from* and *that which he came to save us for*.[38] Inherent in any theory of the atonement is the explanation of how God in Christ makes our sinful human existence his own, so as to do away with it through his life, death and resurrection. As our substitute and representative, Christ brings the divine life into contact with the reality of our sin, making our condition his own, that he might overcome it for the sake of his creatures and their salvation.[39] We consider the substitutionary work of Christ in the next section, and for the time being note that the work of Christ is a negative, judging and destroying work. The death resulting from our sin (Gen. 2:17), the curses of the broken covenant (Deut. 28:15-68), the world powers to which we were subject (Gal. 4:4; Col. 2:20) and so on. We and the world around us are full of the reality of sin and it was the work of Christ to do away with these threats to our flourishing by destroying the boundaries, paying the price, dispossessing the powers, being the ransom, dispelling fears and doing away with death. Every theory of the atonement hinges on some aspect of sin (element three), and in this fourth element, brings that aspect of sin into the divine life through the incarnate Son, so as to do away with it for us and for our salvation.

---

[38]Or, as Campbell puts it: '[T]he retrospective, referring to the evil from which that grace brings deliverance; the other prospective, referring to the good which it bestows.' Campbell, *The Nature of the Atonement*, 37.

[39]Luther tells of the amazing and great things that were to be achieved by Christ: '[T]hat the curse, sin, and death were to be destroyed, and that the blessing, righteousness, and life were to replace them – and that through Him the whole creation was to be renewed.' *LW*26, 282. The key is the life-giving 'replacement'.

But doing away with sin and its consequences is not the purpose of the work of Christ, any more than we open a gift in order to throw away the packaging. The fifth element essential for a theory of the atonement is *that for which Christ saves us*. For while Christ does in fact overcome sin in all its dimensions through his death and resurrection, his purpose is not merely to destroy sin, but to fulfil God's creative purposes. As Gunton notes, '[I]t is easy, particularly in our rather moralistic Western tradition, to hold the realms of nature and grace, of creation and redemption, so far apart that the incarnation is made to appear more "interventionist" than it ought.'[40] Gunton goes on to say 'the "intervention" of God for his world is not isolated from the rest of his action, because it is the mediator of creation who comes to ensure that the original purposes of God do not founder in futility'.[41] Every theory of the atonement, then, develops a vision of the fulfilment of creation, of that for which we are saved, both in terms of (1) the eschaton (life in the new creation) and (2) the life we presently live in anticipation of that reality. Whether it be sharing in the divine immortality, living lives of righteousness or enjoying the beatific vision, every account of the atonement explores in some way how Christ fulfils God's work of sharing the divine life with the creature, for the goal is fundamentally positive and creative in nature.

Together, these five elements comprise the basic features that come to life in the form of metaphors. For instance, penal substitution readily embraces judicial imagery in which we stand before God the (loving) judge (element two) as guilty creatures (element three), and Christ bears our sin and guilt (element four), fully addressing both the problem and its consequences, restoring us to lives of righteousness and justice through his resurrection (element five). A character sometimes added to the plot (element one) is the accuser, Satan, who is divested of what power he may have over sinners through Christ's work. Other theories rely upon different imagery or metaphors: *Christus victor* theories often employ warfare imagery, Athanasius uses the image of a portrait painted by an artist (*De inc*, 14) and Gregory of Nyssa refers

---

[40]Gunton, *Actuality*, 146.
[41]Ibid.

to Christ as a fish-hook.[42] Such imagery, whether Scriptural or otherwise, is an integral feature of our speech, bringing life and colour to our discourse about Christ's work, as well as imaginative connections necessary for development in thought.

This strength of metaphorical language[43] has its attending weaknesses however, for it can guide and bias us to certain emphases or imbalances. *Christus victor*, for instance, can be explored by means of zoological imagery (think of references to Satan as a roaring lion or a serpent) or by means of truth-telling categories, such as deceit (think of the host of questions regarding whether God deceived the devil who had deceived us).[44] Along the same lines, many have claimed that Anselm runs the danger of letting his feudalistic imagery overly determine his approach to the subject matter, impeding what otherwise might have been solid biblical and theological work.[45] When the imagery takes on a life of its own, rooted in cultural rather than biblical soil, we run the risk of producing a bad crop.

Substitution/Representation

These five elements cohere by means of the substitutionary and representative work of Christ, for it is here that all five elements

---

[42]Gregory of Nyssa, 'An Address on Religious Instruction', in *Christology of the Later Fathers*, ed. Edward R. Hardy (Philadelphia: Westminster Press, 1954), 301.

[43]There are those who seem to reduce the power of the atonement to its power as a metaphor or image. E.g. Delores S. Williams, 'Black Women's Surrogacy Experience and the Christian Notion of Redemption', in *Cross Examinations: Readings on the Meaning of the Cross Today*, ed. Marit Trelstad (Minneapolis: Fortress, 2006), 27–8. While Williams is particularly sensitive to the abuses of the cross as an image, she seems to neglect the reality of the cross and resurrection, by which the image can be interpreted and judged.

[44]On the question of deceit, cf. Nyssa, 'An Address on Religious Instruction', 302–4; Anselm, 'The Devotions of Saint Anselm', 106–8; Kevin Vanhoozer, 'Ezekiel 14: "I, the Lord, Have Deceived That Prophet": Divine Deception, Inception, and Communicative Action', in *Theological Commentary: Evangelical Perspectives*, ed. R. Michael Allen (New York: T & T Clark, 2011).

[45]For a valuable corrective to this critique, see: Southern, *Saint Anselm: A Portrait in a Landscape*, 107–14.

coexist in a single person, in a single history and act.[46] In Christ, the triune God becomes man in the person of the Son, joining together the two central characters in the drama (first element). And inasmuch as Christ is a creature, in him all of creation finds a place, for he is the 'firstborn of all creation. For by him all things were created . . . all things were created through him and for him. And he is before all things, and in him all things hold together' (Col. 1:15-17). In Christ, the one who holds all things together has entered that same reality, and the drama takes place in he who is simultaneously the key actor and the one who holds and sustains the stage upon which he acts. But because Jesus is both God and man, we find in him the second and third elements: the fullness of the divine character and attributes on the one hand, and the fullness of human existence on the other, including the reality of sin and its implications. And as Jesus moves towards Golgotha, these elements take on new life, as Christ does away with the sin by suffering its full reality (fourth element), and establishes us in the life of God through the resurrection (fifth element). In Christ, that is, all five elements cohere in a single life and work.

The key is to hold the appropriate balance between substitution and representation on the one hand, and an account of Christ bearing our sin on the other.[47] Scripture states that Christ was our

---

[46]I distinguish between a representational/substitutional theory on the one hand, and a *penal* substitution theory on the one hand. While the former may be filled out in a penal manner via the divine justice, it is a broader and more flexible framework inviting development through a range of diving attributes. Note the difference between 'vicarious substitution' and 'penal substitution' in Michael Horton's systematic theology. The later specifies the former within a judicial framework, not noting the way that this conflicts with earlier statements about divine simplicity. Michael Horton, *The Christian Faith: A Systematic Theology for Pilgrims on the Way* (Grand Rapids, MI: Zondervan, 2011), 499, 514. Cf. Cousar's point that Paul develops the substitutionary motif independently of the penal dimension. Cousar, *A Theology of the Cross: The Death of Jesus in the Pauline Letters*, 79.

[47]As Gunton notes, '[I]t seems unlikely that any conception [of the atonement] that remains true to the Bible can avoid [substitution]. What makes all the difference is the way in which difference theologies conceive substitution.' Gunton, *Actuality*, 130, 164–5. Even Boff, who wants to challenge traditional accounts of substitution, proposes something along those lines with regard to the resurrection of Christ. Boff, *Passion*, 91, 101. For an altogether different understanding of the relationship between representation and substitution, cf. Dorothee Sölle, *Christ the Representative: An Essay in Theology after the 'Death of God'* (London: SCM Press, 1967).

substitute, in that things happened to him so that they would not have to happen to us. For instance, in Romans 3:25, God puts Christ forward as a propitiation/expiation by his blood, since God in his divine forbearance had passed over former sins.[48] While scholars are far from unanimous in their interpretation of this passage, it seems clear that in this particular case something happened to Christ which should have befallen us, but instead fell upon Christ, as in the argument of Romans 3–8. But it states just as strongly that he was our representative in a strong sense – what happened to Christ happened to us because we are in him (Rom. 6). So on the one hand, we are in him and what happens to him happens to us. But on the other hand, what happened to him was a unique experience he underwent so that we might be spared from it. As Torrance puts it:

If representation and substitution are combined and allowed to interpenetrate each other within the incarnational union of the Son of God with us in which he has actually taken our sin and guilt upon his own being, then we may have a profounder and truer grasp of the vicarious humanity in the mediatorship of Christ, as one in which he acts in our place, in our stead, on our behalf but out of the ontological depths of our actual human being.[49]

This substitutionary/representative complex creates space in which our identity is bound up with that of Christ, while also preventing

---

Regarding Christ's bearing of our sin, Crisp suggests that this substitution (at least in accounts of penal substitution) is usually, though not always, accounted for by means of 'forensic fiction'. Oliver Crisp, 'Original Sin and Atonement', in *The Oxford Handbook of Philosophical Theology*, ed. Thomas P. Flint and Michael C. Rea (New York: Oxford University Press, 2009), 436. In my readings, I have not found this to be the case. And, regardless of the historical question, I find it far more profitable to think in terms of Christ taking upon himself our sin, and thereby its consequences, as one finds in: Benedict XVI, *Jesus*, 155, 214–15.

[48]The Greek term is ἱλαστήριον, interpreted either as 'propitiation' or 'expiation'. The debate over this term is extensive. The following two sources provide competing interpretations and helpful sources for further study: Belousek, *Atonement*, 244–52; Donald A. Carson, 'Atonement in Romans 3:21–26', in *The Glory of the Atonement: Biblical, Historical & Practical Perspectives: Essays in Honor of Roger R. Nicole*, ed. Charles E. Hill and Frank A. James (Downers Grove, IL: InterVarsity Press, 2004).

[49]Thomas F. Torrance, *The Mediation of Christ* (Colorado Springs, CO: Helmers & Howard, 1992), 80–1.

us from being entirely absorbed into him, such that we retain our own identity in him. We died in Christ, yet die our own deaths, the latter taking place and being transformed within the former. We are made one with God in Christ, and yet must confess, repent, be baptized and be transformed in him. To be human is to be in Christ, but to be in him in such a way that our identity in him includes our own identity. Christ acts on our behalf and out of the ontological depths of our human being, creating the space within which we are freed to do the same.

And this Christ, our substitutionary/representative Mediator, bore our sin.[50] That Christ acts out of the ontological depths of our actual human being means that he takes our sinful human existence into himself, that he becomes sin (2 Cor. 5:21).[51] He does this by 'taking to Himself the sins of all men' (*CD* IV/1, 94).[52] This is no mere 'forensic fiction' where we speak 'as if' this were true. Christ took upon himself our sin and its consequences, relating to the Father on that basis (*CD* IV/1, 95).[53] In Christ, we have the five central elements essential to the atonement, for in him we have the central characters of the drama united in person, the character of God and the nature of our sin, brought to a climax in the death and resurrection with all that these entail for those represented in the substitutionary work of Christ. These five elements are essential, in other words, because they are constitutive elements of a thorough understanding of the person and work of Jesus; they are who he is and what he did.

---

[50]Luther writes that Christ 'bore the person of a sinner and a thief – and not of one but of all sinners and thieves. For we are sinners and thieves, and therefore we are worthy of death and eternal damnation. But Christ took all our sin upon Himself, and for them died on the cross. Therefore it was appropriate for Him to become a thief and, as Isaiah says (53:12), to be "numbered among the thieves".' *LW* 26, 277 (cf. 277–91). Luther proceeds to distinguish between sins Christ committed (which he rejects) and those which he bore for us (which he affirms).

[51]von Balthasar, *Action*, 4: The Action, 241.

[52]Barth writes that Jesus is rejected by God as a sinner, 'that he not only stands under the wrath and accusation of God, but because this wrath is well-founded, and this accusation is true, he stands under His sentence and judgment' (CD IV/1, 173).

[53]This is in stark contrast to James Alison's parody of substitutionary atonement. James Alison, 'God's Self-Substitution and Sacrificial Inversion', in *Stricken by God? Nonviolent Identification and the Victory of Christ*, ed. Brad Jersak and Michael Hardin (Grand Rapids, MI: Eerdmans, 2007), 172.

5 Key Questions to Ask

To recapitulate the above material, every theory of the atonement builds upon one or more divine attributes to develop its particular perspective on the way Christ's substitutionary/representative death and resurrection changes the relationship between the various members of the cast. Drawing upon these attributes, it accounts for the nature of our sin and its ramifications (which is exposed by these attributes), as well as the nature of our salvation from this reality, and for a life of creaturely fulfilment with God. In order to translate this thesis into a helpful hermeneutic for future studies of the atonement, the present section converts each of the above elements into a question we can use in engaging other theories of the atonement. The questions are as follows:

1 What is the cast assembled in this work on the atonement?

In some ways this is the simplest question, for it is not difficult to discern whether a theory limits itself to the relationship between God and humankind, or whether it includes other members in its cast. However, a nuanced approach to this question yields a far more interesting and demanding task. Is all the emphasis upon humankind, while God merely provides a solution? Or is all the focus upon God and his sovereignty, with only a token role given to his covenant partners? Are demons begrudgingly acknowledged, and quickly transformed into 'social forces of evil'? A different kind of nuance pertains to the way in which the theory provides the resources for thinking of those members of the cast it minimizes, or those it omits altogether. Does it leave room for their inclusion, or even provide resources for such a move? Does it exclude them as a matter of principle? Discerning the members of a cast is a simple task; determining the relative importance of those members, and how this particular theory treats or excludes other potential members is a much more delicate activity, providing excellent resources for expanding, developing and correcting theories of the atonement.

2 What divine attribute, or set thereof, does this particular theory of the atonement emphasize?

At the heart of each of these theories is an account of the divine character. At times, one attribute might seem to be central to the theory, but upon deeper inspection, a second attribute shapes its meaning and significance such that this second attribute proves most influential for the theory as a whole. Determining the attribute (or set thereof) that is most influential for the theory is relatively straightforward, as this tends to be the attribute most spoken of with regard to the character of God, and the one that is most prominent in accounts of why the death of Christ was necessary. Beyond this is a set of more difficult questions to answer: are there attributes that are intentionally omitted or misconstrued in the development of this theory? Is there conflict or tension between attributes that is either necessary for or detrimental to this account? And is this attribute developed in keeping with the full biblical witness to this reality (and if not, how would doing so change not only the understanding of the attribute, but of the whole theory upon which it is built)?

3 What aspect of our sin does this particular theory focus on?

Some theories characterize sin as bondage, others as guilt, while others might focus on shame. Descriptions of sin and the human plight often leap from the page, making this question relatively easy to answer. But this is just the beginning. How does this account of sin relate to the divine attribute highlighted by this theory? How does this account of sin relate to other aspects of sin in the biblical witness? Does this theory explore sin largely in terms of its essence, consequences, or both? And does it think of sin as something we are passively afflicted with, or actively do to others and ourselves? Beyond this, is sin understood individualistically, socially or cosmically? These questions open up a host of possibilities for developing and critiquing theories. Equally importantly, they offer a roundabout way for determining the key divine attribute for a theory, inasmuch as sin simply is a rebellious creaturely perversion of the character or attributes of God. While the theory may not speak much of the character of God, its consistent emphasis upon pride would suggest an emphasis upon the humility of God as the key attribute to consider.

4 How does this theory develop Christ saving us from sin?

Does Christ bear the wrath of God? Does he suffer the shame of being crucified? Is he the outcast, the exile? Is he tempted in our place, or abandoned by God? A full answer includes all of the above, but each theory will highlight one or more of these elements, filling them with detail and significance, relating them to the biblical material on the subject and the Church's subsequent reflections. Is Christ's experience that of Israel's Exodus and suffering in the desert, or the plight of the poor and disposed? Each of these alternatives brings with it powerful resources for the Church to empathize with and challenge similar experiences in the lives of those around us. Even if a theory, such as one might find in Reformed, liberation, medieval scholastic or feminist work, doesn't do justice to other aspects necessary for a full and complete account of the work of Christ in such a way as one might wish, answers to this question provide a foothold – a place from which we can go on to develop the other aspects. Because the doctrine of the atonement is synthetic, finding incomplete theories is an impetus for development, rather than an occasion for blame or censure.

5 *How does this theory develop Christ saving us for life with God and others?*

This may be the hardest question to answer, for the simple and unfortunate reason that theologians throughout the centuries have tended to overlook the significance of the resurrection as the decisive and life-giving dimension of the doctrine of the atonement: the affirmation that Christ saved us for something. How does a theory construe heaven, if it speaks of it? As rest, knowledge, wisdom, obedience or righteousness? And how does it challenge Christians to live in light of that reality? As we will see in Chapter 5, the atonement is first and foremost constructive and life-giving. Being at-one with God is no mere matter of cleansing ourselves from sin or ridding evil from our lives. Rather, it is a matter of being holy as God is holy, righteous as he is righteous and so forth. Regrettably often, this question will go unanswered, or receive only limited attention, awaiting further development at the hand of theologians to come.

These questions offer a well-rounded approach to considering the strengths and weaknesses of various theories of the atonement, as well as avenues for critiquing and developing these theories constructively. Moreover, as we will see in the concluding chapter, these questions provide a framework for extending strictly theological accounts of the atonement into broader areas of thought, such as film, literature, philosophy and other areas of life. The challenge is to use them in a nuanced manner so as to discern the subtle omissions, conflicts and tensions on the one hand, and the brilliant insights, syntheses and applications on the other, rather than mechanically answer the questions based on whatever answer happens to leap off the page most quickly and forcefully. And because of the synthetic nature of the doctrine, the (relative) omission of answers to one or more of these questions is not so much a problem as it is an opportunity for constructive development of doctrine.

As an exercise to familiarize ourselves with these elements (and the respective questions we should ask to access them), we will see how they play themselves out in the thought of Hugo Grotius.

Governmental theory of the atonement[54]

In response to Faustus Socinus, Grotius offered what has become known as the governmental theory of the atonement. Beginning with a clear summary of 'The Catholic Doctrine', he writes:

> God was moved by his own goodness to bestow distinguished blessings upon us. But since our sins, which deserved punishment, were an obstacle to this, he determined that Christ, being willing of his own love toward men, should, by bearing the most severe tortures, and a bloody and ignominious death, pay the penalty for our sins, in order that without prejudice to the exhibition of divine justice, we might be liberated, upon the intervention of true faith, from the punishment of eternal death. (*DCF*, 2)

We find in this statement all the key elements of penal substitution: (1) the cast, consisting of God, Christ and ourselves; (2) the character of God, with particular emphasis upon the goodness and justice of God; (3) our sin, construed as guilt deserving punishment; (4) the vicarious work of Christ in which he pays the penalty for our sins through his suffering and death and (5) our ensuing salvation in

---

[54]In this general outline of Grotius' thought, I overlook a number of important insights and distinctions, some of which are explored in Oliver Crisp, 'Penal Non-Substitution', in *A Reader in Contemporary Philosophical Theology*, ed. Oliver Crisp (New York: T & T Clark, 2009).

the form of liberation from punishment (*DCF*, 13). This much one could find in proponents of penal substitution from Calvin to J. I. Packer,[55] though one might wish for a better account of the fifth element: that for which Christ saves us. It would seem that we have found a neat and tidy summary of Grotius' thought that answers all our questions.

One word stands out in this statement, however, calling for careful attention: the suffering of Christ paid the penalty for our sins without prejudice to the *exhibition* of divine justice. This word, as it turns out, is highly significant for Grotius. Subsequent to this passage, he clarifies:

> The end of the transaction of which we treat, the intention of God and Christ . . . is two-fold; namely, the exhibition of the divine justice, and the remission of sins with respect to us, i.e. our exemption from punishment. For if you take the exaction of punishment impersonally, its end is the exhibition of the divine justice; but if personally, i.e. why was Christ punished, the end is that we might be free from punishment. (*DCF*, 33)

Grotius draws his notion of exhibition from Paul's statement that Christ was set forth by God as a propitiation/expiation (ἱλαστήριον) in his blood 'to declare his righteousness for the remission of sins that are past, through the forbearance of God' (Rom. 3:25-26). The point Grotius grasps in this passage is that it was necessary not only that Christ deliver us from our punishment, but that he do so in such a way as to clearly manifest or declare that he is in fact a just God – one who acts justly precisely because he is the source of all justice. The reality and its promulgation are equally essential, as Grotius understands Paul. Working with the same passage, von Balthasar makes the same point about God's ultimate plan: '"The demonstration of his (covenant-) righteousness" is the pillar of atonement.'[56] But why does Grotius so emphasize terms like 'appearance', 'showing', 'demonstration' and 'exhibition'? Clearly he is no exemplarist – so what is his underlying motive?

---

[55]James I. Packer, 'What Did the Cross Achieve: The Logic of Penal Substitution', *Tyndale Bulletin* 25 (1974): 3–45.
[56]von Balthasar, *Action*, 4: The Action, 206.

The key lies in the divine attribute Grotius highlights in this work (element two). While the above passages might lead one to conclude that the attribute in question would be justice, Grotius locates his treatment of justice within a broader perspective provided by what we might loosely call the Lordship of God: 'Socinus confesses that we are treating of liberation from punishment. We add that we also are speaking of infliction of punishment. From this it follows that in all this subject God must be treated as Ruler' (*DCF*, 51). On this basis he concedes Socinus' point that 'God is not here to be looked at as a judge placed under the law. Such a judge as that could not liberate the guilty from punishment, even by transferring the punishment to another' (*DCF*, 53). But rather than dismissing justice altogether, Grotius locates it in the activity of a ruler rather than a mere judge, who is thus free to enact his justice with a flexibility beyond the pay-grade of a judge.

Within the emphasis of God as ruler, Grotius pairs the justice of God with his wisdom: 'God . . . determined to employ the tortures and death of Christ to set forth a weighty example against the great crimes of all of us with whom Christ was very closely connected by his nature and kingdom and suretyship.' This, he affirms, 'was done not only justly, but also wisely, by a God most wise and most just' (*DCF*, 100–1). This emphasis upon wisdom is significant, for it highlights the way in which God, as ruler, is an exceedingly benevolent ruler: 'benevolence . . . is, of all the attributes of God, the most truly peculiar to him' (*DCF*, 105). A benevolent ruler, as distinct from an absolute ruler, cares not only that his rule or will is followed, but that it is followed freely, with both understanding and appreciation. For this reason he necessarily pairs God's justice with the wisdom befitting a ruler, that the justice of God might enact itself in such a way as to be both fully just, and serve as a wonderful example of his divine attributes. The result is an emphasis on the 'distinguished example' provided by Christ which is so marked as to give the appearance of exemplarism, without succumbing to the weaknesses of that approach.

How does this nuanced examination of Grotius' central attribute (element two) shape our understanding of the other elements of this theory? With regard to the cast (element one), it readily branches out (though Grotius himself does not do this), to include all those things affected by the rule of God, particularly those creatures in addition to ourselves which were created to freely and knowingly relate to the rule of God: angels and demons. That God is ruler highlights our sin (element three) as a wilful and insolent deviation from the will of God, with disastrous consequences for the order necessary to our own and the common good. One thinks here of *The Count of Monte Cristo* and the tragedy of a rule so distorted as to be beneficial to some, but disastrous to others, of *Pride and Prejudice* and our silly and destructive attempts to create artificial social orders, or of *The Tale of Two Cities*, and the nightmare unleashed by the crumbling of order into anarchy.

Grotius' unique perspective subtly alters the way penal substitution thinks about Christ's death, in that the punishment borne by Christ has a distinctively anthropocentric direction (though not in exclusion to the Godward emphasis). 'All punishment has as its object the common good, viz. the preservation of order, and the giving of example' (*DCF*, 64). While vicarious punishment remains, Grotius heightens our awareness of the public and exposed nature of crucifixion; a political punishment intended to secure order through its brutality.[57] Moreover, it calls to mind that in this act Christ was not merely fulfilling justice but being obedient to the will of the Father (Lk. 22:42). Christ fully enters the situation of the insolent and disobedient, suffering the fate of a revolutionary, but does so willingly and obediently, acceding to the rule of God where we only fail to do so.

Positively (element five), this offers us the hope of life in a kingdom in which order and flourishing go hand in hand because the ruler and ruled are of one accord, delightedly participating in an order so keeping with the nature of things that there is no more pain and suffering. This vision, in turn, provokes us to behaviour anticipating that impending reality in the families, schools, neighbourhoods in which we live, not to mention broader international affairs.

But what are we to make of such a 'governmental' theory of the atonement – an account of Christ focusing on God as ruler, which accordingly integrates the benevolence, justice and wisdom of God in such a way as to uniquely emphasize God's longing to make known his justice throughout the creation he rules? The first thing to note is that this is a clearly distinct theory from penal substitution. Sharing many elements in common with penal substitution, it

---

[57]Hengel, *Crucifixion*, 46–50.

is nevertheless distinct at every point, including justice within an overarching concern with the rule of God. Second, we must acknowledge that Scripture concerns itself deeply with questions of the lordship or rule of God, not least in its development of the kingdom theme, and therefore appreciate, as much as possible, the contribution this theory makes to integrating this and related themes to the work of Christ. Third, the question remains how we should understand this (and other theories) in relation to each other, and in relation to the question of orthodoxy. To this question we now turn.

The question of orthodoxy

Such an affirmation of multiple theories begs the question of orthodoxy – for if I treat Athanasius, Anselm and Grotius so charitably, embracing their respective insights, why wouldn't I do the same with Socinus, whose work is typically rejected as unorthodox? In answer, it should be obvious by now that we should reject labelling any single theory of the atonement as *the* authoritative teaching of the Bible and/or Church regarding the saving work of Christ. Orthodoxy is not a matter of a single theory of the atonement. Moreover, we should resist locating orthodoxy at the level of theory at all, as though we could simplistically affirm one theory as orthodox, while rejecting another. While such moves may in fact have their place, orthodoxy is primarily a matter of the constituent elements and their relation to the material and formal witness of Scripture. Orthodoxy supervenes on a theory, one might say, by means of the orthodoxy of its constituent parts. And inasmuch as the Bible offers a manifold answer to each of the questions asked by a theory, the Bible offers resources for an abundance of orthodox atonement theories. Orthodoxy, in this case, is an abundant rather than monolithic orthodoxy; more of a flower-filled alpine meadow than a knife-like ridge.

Theories of the atonement are to be built upon the witness of Scripture, and are to be judged accordingly.[58] The character

---

[58]McIntyre suggests that in addition to '[congruence] with the biblical accounts of the death of Christ', theories must 'cohere' with those models of the atonement developed by the Church as an extension of that norm. McIntyre, *Soteriology*, 85.

of God, the nature of our sin . . . each of the five elements of a theory (and the imagery implicit in and enlivening the theory) – all stand or fall inasmuch as they are supported or rejected by the witness of Scripture. For instance, we should hold Anselm's use of honour accountable to that of Scripture, considering whether (as many critics would have it) the former has departed from the latter in favour of a more medieval feudalistic understanding of the term, or whether, as I find more likely, it was Anselm's way of capturing the biblical notion of honour, particularly as it comes to life in the concepts of 'name' and 'glory'. Likewise, we should explore liberation theology's account of sin as bondage, honouring the biblical witness to bondage both as imposed from without (as in the case of the Israelites in Egypt), and the internal bondage to sin (made so manifest in the post-Exodus story of Israel). No theory is immune from the critique of Scripture, for theology lives with the constant temptation to abstract from the biblical witness, adjusting its concepts and images to suit its own needs. Theories of the atonement have a particularly complex relationship to Scripture and orthodoxy, in that weaving together the five above elements makes for complex, synthetic readings of the biblical material, and therefore an ever-vulnerable claim to orthodoxy, in need of constant revisiting and revision.

Sailing these seas can be relatively straightforward (though sailing is never without its challenges) if Scripture robustly develops all five of the elements of a theory in question. Things get choppier as the wind picks up and theology becomes bolder and more venturesome,[59] for its task is not merely to catalogue and organize the teaching of Scripture into a systematic rather than occasional form. Rather, theology is meant to inhabit the biblical witness in such a way as to draw out its inner logic, delving into its depths and scaling its heights. As Gregory of Nazianzus, writes, we are meant to see 'inside the written text to its inner meaning' and 'perceive the hidden loveliness'.[60] The doctrine of the Trinity, for

---

[59] Or, as Davidson puts it, more 'properly radical'. Davidson, 'Introduction: God of Salvation', 5.

[60] Gregory of Nazianzus, *On God and Christ*, trans. Frederick Williams and Lionel Wickham (Crestwood, NY: St. Vladimir's Seminary Press, 2002), 133. Cf. Kitamori's delightful claim along similar lines in Kazo Kitamori, *Theology of the Pain of God* (Richmond: John Knox Press, 1965), 45.

instance, is nowhere stated in Scripture as such. While the pattern of thinking in terms of Father, Son and Holy Spirit is pervasive in the New Testament, it took the Church centuries to explore and give words to this architectonic feature of the biblical witness. The Church gradually came to discern this aspect of the being and life of God and the way that it shaped and characterized the biblical witness – and once it came to appreciate this logic, used it as one of the key theological tools for interpreting Scriptural passages which themselves did not bear directly on the Trinity.[61]

Much the same is true with the doctrine of the atonement. While certain aspects of the work of Christ are clearly developed, and the coherence of some theories with the Scriptural norm is simple to ascertain, the goal of theology is not merely to categorize these and form them into theories of the atonement.[62] Beyond this, theology strives to fulfil the greater task of delving into the reality of Christ's atonement through Scripture. The reason for this is twofold. First, the Bible, as witness, plays a mediating role, in that our goal is to know and worship the triune God. We honour the authoritative role of Scripture not by focusing *on it*, but by focusing upon the God of our salvation *through it*.[63] Second, the logic of the atonement is so ubiquitous in Scripture that we guarantee that we will misread Scripture if we focus solely upon those passages that seem to speak most clearly about the atonement. By means of those passages, we should develop patterns of thought equipping us for further Scripture reading, characterized at every point by an understanding and appreciation of the death and resurrection of Jesus Christ (1 Cor. 2:2), and the way that it impacted every aspect of creation.

The net effect of such an approach to the question of orthodoxy is dramatic, with significant ecumenical implications. The biggest difference is that such a perspective lends itself to an eager interaction with views foreign to one's own in the hopes of attaining a yet richer orthodoxy, as opposed to a factious approach in which any

---

[61]Cf. Sherman, *King, Priest and Prophet*, 49.

[62]To be sure, we 'acknowledge the priority of biblical concepts and titles, drawing upon them as the normative prophetic and apostolic stock of language and ideas which constitute governing material content of dogmatic reflection', and 'allow [ourselves] only such conceptual inventiveness and argumentative reordering of this material as serves to direct us to the biblical *positum*'. Webster, 'It Was the Will', 16.

[63]C. S. Lewis, 'Meditation in a Toolshed', in *God in the Dock: Essays on Theology and Ethics*, ed. Walter Hooper (Grand Rapids, MI: Eerdmans, 1970).

difference in understanding necessarily means that at least one or the other view is unorthodox and heretical. Proponents of liberation theology, as seen, for instance, in the work of Leonardo Boff, need not approach books on the work of Christ as divinization with fear – for assuming that both views are biblically grounded, they stand to gain by the exchange. The second implication is an extension of the first to the ecclesiological level.[64] Lutheran churches, for example, will benefit by contemplating the insights of Catholic and Pentecostal churches – for at least in the case of the atonement, orthodoxy is a matter of abundance for which we should hunger, rather than a single prize for which we all must struggle. In the slightly adapted words of McKnight, '[W]hat we are most in need of today is not a continuance of the atonement wars for a privileged [theory], but a vigorous discussion of the value of each of the [theories] so that each . . . is invited to the table.'[65] Our contribution is a properly theological account of the nature and basis of this diversity, to equip and fund further efforts towards this task.

Conclusion/Summary

Understanding atonement theories and the conditions for their orthodoxy in this way frees us to delve more deeply into the doctrine, ready to embrace, critique and develop the theories we encounter. In the following chapters we will do this to some extent, though our focus is bringing deeper understanding to the logic of the doctrine, rather than simply moving on to develop our understanding of more theories. The reason for this is that I intend this book to serve as a guide, cultivating ways of seeing, thinking and acting. To do that properly, we must delve into the heart of the matter: the being and life of the triune God.

---

[64]To a limited extent, this point could be extended to inter-religious dialogue.
[65]McKnight, *Community*, 114. To be clear – the theories in question may need to be substantially revised; this is not an argument for a weak 'tolerance' or universalism when it comes to theories of the atonement.

3

Triune Atonement: The Foundation of the Doctrine

Masaccio's fresco *The Trinity* beautifully depicts the Father, Son and Holy Spirit: Christ is in the centre, crucified, while the Father stands behind him, arms supporting the cross. Between them flies the Holy Spirit in the form of a dove. But why label this crucifixion scene 'The Trinity'? As *The Count of Monte Cristo* suggests, 'It is only at [the moment of death] that one can make a study of character' – a point we will explore at length in this and the ensuing chapter.[1] The death and resurrection of Christ is where the character of God reveals itself most fully: where the attributes of God shine forth most brightly, where the depths of God's self-involvement with creation are revealed, and where the reality of God's triune life enacts itself most clearly and efficaciously for us and for our salvation. Masaccio's naming of his piece was most appropriate, for it is in the passion of Christ that the triune life of God manifests itself most clearly, and for this reason the doctrine of the Trinity likewise affords us the best and fullest perspective from which to understand the meaning and significance of Christ's death and resurrection. 'The bedrock of soteriology is the doctrine of the Trinity. The perfect life of the Holy Trinity is the all-encompassing and first reality from whose completeness all else derives.'[2]

---

[1]Alexandre Dumas, *The Count of Monte Cristo*, trans. Robin Buss (New York: Penguin, 2003), 342.
[2]Webster, 'It Was the Will', 18.

The divine dilemma[3]

The atonement is a response to a problem – but whose problem? The temptation is to dive into questions surrounding Christ's death and resurrection as God's way of dealing with sin and evil; but the resolution of this problem, our salvation, takes place within a bigger, all-encompassing mystery. As Migliore notes, 'Christian theology begins, continues, and ends with the inexhaustible mystery of God.'[4] Our task in the present chapter is to explore some of the ways in which this is the case: the ways in which the atonement begins, continues and ends with this mystery, the ways that 'the perfect life of the Trinity' is 'the bedrock of soteriology'.[5] Approaching the doctrine of the atonement from within this mystery affords us a unique vantage point for perceiving the 'problem' of the atonement.

There are many different ways to express the dilemma underlying the atonement – the crisis for which Christ's saving work is the solution. Typically, explanations canvas some aspect of the human plight: our inability to partake of everlasting life and happiness due to our guilt and uncleanness, our incapacity to offer satisfaction to God, our failure to obey the law and consequent disobedience and necessary punishment, and our bondage to Satan are commonplace answers. In a markedly different approach, Athanasius draws attention to the surprising way in which these different aspects of the human problem take place within an account of God's own dilemma.

> What was God to do? Be silent before such things and let human beings be deceived by the demons and be ignorant of God? But then what need was there in the beginning for human beings to come into being in the image of God? . . . Or what profit would there be to the maker God, or what glory for him, if human beings, brought into being by him, did not revere him but reckoned others to be their maker? For God would be found

---

[3]To balance this emphasis upon the divine dilemma, we would need to expound upon the delight God takes in sharing himself with the creature, in this act of unrestrained freedom and grace.

[4]Migliore, *Faith Seeking Understanding*, 64.

[5]Webster, 'It Was the Will', 18.

creating them for others and not for himself. . . . What then was God to do? (*De inc*, §13)

Why does Athanasius put it this way? Are not our dehumanization, ignorance, deception and death *our* problem? Surely they are the result of our actions, and we suffer their disastrous consequences. Why turn the tables, burdening God with our problem?[6] This seems like the antic of a rebellious teen, blaming her parents for her problems and angst. Is this not the height of impiety, burdening God with a dilemma that is ours and ours alone?

The answer lies within the will of God, for our dilemma, and the whole of creaturely reality within which this dilemma occurs, takes place only because of the prior and fundamental reality of the life and will of the triune God.[7] This God is the maker of heaven and earth: 'All things were made through him, and without him was not anything made that was made' (Jn 1:3). All of reality, all things in heaven and earth receive their nature, existence and purpose from God – a fact entailing far more than the negation of a creative source other than God. For instance, *creatio ex nihilo* means that the resources, inspirations and motives for creating all things were God's alone – God himself, to be precise. As Thomas puts it, '[T]he entire universe, with all its parts, is ordained towards God as its end, inasmuch as it imitates, as it were, and shows forth the Divine goodness, to the glory of God' (*ST*, 1.65.3). God was not motivated

---

[6]McCall rejects the idea that we can 'posit an internal struggle within God's own life'. Thomas H. McCall, *Forsaken: The Trinity and the Cross, and Why It Matters* (Downers Grove, IL: IVP Academic, 2012), 81. While this may seem to contradict the divine dilemma outlined here, that is not the case. McCall is working with struggle within the character of God, between his attributes. This we both reject. I locate the struggle not within the character of God, but between God's purposes and their fulfilment in creation, noting that ultimately all struggle gives way to the efficacy of God's will.

[7]And because it lies within the will of God, at the same time it is a dilemma, it is simultaneously his joy. Julian of Norwich writes of Christ's passion: '[W]hat I am describing now is [such] a great joy to Jesus that he counts as nothing his labour and his sufferings and his cruel and shameful death. . . . The love which made him suffer it surpasses all his sufferings, as much as heaven is above earth. . . . This deed and this work for our salvation were as well devised as God could devise it. It was done as honourably as Christ could do it, and here I saw complete joy in Christ, for his joy would not have been complete if the deed could have been done any better than it was.' Norwich, *Showings*, 216–18. Cf. 279.

by an inspiration external to himself, a competitive desire to outdo someone, or by any lack on his part. His fundamental motive in creation was the grace of sharing himself with that which was yet to be, or as Thomas puts it, for the 'fruition of God' (*ST*, 1.65.3) for the benefit of the creature. In doing so, God glorifies himself anew by sharing his glory.[8]

But since God is the only source for creation, its failure and shame rests first and foremost on him as well. For where the triune God binds to himself a purpose, the fulfilment (or failure) thereof becomes a part of God's identity due to the strength of that bond. Not only is God not honoured when we sin – he is dishonoured by us.[9] Not only is God's name not magnified when we sin – it is taken in vain. God's binding a purpose to himself through both creation and covenant entails God making himself vulnerable in certain ways – vulnerable to being sinned against, being dishonoured and being confronted with dilemmas. Take, for example, the doctrine of the *imago Dei* – that as men and women we are made in the image of God. We typically explore this doctrine anthropologically, attending to those unique characteristics of our creaturely being and vocation. Another way to approach this doctrine is to explore what it means for God to be imaged, or portrayed, by the creatures he has made.[10] In our misrepresentation of God we nonetheless continue to represent him, but do so poorly. And while we may think that this would not affect God, Scripture suggests otherwise. This is the mystery of the self-imposed dilemma of God – where God in his freedom chooses to bind himself to creatures, thereby in a sense binding their failures to himself.

After the incident of the Golden Calf, the Lord tells Moses: 'Now therefore let me alone, that my wrath may burn hot against

---

[8] Jonathan Edwards, 'Dissertation on the End for Which God Created the World', in *The Works of Jonathan Edwards*, ed. Henry Rogers, Sereno Edwards Dwight and Edward Hickman (Peabody, MA: Hendrickson, 1998).

[9] Anselm was wrong to argue 'nothing can be added to, or subtracted from, the honour of God, in so far as it related to God himself. For this same honour is, in relation to him, inherently incorruptible and in no way capable of change.' (*CDH*, 288). The division between God's honour 'in so far as it related to God himself' and in so far as it relates to us is one which should at best be a distinction.

[10] Kathryn Tanner, *Christ the Key* (Cambridge: Cambridge University Press, 2010), 1–57.

[the people] and I may consume them, in order that I may make a great nation of you.' To this, Moses replies: 'O Lord, why does your wrath burn hot against your people, whom you have brought out of the land of Egypt with great power and with a mighty hand? Why should the Egyptians say, "With evil intent did he bring them out, to kill them in the mountains and to consume them from the face of the earth?"' In response, 'The Lord relented from the disaster that he had spoken of bringing on this people' (Ex. 32:10-14). The logic with which Moses pled his case to God is fascinating: a form of national pressure based on what the Egyptians would think. But why would God care about what the Egyptians thought, when he had just devastated them with the plagues, rescuing the Israelites from their grasp?

The answer has to do with how God seeks to be known by his creation. By creating free and rational creatures out of nothing, God bound himself to his creation, vesting himself fully (*TD*, 174) in this enterprise, that his creatures might reflect his glory through knowledge and worship. But failure in the creative project, failure on the part of the creature's understanding and reverence, sully the glory of God, in addition to its consequences for the creature.[11] What does it mean for God to have free and rational creatures failing to know and delight in him? This failure transcends disappointment, or jealousy. If God has bound his purpose to himself and his purpose is failing, then God is failing; our failure to know and worship God is for God to fail to be who he has set out to be, to fail to be worshipped by us.[12] This is why God was so concerned about the reaction of the Egyptians (Ex. 32:12), and why the problem of our misdirected worship (Rom. 1:25) is first and foremost the Creator God's concern: Father, Son and Holy Spirit. The failure of the creature is the failure of the Creator whose creature this is.

---

[11]As we will see in Chapter 6, the glory of God can be sullied to the extent that God puts his glory at stake within creation.

[12]That God is failing does not mean that God fails, for his failing is an act of his patience, ordered towards the fruition of his purposes. That is to say, God is not a God who fails. But as one who fulfils his purposes patiently in relationship with his free creatures, there is a nuanced way in which we can affirm that God and his purposes, can, for a time, be failing, within the overall providence he exercises so as to bring his works to completion.

Why a Mediator?

Our problem is God's problem because God has bound himself to our creaturely thriving in such a way as to make our failure redound to himself. But as Thomas notes, there were any number of possible solutions to this dilemma (*ST*, 3.46.1) – so why the incarnation? Why did the Son come as Mediator? Athanasius suggests that neither men nor angels could have accomplished the work of reconciliation, for men are made after the image of God but are not the image itself, and angels are not made after the image at all – so only the incarnate Son, the Image of God himself, would serve to remake us in the image of God once more (*De inc*, §13). Anselm notes, 'Supposing any other person were to rescue man from eternal death, man would rightly be judged his bondslave. . . . If he were this, he would in no way have been restored to that dignity which he would have had in the future, if he had not sinned' (*CDH*, 1.5). While good answers to the question 'why the incarnation?' abound, we will explore several related answers, providing an entry into the relationship between the Trinity and atonement.

As triune, God is self-knowing, and seeks to involve his creatures in the self-knowing proper to himself (Mt. 11:27) – an involvement redounding to the joy of Creator and creature alike. In our sin we rejected knowledge of God, becoming ignorant and foolish (Gen. 3; Rom. 1). Why did God not choose a means other than himself to accomplish atonement? Because the atonement is not simply a matter of overcoming our plight, but also and primarily a matter of undoing the dilemma by re-establishing God's creative purpose: of involving the creature in his self-knowledge. Why did the Son become our Mediator? That overcoming our sin, bringing us to creaturely fulfilment and sharing with us the divine life might together find their completion in a single source: the life of Jesus Christ. Why did the Son become the Mediator? He did so that the self-investment at the beginning of creation might be equalled or exceeded in bringing that same creation to fulfilment. He did so that the means of overcoming our sin and ignorance might itself be the end for which he saves us: himself.[13]

---

[13]An example of this line of thinking is Jeremy Treat's integration of kingdom and cross theology, where 'God's kingdom is qualified by the cross *and* Christ's death is characterized by God's reign'. Treat, *The Crucified King: Atonement and Kingdom in Biblical and Systematic Theology*, 141. Treat's whole project is oriented towards integrating the cross (as means) and the kingdom (as end).

As triune, God is glorious, eternally glorifying himself as Father, Son and Holy Spirit. Creation was the act of God opening up this self-glorifying work, that God's creatures might enter this exchange of glory. However, in our sin we dishonour God, bestowing glory on ourselves and other creatures (Rom. 1), rejecting the Creator whence all glory comes. Why did God not send someone other than himself to accomplish atonement? Because the atonement is God's reaffirmation of his glory in the face of his dilemma in such a way as to glorify himself, glorify his creatures and free them to join once more in this process of ongoing glorification. Why did the Son come to be the Mediator? To bind himself once more to creation: that the means of overcoming our shame might itself be the entry into and the very locus of the fulfilment of God's original plan to share his glory and honour. Christ's atonement is not simply a means to some distant end, but is itself the reality of God's self-glorification into which we are brought through Christ.

As triune, God is self-loving, eternally loving himself as Father, Son and Holy Spirit. Creation was the act of God sharing this love, that God's creatures might delight in and reciprocate this love to their Creator and each other. In our sin and perversion we elevate ourselves as the chief object of our love, hating our neighbours and Creator. Why did God not send someone other than himself to accomplish atonement? Because the atonement is God's reaffirmation of his love to us in the face of his dilemma by means of bringing his life of love into the circumstances of our life of hate. Why did the Son come to be the Mediator? Because the atonement is not only the means for God to love us, but the love of God itself, enacted for us and for our salvation. The atonement is therefore the means to God's love precisely because it is itself the love of God, shared with us in face of our hate.

Why did God make himself the Mediator? Why did the Son become incarnate, so to accomplish our atonement? And was this necessary? God chose to make himself the Mediator because the atonement is God's reaffirmation of the bond with which he committed himself to his creative purposes.[14] Christ is the reality into which he invites us, rather than a mere means to it, because God's goal always was that he might be the means

---

[14]As Adam Kotsko puts it, 'In Jesus Christ, the purpose of creation persuasively reasserts itself.' Kotsko, *Politics*, 199.

to himself: that he might be in relationship with us. In short, the atonement is God's chosen means of fulfilling his original purpose while simultaneously being that reality into which he invites us. Anything less would be unworthy of the intensity and completeness with which God bound himself, his life, his purposes to the creative project, to us.[15] Only the significance of this choice and the depth of this bond sufficiently explain the jealousy, zeal and even violence of God.

The necessity of Christ's atonement lies not in the nature of our sin, for there are other ways that sin could be dealt with. Neither did it lie in the prophecies needing fulfilment, for these need not have been made. The necessity lies in the divine will itself. To be clear, this necessity does not force God into an undesired path; rather, it is the necessity of relentlessly self-giving divine love, the necessity of the delight God takes in the most fitting or appropriate way to fulfil his creative purposes: sharing the divine life with the creature.[16] The mechanics creating the divine dilemma are the same as those operative in its resolution: the completeness with which God seeks to share himself with his creation. Was Christ's atonement necessary? As Thomas says, it was 'necessary from the necessity of the end proposed' by God (ST, 3.46.1), the necessity of the freedom, grace and love God holds out for us and which we can have, in him.

And in writing of this necessity, we are already working within the sphere of the doctrine of the Trinity, for assumed throughout all this material is the belief that as Father, Son and Holy Spirit, God 'is self-expending, other-affirming, community-building love', and that it is this 'exchange of love' within the triune life that constitutes the basis of both that for which God saves us and the means by which he does so.[17] The business of the doctrine of the Trinity is to explore precisely this: to 'describe God in terms of shared life and

---

[15]Sanders, while noting that there may have been other ways that God could have accomplished the same result, affirms that 'the one thing we know is that what God in fact chose to do was to give himself to us personally to be our salvation. Apparently that self-giving is what counts for God as the kind of salvation he wants to extend to fallen humankind.' Sanders, *The Deep Things of God: How the Trinity Changes Everything*, 120.

[16]'The Trinity and the gospel have the same shape! This is because the good news of salvation is ultimately that God opens his Trinitarian life to us.' Ibid., 98.

[17]Migliore, *Faith Seeking Understanding*, 72.

love' as Father, Son and Holy Spirit,[18] to ponder what it means to affirm that 'in himself and without any reference to a created world or plan of salvation, God is that being who exists as the triune love of the Father for the Son in the unity of the Spirit'.[19] And it is the business of the doctrine of the atonement to unpack the reality of God's triune life as basis for God's saving activity in Christ.

Divine violence

But to bring up the Trinity in this context is a highly contested matter. Recent decades have witnessed a manifold attack on traditional understandings that the death of Christ was an intentional act on the part of God, a chosen means for responding to the divine dilemma.[20] This critique contends that if Christ's death and resurrection accomplishes atonement, then it is by means of an act on the part of the Father that is violently antithetical to the shared life and love of God. Christ's death, understood this way, is a shameful, hateful and violent act on the part of God, and therefore to be rejected.[21] Given the force of this critique in present work on the doctrine, it is impossible to overlook this material precisely at this point in the book. I will briefly sum up these concerns, allowing the constructive arguments that follow to provide a response largely free of polemic.[22]

Feminist theologians have launched a vigorous critique against *Christus victor*, satisfaction (especially penal substitution) and

---

[18]Ibid., 73. I have sought to integrate what Migliore refers to as the 'surface' and 'depth' grammar.

[19]Sanders, *The Deep Things of God: How the Trinity Changes Everything*, 62.

[20]For a recent work highlighting many of the key figures and concerns of this movement, cf. Marit Trelstad, *Cross Examinations: Readings on the Meaning of the Cross Today* (Minneapolis: Fortress, 2006).

[21]Along the lines of Feuerbach, such a move could be little but a projection into the infinite of our own patterns of violence. Ludwig Feuerbach, *The Essence of Christianity*, trans. George Eliot (Amherst, NY: Prometheus Books, 1989), 60–1.

[22]In other words, I will address feminist concerns indirectly, allowing a constructive proposal to take the place of polemic interaction with key feminist texts. As Webster notes, we should 'be cautious about ordering [our] material around some theme (such as "facing" or "hospitality"), or as a response to a perceived problem (such as violence)'. Webster, 'It Was the Will', 16–17.

exemplarist theories of the atonement, rejecting the work of Christ as being in any way a substitutional or surrogate work, opting instead to find in the life of Jesus a 'new vision to see resources for positive, abundant relational life'.[23] They abhor any explanation of the death and resurrection of Christ by means of a dynamic between himself and the Father in which the Father intends the crucifixion of the Son and relates to him as a sinner or as bearing our sin. These theologians deny any such reality within the life of God, understanding any violence or punishment on the part of the Father towards the incarnate Son to be of a wicked and abusive sort.[24] 'If God is imagined as a fatherly torturer, earthly parents are also justified, perhaps even required, to teach through violence. . . . The child or the spouse who believes that obedience is what God wants may put up with physical or sexual abuse in an effort to be a good Christian.'[25]

There are many genuine and valuable insights offered by feminist theology, some of which we will explore elsewhere.[26] For the time being, we focus on the question feminist reflection on the cross raises regarding the role of the Trinity in Christ's death. Feminist theologians largely agree in rejecting the death of Christ as a theologically necessary event, a '*necessary* . . . part of an overall plan of God to reconcile Godself with the world'.[27] This is due to the fact that such an image is said to create a dynamic of violence, oppression and dominance within the Godhead (a dynamic spilling over into deeply harmful social relations). Even granting Moltmann's efforts at making the role of the Trinity in

---

[23]Williams, 'Black Women's Surrogacy', 31.

[24]A recent defence of different kinds of violence can be found in Boersma, *Violence*. Cf. a counter argument in Kotsko, *Politics*, 53–70.

[25]Rita Nakashima Brock and Rebecca Ann Parker, *Proverbs of Ashes: Violence, Redemptive Suffering, and the Search for What Saves Us* (Boston: Beacon Press, 2001), 30–1. On a personal note, I have witnessed the doctrine of the atonement abused in an attempt to keep victims of abuse in dangerous situations. While I am wholly sympathetic with the feminist outrage at this abuse, I am inclined to offer constructive alternatives from within the tradition, rooted in a properly Trinitarian account.

[26]For works which highlight these insights, cf: Arnfríður Guðmundsdóttir, *Meeting God on the Cross: Christ, the Cross, and the Feminist Critique* (Oxford: Oxford University Press, 2010); Tanner, *Christ the Key*, 247–73.

[27]Trelstad, *Cross Examinations*, 15.

Christ's passion a viable alternative within the feminist movement,[28] the question remains for many: 'Can there be salvific power in Christian images of oppression (for example, Jesus on the cross) meant to teach something about redemption?'[29] The question to which we now turn lies at the heart of this critique: in what sense can we describe the death and resurrection of Jesus Christ as a work willed and accomplished by the triune God, without introducing violence and oppression into the life of God and his followers?

The atonement as the work of the one God

Not every critique of the role of the Father, Son and Holy Spirit within the atonement critiques the Christian faith – for not all who speak of a father, a son and a holy spirit are in fact speaking of the triune God of the Gospel. At the heart of many feminist critiques is an account of God bordering on, if not fully embracing, a tritheistic interpretation of the Father, Son and Holy Spirit as distinct entities or personalities, in which the Father relates to the Son in a violent and abusive manner.[30] They employ these words in the way one might when one person acts towards another: a father towards a son, a coach to a player, a robber to a victim. But the Father and the Son are not distinct in the same way that a boss and an employee are distinct entities, for the God of the Gospel is one God, and monotheism is a fundamental commitment at the core of its message: 'Hear O Israel, the Lord our God the Lord is one'

---

[28] Jürgen Moltmann, *The Crucified God: The Cross of Christ as the Foundation and Criticism of Christian Theology* (Minneapolis: Fortress, 1993); 'The Motherly Father: Is Trinitarian Patripassianism Replacing Theological Patriarchalism?', in *God as Father*, ed. Johannes-Baptist Metz, Edward Schillebeeckx and Marcus Lefébvre (New York: Seabury, 1981).

[29] Williams, 'Black Women's Surrogacy', 28.

[30] One finds many such instances in these collections: Trelstad, *Cross Examinations*; Brad Jersak and Michael Hardin, eds, *Stricken by God? Nonviolent Identification and the Victory of Christ* (Grand Rapids, MI: Eerdmans, 2007).

(Deut. 6:4; cf. Mk. 12:29). Concerning the oneness of God, Gregory of Nazianzus writes:

> Monotheism, with its single governing principle, is what *we* value – not monotheism defined as the sovereignty of a single person . . . but the single rule produced by equality of nature, harmony of will, identity of action, and the convergence towards their source of what springs from unity – none of which is possible in the case of created nature.[31]

There is a single nature, substance or essence in God. What it means for God to be God is for God to be a simple rather than composite reality, incapable of division or corruption. What it means for God to be God is for him to be of a single, harmonious will – a will that does not work to accomplish different or conflicting ends, or stem from different or conflicting motives. And because God's nature and will is such, his action is also one: rooted in and utterly faithful to his nature, incapable of failing in this regard as is possible with a composite being made up of parts. Such is the unity between God's acts and his nature that Barth has gone so far as to say that God's being is in his act (*CD* II/1, 257–72): God's being is a living and active being, in which there is no separation between what it means for God to be God (his nature), and the enacted identity of God's life (his act); God is what he does and vice versa. In contrast to all forms of polytheism or tritheism on the one hand, and to any account of unity or oneness inclusive of parts or divisions capable of discord, conflict or separation on the other, God is one.[32]

With that said, the doctrine of the Trinity does not stop with the oneness of God, for this one 'eternally changes to a two and stops at three – meaning the Father, Son and Holy Spirit'.[33] As Thomas puts it, these three objects of belief and worship, these three persons 'signif[y] in God a relation as subsisting in the divine nature [by relation of origin]. . . . There are several real relations in God; and hence it follows that there are also several realities subsistent in the divine nature; which means that there are several persons in God'

---

[31]Nazianzus, *On God*, 70.
[32]As John Stott writes, 'Any notion of penal substitution in which three independent actors play a role . . . is to be repudiated with the utmost vehemence.' John R. W. Stott, *The Cross of Christ* (Downers Grove, IL: Inter-Varsity Press, 1986), 158.
[33]*On God*, 70.

(*ST*, 1.30.1). To account for this feature of the divine life is one of the great challenges of the doctrine of the Trinity, well beyond the scope of the present work. For our purposes, we presuppose as axiomatic the oneness and threeness of God, such that this one, undivided and living God lives, from eternity, in eternal repetition of himself, and therefore in relation to himself. That is to say, because the one God is living, active and personal, in his threefold self-repetition he relates to himself in a living, active and personal way. As Migliore puts it, 'the Trinitarian persons are precisely not self-enclosed subjects who define themselves in separation from and opposition to others. Rather, in God "persons" are relational realities and are defined by intersubjectivity, shared consciousness, faithful relationships, and the mutual giving and receiving of love.'[34] We thus speak 'not of three divine I's', three Gods, 'but thrice of the one divine I' (*CD* I/1, 351). We speak of God relating to God, relating God; and inasmuch as Scriptural names inform this language, we speak of Father, Son and Holy Spirit: one fully relational God.[35]

What happens if we explore the violent death of the incarnate Son from a consistently Trinitarian perspective? We begin by emphasizing the fact that the triune God is one, which means, among other things, that he is of one will: they 'have one will as [they] have one Godhead'.[36] There is no struggle, no difference of will within the Godhead, as if the Father wills one thing, and the Son wills another.[37] Whatever God wills, God wills it as one, whether that is creation, the election of Israel, or the substitutionary death of Christ. This does not mean, of course, that God wills everything he wills monolithically, in the same way – for he wills what he wills in the oneness of the Father, Son and Holy Spirit. Accordingly, we might say that the one God wills the passion of Christ triunely – which is to say, the one God willed the suffering, death and resurrection of Jesus Christ, and yet did so according to his triune mode of living as

---

[34]Migliore, *Faith Seeking Understanding*, 77.

[35]I develop this material in greater depth in relation to Barth's theology in Johnson, *God's Being*, 57–84.

[36]Nazianzus, *On God*, 103.

[37]Even the affirmation that 'God required Jesus' death' goes too far, and is inadequate in its summation of the logic of traditional theories of the atonement. God is not a distinct personality from Jesus, that he might require him to do something. Such language presupposes too much divergence of will. JoAnne Marie Terrell, 'Our Mothers' Gardens: Rethinking Sacrifice', in *Cross Examinations: Readings on the Meaning of the Cross Today*, ed. Marit Trelstad (Minneapolis: Fortress, 2006), 40.

Father, Son and Holy Spirit: the Father by willing the death of the Son, the Son by willing his own death and suffering and the Spirit by willing to accompany the Son in obedience to the Father.[38]

In this we do not suggest that Father, Son and Holy Spirit are three independent persons, such that the Father willed to send someone other than himself to suffer a horrible death. Rather, the one God willed to send himself by means of a threefold willing: as Father he willed to sacrifice; as Son he willed to be sacrificed; and as Spirit he willed to accompany and enable the sacrifice.[39] Willing, sending, sacrificing: God does these things, not as one wills another to do something, or sends a servant to fulfil a task, but as one wills oneself to do a task. The difference between God and ourselves is that God exists in this threefold repetition, so that he can relate to himself as another, without in fact relating to another which is a distinct and separate person. If anything, as McCormack notes, feminists should critique the cross as an instance of masochism, for this is an event God willed for himself, rather than event he willed for another.[40]

Rather than speaking of the violence of Father against Son, it is best to affirm something along Kitamori's claim that 'God himself was broken, was wounded, and suffered, because he embraced those who should not be embraced'.[41] Of course this breaking, wounding and suffering of God occurs in a differentiated manner fitting to the threefold way of being proper to God as Father, Son and Holy Spirit – but it was a genuine suffering of the one God. We speak of this event improperly if we refer to the Father abusing or pouring out his anger upon the Son as though the latter were an entity or being distinct from himself. As Benedict XVI writes:

> It is not a case of a cruel God demanding the infinite. It is exactly the opposite: God himself becomes the locus of reconciliation,

---

[38]Bruce L. McCormack, 'The Ontological Presuppositions of Barth's Doctrine of the Atonement', in *The Glory of the Atonement: Biblical, Historical and Practical Perspectives*, ed. Roger R. Nicole, Charles E. Hill and Frank A. James (Downers Grove, IL: InterVarsity Press, 2004), 362. I use the word 'mode' in the qualified sense employed by Barth – not as a movement towards modalism.

[39]Cf. Nazianzus, *On God*, 96; Davidson, 'Introduction: God of Salvation', 3.

[40]McCormack, 'Ontological Presuppositions', 364.

[41]Kitamori, *Theology of the Pain of God*, 22. von Balthasar grounds this suffering by means of positing a distance or primal kenosis within the immanent Trinity so comprehensive as to ground and allow for 'all we mean by separation, pain and alienation' (*TD*, 319–28).

and in the person of his Son takes the suffering upon himself. . . . God himself 'drinks the cup' of every horror to the dregs and thereby restores justice through the greatness of his love, which, through suffering, transforms the darkness.[42]

It is for this reason that the Father, like the Son, stands with arms outstretched at the cross, with an expression akin to that of his Son, in Masaccio's fresco mentioned at the beginning of the chapter: it affirms the fatherly suffering of God.[43] The cross, we affirm, is the work of the triune God.

The implications of such a vantage point for viewing the Gospel are momentous, particularly in allowing us to reaffirm God's bond with his creation in the form of his utter self-involvement in Christ's atoning work. In sending the Son, the Father does not hold himself back but gives himself fully in giving the Son (cf. *TD*, 52). In coming to us, the incarnate Son does not leave behind the Father, but is the mode of the Father's presence with us. In the death of Christ the Father is not hidden, for his death is the revelation of the Father – the Father who suffers in the suffering of the Son. The death and resurrection of Jesus Christ, in other words, is a threefold act of the triune God – one in which the one God fully enters our situation, making it his own, according to his threefold way of living and willing. There is no room whatsoever within this view of a father who wills for his son what he would not will for himself, who abuses or takes out his frustration upon his son. Rather, we have a God who fully invests himself in this project to overcome its manifold dilemma, as the one who simultaneously sends, is sent and accompanies the sending, that he might fully enter our situation so as to redeem it. Out of the resources of the divine life, God both makes us fit for, and brings us into, that same divine life: 'If the triune God is self-giving love that liberates life and creates new and inclusive community, there is no salvation for the creature apart from sharing in God's agapic way of life.'[44]

Critiques of the atonement as intra-divine abuse fall radically short of the threefold self-involvement of the one God of the Gospel. At the same time, this means that we must chastise the language

---

[42]Benedict XVI, *Jesus*, 232.

[43]The same expression on the faces Jesus and his Father further warrants this interpretation. Cf. Julian's affirmation that 'of all the pains that lead to salvation, this is the greatest: to see the lover suffer'. Norwich, *Showings*, 209.

[44]Migliore, *Faith Seeking Understanding*, 81.

sometimes employed by adherents to more traditional views of the atonement in which Christ transforms the wrath of the Father into love through his sacrifice.[45] Such a view presumes a wrathful Father and a loving Son – a difference within the life of God unpalatable for any consistently Trinitarian account of the atonement. Any time we speak of the Father, Son and Holy Spirit as though they were opposed, we do so at the expense of the doctrine of the Trinity and therefore at the expense of the Gospel – and this is just as true of those critical of the tradition as it is of its overzealous adherents.[46] Much better to follow George Herbert, who writes in his poem *Prayer (2)*:

> Of what unmeasurable love
> Art thou possessed, who, when thou couldst not die,
>   Wert fain to take our flesh and curse,
> And for our sakes in person sin reprove,
> That by destroying that which tied thy pursue,
> Thou mightst make way for liberality![47]

---

[45]In the current climate of bias against traditional interpretations, it is important to heed Marshall's challenge to name the scholars and the sources, rather than generically deploring 'abuses'. I. Howard Marshall, 'The Theology of the Atonement', in *The Atonement Debate: Papers from the London Symposium on the Theology of Atonement*, ed. Derek Tidball, David Hilborn and Justin Thacker (Grand Rapids, MI: Zondervan, 2008), 63.

I am sceptical that this happens as often as critics would suggest. Stephen Finlan, for example, quotes Don Carson as making such a move. In context, however, Carson is affirming both the love and wrath of the Father, addressing precisely Finlan's question in a nuanced and theologically informed way. Cf. Stephen Finlan, *Problems with Atonement: The Origins of, and Controversy About, the Atonement Doctrine* (Collegeville, MN: Liturgical Press, 2005), 2 n.9; Carson, 'The Glory of the Atonement', 130–1.

Perhaps this view owes more to the critics of traditional views than its proponents. Troeltsch, for instance, writes of the holy love of God, critiquing the old school, wherein 'God was the essence of righteousness, and only Jesus' substitutionary sacrifice for sin could mitigate God's righteous condemnation of humanity and transform divine punishment into mercy. But Jesus held no such view.' Ernst Troeltsch, *The Christian Faith: Based on Lectures Delivered at the University of Heidelberg in 1912 and 1913*, trans. Garrett E. Paul (Minneapolis: Fortress, 1991), 182–3.

[46]A delightful text to contemplate in this regard is Luke 22:39-46.

[47]George Herbert, *The Complete English Poems*, ed. J. J. M. Tobin (New York: Penguin, 1991), 95. As McCall notes, '[T]he death of Jesus does not make it possible for God to love us.' McCall, *Forsaken*, 91. Forgiveness precedes atonement, for the atonement is an act of love. Or, to be more precise, atonement is an act of forgiveness.

But we have far from exhausted the significance of the oneness of God for the doctrine of the atonement. A further implication of God's oneness within the saving work of Christ hearkens back to the first chapter of the book, and the way in which Jesus Christ accomplished atonement that we might know the Father. If we depend upon a tri-theistic account of God, the life, death and resurrection of Jesus Christ do not reveal anything about the character of the Father – we are left entirely in the dark. If the Father is a second god over and against the Son, and thus is a hidden god, how could we possibly discern whether this 'Father', if there was any such reality, approved or disapproved of the work of Jesus? And if this 'Father' could change his mind (and who would say that he could not?), then how would we know that through the work of Christ we had a secure relationship not only with Christ, but with the Father as well? It is because God is one God as Father, Son and Holy Spirit, that in Christ and through his Spirit we know the Father – not in part, not a knowledge in passing, a mere acquaintance, but a genuine, abiding and saving knowledge of the Father. To put it differently, because God as Father, Son and Holy Spirit is one God, in Jesus Christ we know God himself – who he is, what he thinks of us, what he has done for us and who we are in him.[48] And this knowledge, as we saw in Chapter 2, is no inconsequential matter!

But just as the oneness of God has radical implications for how we understand the doctrine of the atonement, so, upon that basis, does the atonement have radical implications for how we understand God, particularly God the Father. Typically, the atonement highlights the suffering of Jesus Christ, the creaturely suffering of the Son. God brings suffering into the divine life in the person of the Son by means of the incarnation: '[W]e are saved by the sufferings of the impassible [One],' as Nazianzus says.[49] But if God is one, and the Son suffers by means of the incarnation, what does that say of the Father? The past century or so has witnessed an increased interest in what we might call the fellow suffering of the Father (CD IV/2, 357), in which the 'Son suffers dying, [and] the

---

[48]'Salvation is secure because the works of the redeemer and the sanctifier can be traced to the inner life of God, behind which there lies nothing.' Webster, 'It Was the Will', 27.

[49]Nazianzus, On God, 97.

Father suffers the death of the Son.'[50] That is to say: in some sense the Father suffers in the sending and the suffering of the incarnate Son, for the love and unity between God the Father and God the Son is not such as to allow the suffering of one without the suffering (in some form) of the other.

It is at this point more than any other that the eternal act of the living and loving God, what Hegel calls the 'play of love with itself, which does not arrive at the seriousness of other-being, of separation and rupture', becomes, as Hodgson says, 'deadly serious' – where the love between Father and Son brings a new dynamic into the divine life, a dynamic of suffering and pain.[51] It is here that we see the full resources of the divine life, of the divine play, in terms of what this life is capable of in terms of entering our situation, and grappling with pain, suffering and evil.[52] We are powerfully reminded of this by the tiny sketch of the passion by St John of the Cross, which for the first time in the history of the Church portrays the passion from the vantage point of the Father, looking down on his beloved Son.[53] The physical suffering of the incarnate Son is the vehicle by means of which suffering enters the divine life to the fullest possible extent, a suffering made possible or given room only because of the love proper to the life of God.

---

[50]Moltmann, *The Crucified God*, 243. For current scholarship which also serves as a wonderful guide into the historical figures and debates, cf. James Keating and Thomas Joseph White, *Divine Impassibility and the Mystery of Human Suffering* (Grand Rapids, MI: Eerdmans, 2009). On Barth's formulation of the fatherly suffering of God, and its distinction from Moltmann, cf. Johnson, *God's Being*, 81–3; Paul D. Molnar, *Divine Freedom and the Doctrine of the Immanent Trinity: In Dialogue with Karl Barth and Contemporary Theology* (New York: T & T Clark, 2005), 225.

[51]Peter C. Hodgson, 'Alienation and Reconciliation in Hegelian and Post-Hegelian Perspective', *Modern Theology* 2, no. 1 (1985): 51; Hegel, *Lectures on the Philosophy of Religion: The Lectures of 1827*, 292.

But play and seriousness are one for God. For in this event 'the Father is pleased, the Son is honoured, the Holy Spirit takes delight', as Julian of Norwich writes. Norwich, *Showings*, 146.

[52]It is here, according to von Balthasar, that we see the 'seriousness' of the immanent Trinity, the initial or 'primal "kenosis" [emptying] within the Godhead that underpins all subsequent kenosis' (*TD*, 320, 323).

[53]Graham M. Schweig, 'Imagery of Divine Love: The Crucifix Drawing of St. John of the Cross', in *John of the Cross: Conferences and Essays by Members of the Institute of Carmelite Studies and Others*, ed. Steven Payne (Washington, DC: ICS Publications, Institute of Carmelite Studies, 1992).

This brings us to the conclusion of our treatment of the oneness of God. In Christ's atonement we see the full self-investment of God which began at creation and awaits fulfilment in the new earth – an investment so complete as to bring suffering into the life of God. To be clear, generic suffering as such is not and never will be saving, but in this case it is the chosen and effective means by which we are brought into the saving life of God through the mediatorial work of the same.[54] We thus honour the basic insight of the feminist perspective 'that redemption had to do with God, through Jesus, giving human-kind . . . positive, abundant relational life' – but do so via a pro-perly Trinitarian account of the one God embracing us through the way of the cross and suffering.[55] The death of Jesus is saving because it is the way to life – the effective means of God dealing not only with our sin, but of bringing us into the life he always intended for us.

The atonement as work of Father, Son and Holy Spirit

Thus far we have emphasized the oneness of God, though in constant awareness that God is one as Father, Son and Holy Spirit. We now explore the atonement once more, from the other vantage point: that God is Father, Son and Holy Spirit and only as such is he one. In doing so, we delve further into the Trinitarian logic of the doctrine of the atonement, particularly in the way that through Jesus Christ the triune God brought the reality of sin into his own proper life, that he might deal with it in and through himself.

---

[54]Tanner, *Christ the Key*, 261. As Dillistone says, 'Jesus is not to be regarded as a hero in the sense of one who engages in a conflict for conflict's sake . . . he is a hero in the sense that his whole struggle is directed toward the achievement of a worthy end.' F. W. Dillistone, *Jesus Christ and His Cross: Studies on the Saving Work of Christ* (Philadelphia: Westminster Press, 1953), 21–2. Campbell writes in a similar vein: 'Love cannot be conceived of as doing anything gratuitously, merely to shew its own depth, for which there was no call in the circumstances of the case viewed in themselves.' Campbell, *The Nature of the Atonement*, 49.

As Luther writes in a 1530 sermon, '[Y]ou should accustom yourself to distinguish carefully between the suffering of Christ and all other suffering and know that his is a heavenly suffering and ours is a worldly, that his accomplishes everything, while ours does nothing except that we become conformed to Christ.' *LW* 51, 208.

[55]Williams, 'Black Women's Surrogacy', 30–1.

From eternity, the one God lives out his life in a threefold way, as Father, Son and Holy Spirit. One could never reach behind this threefold life to reach the one God, because the one God lives out his identity as the one God only and exclusively, from eternity, in this threefold repetition. In the incarnation, death and resurrection of Jesus Christ, God brings this threefold self-repetition to bear upon sin and need, enacting the resources proper to the divine life for us and for our salvation. We often hear this incarnation described as the downward movement of the Son of God, as he leaves the glory of heaven that was rightfully his, to dwell with us.[56]

This is a fully valid way of exploring the reality of the incarnation, bringing to light certain vital aspects of the glory and life of God, particularly the way that God is capable of self-humiliation. For our present purposes, however, we will take a quite different approach, following an altogether different movement, exploring the incarnation as an *ascent* – not of the Son of God, but of our human nature.[57] Given that God is omnipresent, it is just as appropriate to think of the descent of the Son of God as it is of the ascent of our human nature in the incarnation, for through the Virgin birth by the power of the Holy Spirit, God brought human existence into his own proper being and life in the person of the Son. To be more specific, in this event God brought our sinful condition up into his own life, that he might bear this reality in himself so as to deal with it as Father, Son and Holy Spirit.[58]

To say that God brings our sinful condition up is to affirm that he 'takes this human experience into his own life; he "drinks it to the dregs"'.[59] As von Balthasar writes, '[T]his dramatic aspect does not entangle the immanent Trinity in the world's fate . . . but it *does*

---

[56]While 'descent' is not mentioned in Philippians 2:5-11, the twofold movement of servant-hood, paired with his subsequent exaltation clearly implies a descent of sorts. But what does it mean for an omnipresent God to descend? Obviously we cannot explain such a claim with a simplistic literalism, for a descent would imply movement from a higher place to a lower, implying a vacation of the former place and a denial of omnipresence. Thus, while the notion of descent is a valuable resource for thinking about the incarnation, it is not exhaustive.

[57]Put somewhat differently, Nazianzus notes that the Son 'remained what he was; what he was not, he assumed'. I take this 'assumption' to be roughly equivalent to the upward movement I develop in this section. Nazianzus, *On God*, 86.

[58]Marshall, *Aspects*, 66.

[59]McCormack, 'Ontological Presuppositions', 364.

lift the latter's fate to the level of the economic Trinity, which always presupposes the immanent' (*TD*, 362). While the descent of the Son means God's gift of himself to us, the ascent we emphasize here is a matter of God making his own, or taking to himself our fate, our condition and the reality of our sinful existence. Guilt, shame, death . . . the full horror and reality of sin is not something foreign to God, alien to himself, to which he relates as a third party, as an unaffected judge. God enters our condition. He makes it his own. Without himself sinning, without himself willing and creating these dynamics, he lifts their reality up into his divine life in the person of Jesus Christ, the incarnate Son of God. As Kitamori puts it, '[T]he cross is in no sense an external act of God, but an act within himself.' Accordingly, '[T]he question in regard to the salvation of the world . . . is not the relation between God and the world, or God and Satan, but the relation between *God* and *God to the world*,' a matter of God's faithfulness to himself in his faithfulness to his creation.[60] The remainder of this section explores two related questions we can ask of this line of thought: (1) why deal with sin in this way and (2) how is dealing with sin in this way possible without leading to a disastrous understanding of a deeply conflicted and divided God?

Why deal with sin in this way? Why would God bring sin into his own life through the incarnation? The motive of Christ's saving work is for God to reaffirm his creative purposes in the face of sin, bringing his fallen creatures into a restored relationship with himself, with all the blessings entailed therein. 'In the face of sin', however, is a monumental qualification, for sin opposes the being and will of God, distorting and rejecting him in every possible way. God's reaffirmation of his purposes accordingly had to take into account in some way this holistic opposition to himself on the part of his creation – an opposition consisting of a matrix of personal and social intentions, actions, habits and consequences. In Genesis, God comes close to rejecting and destroying his sinful creation in the story of Noah, but ultimately rejected this as a viable alternative, given his unrelenting commitment to his creation

---

[60]Kitamori, *Theology of the Pain of God*, 45. Kitamori follows Moltmann in his account of 'God against God'. This is unfortunate, for it goes beyond the bounds of a properly Trinitarian account, suggesting that there is a '*stasis* within God – "God against God"', and that 'the cross of the Son divides God from God to the utmost degree of enmity and distinction'. Moltmann, *The Crucified God*, 152.

(Gen. 6:11-13; 8:20-22). The challenge was to reject and destroy sin while simultaneously preserving the integrity of the creature. God's answer was to make sin his own, so that he could fully reject and destroy sin and evil, while ultimately safeguarding his beloved creatures from that same rejection and destruction.

And how does God do this? Simply put, he does this, he can do this, because he is the one God, Father, Son and Holy Spirit, and in the space contained within these relationships he has the resources necessary for the work of atonement accomplished in Jesus Christ. 'The Son's eternal, holy distance from the Father, in the Spirit, forms the basis on which the unholy distance of the world's sin can be transposed into it, can be transcended and overcome by it' (*TD*, 362).[61] It is this 'holy distance', the otherness within which God relates to himself, the room or space within which the living and active God loves and relates to himself as Father, Son and Holy Spirit, which contains within itself the dynamics and realities amply sufficient for the work which was to be done for us.

As Father, God is free to respond to the sin borne by the Son in a way fully in keeping with his nature as God: to deny, reject, punish and destroy that which opposes him. God is free to exercise his love, righteousness and holiness towards sin, which is to say that he is free to hate, judge and cast it away, to destroy and abolish this wilful and destructive opposition to and perversion of himself. While divine violence has rightly been questioned in some contexts, it is here that it finds its proper place: the full unleashing of the gentleness, compassion and peacefulness of God against that which is utterly opposed to these things, an unleashing which takes the form of violence, destruction and unrestrained conflict, because that which it confronts is inherently and essentially opposed to the life and will of God.[62] But as Kierkegaard notes, this violence takes a

---

[61]As Migliore puts it, 'God can enter into vulnerable interaction with the world, even to the depths of temporality, deprivation, suffering, and death, because as Father, Son and Holy Spirit God is essentially an inexhaustible history of mutual self-surrendering love.' Migliore, *Faith Seeking Understanding*, 81.

[62]'The fact that God's love reacts violently to the violence done to it by men is explained by God's total investment of himself and by the utterly astonishing indifference, rejection and hardness of heart on man's part' (*TD*, 174). While divine violence is an important topic, its dogmatic location should be kept in mind – precisely at the intersection of God's loving self-involvement with creation, and the astonishing nature of sin.

surprising form: 'Only one who knows anguish finds rest, only one who descends to the underworld saves the loved one, only one who draws the knife gets Isaac.'[63] Wrath is an expression of the divine love,[64] for only a divine love is so intense as to destroy that which is evil, uncompromisingly given over to the good of the creature.

As the incarnate Son, God is free to bear his own judgement, opposition and destruction of sin, without himself being utterly overthrown and destroyed.[65] As man, God is able to suffer and die, experiencing in himself the full consequences of the sin he bears, the full reality of this curse, while as God he is able to withstand this reality without suffering dissolution, and ceasing to be altogether. As the incarnate God he is able on the one hand to repent, confess and acknowledge the goodness of the wrath, jealousy and forsakenness he directs towards himself, to 'appropriate [our] want of submission . . . effect[ing] our submission, mak[ing] it his own and present[ing] it to God'.[66] On the other hand, as the incarnate Son bearing our sin he 'expresses our condition' in the 'sufferings of the impassible'.[67] As Nazianzus puts it, 'He bears the whole of me, along with all that is mine, in himself, so that he may consume within himself the meaner element, as fire consumes wax or the Sun ground mist, and so that I may share in what is his through the intermingling.'[68] The second movement, our sharing what is his, we will consider shortly. In the meantime, we acknowledge that because God is the incarnate Son, he is able to bear in himself the whole of what we are, consuming within himself that which is evil.

And as the Holy Spirit, God is free to accompany and enable this process in which he deals conclusively with our sin. The Spirit, the

---

[63] Sören Kierkegaard, *Fear and Trembling: Dialectical Lyric by Johannes De Silentio*, trans. Alastair Hannay (London: Penguin, 1985), 57.

[64] McCall, *Forsaken*, 86.

[65] But this is true only because of who he is: the incarnate Son of God. As Torrance puts it, '[E]verything depends on *who* He was, for the significance of His acts in life and death depends on the nature of His Person . . . we must allow the Person of Christ to determine for us the nature of His saving work, rather than the other way around.' Thomas F. Torrance, *God and Rationality* (London: Oxford University Press, 1971), 64.

[66] Nazianzus, *On God*, 96.

[67] Ibid.

[68] Ibid., 97.

Lord and giver of life, is free to accompany the crucified and risen Christ. Inasmuch as Christ bore the burden of our sin, on the cross and over the course of Holy Saturday, the Spirit mediated to Jesus the presence of the Father. And because Jesus was bearing our sin, the experience of the Father mediated by the Spirit could only be the experience of death, forsakenness, judgement and expulsion.[69] But inasmuch as the reality of sin and evil was exhausted in this event, God continues to accompany himself, sharing himself as Spirit with himself as incarnate Son, filling him who was now free of sin with the life of God, an experience which sinless man could experience only as resurrection, the fullness of human life and graced existence.

In short, because God is triune, God is free to take our sin up into his own life, and deal with it as God by means of the relationships proper to his own being and life. The bearing of and doing away with our sin is thus a thoroughly Trinitarian event. This is so much the case, in fact, that were it not for God's triunity, such an event would be impossible – for it is God's freedom to relate to himself as himself by means of himself that enables him to bring sin into his own life, and relate to it as such on the basis of his own being and life.[70] Were God monolithic, a single God, he would not be free to relate to himself in this way. However, were God three individual and distinct gods, he could relate only to others which were not himself, thereby inflicting on other gods that which he himself was not willing to do, a position readily and rightly condemned in feminist critiques.

Because God is one, the action he accomplishes and effects in Christ is willed and accomplished in and through himself without division, without conflict.[71] And it is because the one God is Father,

---

[69]Death is not the cessation of existence – Scripture does not tend to explain death in such a way. Rather, death is the experience on the part of the sinner of the living God, which includes the cessation of bodily life, but transcends it.

[70]As Hegel writes, from the incarnation and atonement 'develops the consciousness that knows that God is triune. The reconciliation in Christ, in which one believes, makes no sense if God is not known as the triune God, [if it is not recognized] that God *is*, but also is as the other, as self-distinguishing, so that this other is God himself.' Hegel, *Lectures on the Philosophy of Religion: The Lectures of 1827*, 469.

[71]Cf. Bruce McCormack's excellent account, rooted in the continual emphasis that the atonement is a matter of the work and relationships of the Father, *incarnate* Son and Holy Spirit, and therefore not to be read back directly into the modes of relating between the Father and Son. McCormack, 'Ontological Presuppositions', 363–5.

Son and Holy Spirit, eternally living with and relating to himself, that he is able to enact the dynamics of these relationships, of the divine life, for us, bearing our sin and re-establishing us as his creatures. That is to say, it is because God is triune that he is able to be both *God* and *our God*, to do away with our sin without being faithless to himself or destroying us, and in that same act, able to establish us in eternal life with himself.

The triumph of the life of God: Atonement as theōsis

But our life with God is key, for it is without question the focus of the atonement; this is why Christ came, that we might have abundant life (Jn 10:10). God deals with our sin through the resources proper to his being and life, and it is the positive and creative triumph of this life of God in the resurrected Jesus Christ that gives the atonement its definitive character and meaning. God's intent was not merely to overcome sin, 'but rather a profound reworking and *anakephalaiosis* [recapitulation, or transformative summing-up] of the terms of ordinary humanity, into a divinely graced life-form that would experience an ascentive metamorphosis', an 'abundantly energized life' in relationship with the giver of life himself.[72] That is to say, the goal of atonement is our ongoing transformation in Christ, into a life that is so filled with the grace, power and character of God that it pushes the boundaries of what we now recognize as human. The goal of the atonement is that we participate in the life of God as completely as possible, without ceasing to be the distinct and unique creatures God made us to be.

Current scholarship capitalizes on the life-giving aspect of Christ's work by means of a range of more or less related theories traditionally known as *theōsis*, divinization and union with Christ.[73]

---

[72]J. A. McGuckin, 'The Strategic Adaptation of Deification in the Cappadocians', in *Partakers of the Divine Nature: The History and Development of Deificiation in the Christian Traditions*, ed. Michael J. Christensen and Jeffery A. Wittung (Grand Rapids, MI: Baker Academic, 2007), 96–7.

[73]This is not to suggest that these theories are identical. They vary widely, both in terms of how the terms are to be understood, and within theological traditions, particularly when it comes to their metaphysical presuppositions.

This emphasis draws considerable energy from Patristic and particularly Orthodox theology, and is partly intended to overcome contemporary theology's perceived overemphasis upon the death and suffering of Christ (at the expense of his life before and after his passion). The basic insight is that the atonement, while dealing with sin and its consequences, brings us into the life of God, that we might be creaturely sons and daughters of God, and co-heirs with Christ (Rom. 8:14-16).[74] The benefit we receive from Christ is not abstracted from or unrelated to his life as the incarnate Son of God, a whimsical vision of life on a paradisiacal beach. Rather, the good that God has in store for us is his very self, his life, such that he is both the means and the end of our salvation, of our filial relationship with him.

There are several ways to employ this constellation of theories (which I refer to simply as *theōsis*), two of which we explore here. One is to develop them as models of salvation inherently opposed to theories of the atonement, exploring the saving nature of the incarnation and life of Jesus (often while deploring the cross as an unfortunate political event). We see such an approach in the work of Stephen Finlan, who asks:

> What happens if we restate the divine Incarnation of Jesus, thereby highlighting the fact of God's near approach to humanity and to human suffering through the Incarnation of Jesus through his *whole* life, but drop the idea of any magical transaction taking place at the cross [i.e. any traditional theory

---

For an introduction to this family of thought in a wide variety of traditions, see: Stephen Finlan and Vladimir Kharlamov, *Theōsis: Deification in Christian Theology* (Eugene, OR: Pickwick, 2006); Christensen and Wittung, *Partakers of the Divine Nature: The History and Development of Deificiation in the Christian Traditions*; Vladimir Kharlamov, *Theōsis: Deification in Christian Theology*, vol. 2 (Eugene, OR: Pickwick Publications, 2011); Norman Russell, *The Doctrine of Deification in the Greek Patristic Tradition* (Oxford: Oxford University Press, 2004).

[74]Pseudo-Dionysius writes, for instance, that: 'God has come down to us and that, like a fire, he has made one with himself all those capable of being divinized,' citing John 1:12f. as support of his claim: '[F]or to all who received him, who believed in his name, he gave power to become children of God.' Pseudo-Dionysius, *Pseudo-Dionysius: The Complete Works*, trans. Colm Luibheid (New York: Paulist Press, 1987), 201.

of atonement]? – What happens is that we return to Jesus' parental God who wants only spiritual progress and maturation for God's offspring.[75]

Finlan touts spiritual progress and maturation, making the incarnation the original and central doctrine of the Christian faith, relegating the atonement to the status of an impure accretion.[76] An altogether different approach explores *theōsis* as a comprehensive model of salvation, including a definite place for the atonement. 'Deification,' Andrew Louth writes, 'is not to be equated with redemption. Christ certainly came to save us, and in our response to his saving action and word we are redeemed; but deification belongs to a broader conception of the divine [economy]: deification is the fulfillment of creation, not just the rectification of the Fall.'[77] For Louth, *theōsis* is a model of salvation that honours the role of redemption while focusing on eschatology and the sanctification anticipating it.

We can and should take a further step in relating *theōsis* to atonement, partly to counteract the tendency of some contemporary thought to pit these two against each other. More importantly, while there is much to appreciate in Louth's claim that atonement is a matter of redemption from the consequences of the Fall, this book argues for a far more comprehensive understanding of the atoning work of Christ, one which emphasizes the at-one-ment so prized by *theōsis*: our creaturely oneness or union with God through our reconstitution in Christ. How then might we develop *theōsis* as itself

---

[75]Finlan, *Problems with Atonement: The Origins of, and Controversy About, the Atonement Doctrine*, 119. While Finlan commends the antiquity of this view, note the deplorably selective reading he offers of the history of the Church, endorsing choice quotes from figures such as Irenaeus and Athanasius, while rejecting the overall shape of their soteriology which includes, of course, robust doctrines of the atonement. Regarding his rejection of the atonement as the central doctrine of the Christian faith, see Athanasius' claim: 'The next step is to recount the end of his life and dealings in the body and to relate also of what kind was the death of the body, especially because this is the chief point of our faith' (*De inc*, §19).
[76]Ibid., 117–20.
[77]Andrew Louth, 'The Place of *Theosis* in Orthodox Theology', in *Partakers of the Divine Nature: The History and Development of Deificiation in the Christian Traditions*, ed. Michael J. Christensen and Jeffery A. Wittung (Grand Rapids, MI: Baker Academic, 2007), 34–5.

a theory of the atonement? History is on our side, for the author of one of the most famous Patristic affirmations of divinization provides us with precisely such an integration of atonement and *theōsis*.

Athanasius claims that '[the Son] was incarnate that we might be made God' (*De inc*, 54), embedding this affirmation within the context of several statements concerning Christ's work: '[T]hrough death incorruptibility has come to all,' '[H]e endured the insults of human beings, that we might inherit incorruptibility,' and '[H]e held and preserved in his own impassibility the suffering human beings, on whose account he endured these things.' Amid such claims, Athanasius writes, 'He himself was harmed in no way, being impassible and incorruptible.' This context – particularly the themes of corruption and incorruption – provides us with the necessary tools for exploring Athanasius' view.

Throughout *De incarnatione*, Athanasius consistently refers to the incorruption of God as one of his chief attributes. In his grace and by the Word, God made us out of nothing and 'granted us by the grace of the Word to live a life according to God'. However, by turning away from him, humankind became corruptible – a corruption unto death (*De inc*, §§4–5). The purpose of the incarnation of the Son was that the incorruptible God might clothe himself with mortality, enduring corruption and death in our place (*De inc*, §§8, 20) that he might bring 'the corruptible to incorruptibility' in such a way as to 'maintain for the Father His consistency of character with all' (*De inc*, §7). Such a goal meant that Christ not only dealt with the source of our corruption (guilt, shame, debt, punishment etc.) but above all gave us life and incorruption once more, through the resurrection (*De inc*, §§21–2). In this way, he brought resurrection and immortality to all, through union with himself (*De inc*, §§34, 56). In sum, Athanasius develops the atonement in light of God's incorruptibility and our corruption, exploring the way in which Jesus Christ suffers the latter in his death that he might bring us to the former through his resurrection, sharing with us the life, or incorruptibility, of God.

Theōsis, we might therefore say, is (at least in this instance) a theory of the atonement developed in light of the incorruptibility of God, rather than an account of salvation which leaves room for a doctrine of redemption – Athanasius integrates the two much more closely than that. While not every theory of *theōsis* focuses on this attribute, and many theologians may develop *theōsis* largely as a vision of salvation including within it an account of Christ's death and resurrection, this is not the case here. In Athanasius we find a more integrated vision of atonement and *theōsis* – one which powerfully brings to light the central claim of this chapter: that in and through the atonement the triune God reaffirmed his creative purposes in order to share his own proper life with us through union with Jesus Christ, the incarnate Son.

Conclusion

The atonement is an event within the life of God. It is because God is triune that the life, death and resurrection of the incarnate Son is meaningful and effective for us; it is because God is triune that he is able to take up our plight into himself, so as to deal with it on the basis of the resources and relationships proper to the divine life. And it is precisely this divine life that is the goal of the atonement: that which God seeks to share with us, as he reconstitutes our creaturely being in Christ. At every step it is this fact which is determinative for shaping the structure, determining the motives and explaining the outcomes of Christ's work: the fact that the life, death and resurrection of Jesus Christ is the work of the triune God, Father, incarnate Son and Holy Spirit. In the next chapter we continue to develop this line of thought by attending more carefully to the life or attributes of the holy Trinity, and the determinative role they play in the atonement of Jesus Christ.

4

Atonement and the Divine Attributes

Delving further into the doctrine of the triune God, in this chapter we concentrate on the deeply formative role of the divine attributes within theories of the atonement.[1] Every theory focuses our attention on one particular aspect (or subset thereof) of the character of God who comes among us, shaping our understanding of different nuances within the work of Christ, of human sin and of the nature of his saving benefits. The influence of the divine attributes within every element of theories of the atonement is so determinative, that attending to their role is the most decisive element in the study of the doctrine.[2] To bring this thesis to life, we begin by exploring the role of the divine attributes in two different works by Jonathan Edwards.

Edwards on justice and wisdom

In his essay 'Concerning the Necessity and Reasonableness of the Christian Doctrine of Satisfaction for Sin' Edwards builds on the

---

[1] The connection between the doctrines of the Trinity and divine attributes is that 'God's perfection is the fullness and inexhaustibility in which the triune God is and acts as the one he is.' Webster, 'It Was the Will', 18.

[2] Though I do not develop this line of thought in the present work, it is vital that these attributes be properly construed, in keeping with God's self-revelation. It is in the death and resurrection of Jesus that we receive the fullest revelation of God's character. Cf. *CD* II/1, 257–677, and the salutary but much shorter: Cousar, *A Theology of the Cross: The Death of Jesus in the Pauline Letters*, 45–8.

premise that 'justice requires that sin be punished, because sin deserves punishment'.[3] In doing so, he draws upon one of the foremost characteristics of the Reformed understanding of the atonement – its emphasis upon the necessity of upholding God's *justice*. Turretin, for example (upon whom Edwards draws heavily), affirms the absolute necessity of the atonement in the following manner: 'God neither has willed, nor could have willed to forgive sins, without a satisfaction made *to his justice*.'[4] Our sin, in this system, is 'a debt which we are bound to pay to divine justice' and 'a crime against the government of the universe by which before God, the supreme governor and judge, we become deserving of everlasting death and malediction'.[5] From the very beginning, judicial terminology and distinctions dominate the scene, depending on an understanding of the nature and pre-eminence of the divine justice. Given this judicial emphasis, the problem raised by sin is threefold: payment of our debt of punishment, appeasing the divine wrath and expiation of our guilt. Because God is the just ruler of the universe and we have sinned, Turretin and others formulated a solution guaranteeing that God remains the just ruler of the universe by destroying the sin, guilt and debt of humanity that affronted him. Every other consideration falls under this fundamental rubric.

Adhering to this model of the atonement, Edwards begins the aforementioned essay with the claim that 'justice requires that sin be punished, because sin deserves punishment'.[6] He secures this fundamental premise in the nature of divine justice:

> The justice of God obliges him to punish sin: for it belongs to God as the supreme Rector of the universality of things, to maintain order and decorum in his kingdom, and to see to it that decency and right takes place at all times, and in all cases. That perfection of his nature whereby he is disposed to this, is his justice; and therefore, his justice naturally disposes him to punish sin as it deserves.[7]

---

[3] Edwards, 'Of Satisfaction for Sin', 565.
[4] Francis Turretin, *Institutes of Elenctic Theology*, vol. 2. Phillipsburg: P&R Publishing, 1992, 418.
[5] Ibid.
[6] Edwards, 'Of Satisfaction for Sin', 565.
[7] Ibid., 566.

As the universal rector or ruler, God must act justly. Following this path, Edwards gives a judicial or 'forensic' account, which agrees in almost every respect with that of Turretin.[8] While the details of this account are intricate, it suffices for our purposes to note that the sin of humankind was imputed to Jesus, so that he might suffer 'the full punishment' which 'we owed to divine justice for our sins'.[9] This mediatorial work was an act of great love and mercy, to be sure – but an act in which the God, who had to be just, freely chose to be both just and merciful. Justice, in this case, provides the architectural features of the work, which is then supplemented by other attributes (such as mercy). It would be a mistake, however, to claim this as Edwards' definitive account of the atonement, for in looking at another of his writings on the subject, we find a strikingly different portrayal.

In an edited collection of sermons known by the name 'The Wisdom of God Displayed in the Way of Salvation' we find Edwards once again dwelling upon the doctrine of the atonement, but from a radically different perspective.[10] Rather than starting with the concept of God as the just ruler of the universe, he begins his reflection with Ephesians 3:10: 'To the intent that now unto the principalities and powers in heavenly places, might be known by the church the manifold wisdom of God.' That is to say, Edwards uses the 'manifold Wisdom of God' as the key attribute for exploring the work of Christ.

It is called *manifold wisdom*; because of the manifold glorious ends that are attained by it. The excellent designs, hereby accomplished, are very manifold. The wisdom of God in this is of vast extent. The contrivance is so manifold, that one may spend an eternity in discovering more of the excellent ends and designs accomplished by it; and the multitude and vast variety of things that are, by divine contrivance, brought to conspire the bringing about those ends. (*Wisdom*, 141)

---

[8]Dorus Paul Rudisill, *The Doctrine of the Atonement in Jonathan Edwards and His Successors* (New York: Poseidon Books, 1971), 15.

[9]Edwards, 'Of Satisfaction for Sin', 576.

[10]A number of textual difficulties present themselves with this particular collection. While I refer to them as Edwards' work, I take due note that the text was edited, and not intended for publication as such by Edwards.

To expound God's manifold wisdom is to dwell on that aspect of God's character which brings God's counsels and purposes together in completion and fulfilment, or as Edwards puts it, which attains the 'manifold glorious ends' of God (*Wisdom*, 141). The emphasis here is upon the source within the character of God which discerns the course of action most suitable for attaining a wide array of purposes, simultaneously highlighting the biblical theme of God's wisdom and the range of goals behind God's (re)creative activity.

What might these goals of God be? In *The End for Which God Created the World*, Edwards suggests that God created in order to glorify himself by exercising his glorious attributes towards creation (99), communicating God's fullness to creation (117), so that it might delight in and glorify him in return (119–20).[11] While in this treatise Edwards emphasizes the divine glory, this does not make for a one-dimensional account. This is because for Edwards, the divine glory is the fullness of the divine attributes; emphasizing divine glory means simultaneously emphasizing the fullness of God's character, which is then communicated to the creature. Integrating the insights from these two works, to expound God's manifold wisdom is to expound the ways in which it brings to fulfilment the communication of the divine attributes (the divine glory) to the creature, in fulfilment of God's promises.

God's mercy, justice, honour, knowledge, goodness . . . all these and others beside attain their end within creation by means of the wisdom of God. And God decisively displays his wisdom in the way of salvation, for:

> All [God's] works praise him, and his glory shines brightly from them all: but as some stars differ from others in glory, so the glory of God shines brighter in some of his works than in others. And amongst all these, the work of redemption is like the sun in his strength. The glory of the author is abundantly the most resplendent in this work. (*Wisdom*, 144)

In short, Christ's redeeming work is that act of God which most completely sums up and fulfils God's creative purpose of glorifying himself by communicating that same glory, by communicating the

---

[11] Edwards, 'Dissertation on the End for Which God Created the World.'

fullness of the divine life to the creature. This being the case, justice is an essential component of any account of the wisdom of God displayed in our salvation (as developed, for instance, in Edwards' *Of Satisfaction for Sin*), but it plays its role alongside a host of other divine attributes, each with their respective role and insight.

And because each attribute has its role and insight, the more divine attributes we integrate into our account of the Passion, the fuller an understanding we will have of Christ's work and its meaning. We see this clearly in Edwards' sermons on wisdom, distinctive for how they cultivate appreciation for a multiplicity of ends accomplished by Christ's death on the cross. At the level of divine attributes, Edwards considers the role of the divine mercy, justice, honour, knowledge, goodness and others. While God still requires satisfaction of his justice,[12] we now see the infinite love, pity, wisdom, power and merit of God in Christ's redeeming work. As Edwards says, 'each *attribute* of God is glorified in the work of redemption'[13] In addition to the various attributes, each person of the Trinity is exceedingly glorified in this work: Father, Son and Holy Spirit.[14] Focusing specifically on humankind, a wide variety of goods were procured for us, extending far beyond the removal of guilt. We now stand in peace with God, have the favour of God, are bestowed with satisfying happiness and have great enjoyment and every sort of good for soul and body among a great number of other goods.[15] Beyond the implications of the cross and empty tomb for God and humans, Edwards extends these reflections to the fate of the fallen and unfallen angels (cf. Chapter 6) – yet another instance of the increased breadth and scope which Edwards gives to the doctrine of the atonement in these sermons.

In sum, we find a startling difference between two of Edwards' treatments of the atonement – an essay in which he advances a finely honed summary of Turretin's theory of penal substitution, and a set of sermons which canvas the breadth of the doctrine of the atonement and those things impacted by it in a way which is to my knowledge unprecedented in the history of theology.

---

[12]'The Wisdom of God Displayed in the Way of Salvation', 142.
[13]Ibid., 144–5.
[14]Ibid., 145.
[15]Ibid., 145–7.

The role of attributes

Why do Edwards' accounts different so greatly? Why is Edwards' treatise on satisfaction so one-dimensional, whereas the collection of sermons is so rich and diverse? It is as though one attended a lecture focusing on marriage as a financial institution integral to national economies, and then attended a second lecture by the same speaker, which expounded on marriage as a romantic union, covenantal bond, foundation for the family, political organization, economic institution and educational establishment. In these lectures on marriage and the works of Edwards we just explored, a far more comprehensive second account includes within it the content of the first one-dimensional lecture. Both approaches are of great interest, for a sustained exploration of a single element of a complex reality is of great value, while a broader and fuller account, though less thorough in the details, paints a compelling vista, providing numerous connections and avenues for further exploration. What then might account for the difference in the scope of the two accounts?

We must not rule out the role of context – for perhaps in the treatise on satisfaction Edwards was responding to a specific question or disputation, just as the expert on marriage in the first lecture may have been addressing students majoring in economics. For our present purposes, however, I would like to attend to a conceptual rather than contextual feature. In the lectures on marriage and Edwards' two works, the second instance in each case offers a far greater breadth of approach than the first. In the case of the marriage lectures, the second lecture explores a fuller range of elements properly considered dimensions of a robust anthropology. In Edwards' case, the breadth flowed from a heightened awareness of different dimensions of the character of God. For while Edwards emphasizes a single divine attribute, the nature of divine wisdom and the way in which it turns one's attention to the other divine attributes has a markedly different effect than the selection of many other attributes. This decision is of immense significance for the shape of Edwards' respective accounts, and guides us deep into understanding the nature of 'theories' of the atonement and the Church's vocation regarding them.

Theories of the atonement, as we have seen, are synthetic in nature, explaining the death and resurrection of Jesus Christ through an integrated account of the character of God, the nature of our sin, and the fulfilment of God's creative purposes. But for two reasons the divine attribute we choose to emphasize shapes a theory more decisively than any other element. First, this is the case because the Gospel is first and foremost a matter of God, and the good news that God has chosen to be with us (Emmanuel), to make our dilemma his own and to make himself both the means and goal of our salvation. For this reason, properly theological concerns, matters pertaining to the doctrine of God, should always be primary in our thinking about the atonement. As Barth puts it, the atonement is 'primarily a statement about God and only then and for that reason a statement about us men' (*CD* IV/1, 5).[16] For this reason alone, the role of the divine attributes is necessarily one of, if not the, most important feature of any theory of the atonement, as the account of the character of God who is the central agent in this drama. Building upon this, we note the second reason: each of the main components of any theory of the atonement derives, in one way or another, from the antecedent reality of the divine life, the divine attributes.

Regarding sin, what is it but creaturely opposition to the character of God? As Augustine notes in a beautiful passage:

> Pride imitates what is lofty; but you alone are God most high above all things. What does ambition seek but honour and glory? Yet you alone are worthy of honour and are glorious for eternity. The cruelty of powerful people aims to arouse fear. Who is feared but God alone? What can be seized or stolen from his power? When or where or how or by whom? Soft endearments are intended to arouse love. But there are no caresses tenderer than your charity, and no object of love is more healthy than your truth, beautiful and luminous beyond all things. Curiosity appears to be a zeal for knowledge; yet you supremely know all. Ignorance and stupidity are given the names of simplicity and

---

[16]As Holmes puts it, '[N]ecessarily, the whole volume [on soteriology] must deal with the divine perfections, since soteriology is grounded and built upon accounts of divine perfection, in its biblical and historical foundation, and in its contemporary expression.' Stephen R. Holmes, 'A Simple Salvation? Soteriology and the Perfections of God', in *God of Salvation*, ed. Ivor J. Davidson and Murray A. Rae (Burlington, VT: Ashgate, 2011), 37.

innocence; but there is no greater simplicity than in you. And what greater innocence than yours, whereas to evil men their own works are damaging? Idleness appears as desire for a quiet life; yet can rest be assured apart from the Lord?[17]

Every sin in some way parodies the character of God, corrupting our portrayal of it. Creation is the gift of God by means of which we can partake of the divine life in creaturely form. And just as our words and deeds are the tools and stage of our creaturely partaking of the character of God, so also they are the occasion for the terrifying and disastrous corruption or perversion of that possibility. But just as the atonement presupposes sin, so it aims towards salvation, the fulfilment of God's creative purposes. And these too are necessarily bound up with the divine character: for what else could God share with us than the divine character in a context and mode appropriate for the creature?

In short, the divine character is at the heart of the atonement: in Christ, God is present to us in the fullness of his perfection, so as to take sin (the opposition to that perfection) into account in himself, and to bring about our salvation (creaturely participation in that perfection) in the same way. The key to every aspect of the atonement is the divine character: the perfection of the triune God who in and of himself is the source of all goodness, love, power and wisdom (to name but a few). And as the Church seeks to witness to this reality, and as it cannot say at once all that it must say, it must offer glimpses into this reality in the shape of concrete theories which speak truly, though incompletely, of Christ's saving work. And it is the selection of the divine attribute at the heart of this work that exercises the greatest shaping influence on the account as a whole. *The divine attribute(s) stand at the centre of any theory of the atonement, shaping its constituent parts and determining its insights and limitations.*

For this reason, the single best vantage point from which to appreciate the nature, strengths and limitations of any given theory of Christ's saving work is to explore the role of the attribute(s) emphasized within that theory. While a host of other factors converge in each theory, the divine attributes provide the

---

[17]Augustine, *Confessions*, 31.

fundamental structure and integrity to the whole, calling for our most careful attention.

Atonement and divine simplicity

A second example of the role of the divine attributes in the atonement will further establish our thesis, while pushing us to a deeper level of reflection. We have already seen how Turretin's account of satisfaction revolves around divine justice. On this account, 'God neither has willed, nor could have willed to forgive sins, without a satisfaction made *to his justice*,'[18] but chose to be merciful as an 'exercise of a gratuitous power'.[19] We see precisely the opposite approach in a recent book by Belousek, who argues, 'retribution is the right, not a necessity, of God'.[20] Rather, 'God's steadfast love and faithfulness belong to God's character in an essential way that anger or wrath does not; anger or wrath is not the dominant side or controlling element of God's character, but love and mercy.'[21] To rephrase Belousek's position in a mode akin to Turretin and Edwards, we might say that 'God neither has willed, nor could have willed to act toward sinners without love and mercy', and any incorporation of retributive justice, wrath or anger would be an 'exercise of gratuitous power' belonging to God by right, though not demanded by nature. In short, the two positions are strongly if not diametrically opposed to each other, due to opposing conceptions of the nature and role of divine mercy and justice.[22]

One possibility is that one or both understandings are deeply flawed. Another is to note the difference between Edwards' focus on *sin* and Belousek's focus on the *sinner*. At present, we will take a third alternative, inquiring into the way both Edwards and

---

[18]Turretin, *Institutes of Elenctic Theology*, vol. 2. Phillipsburg: P&R Publishing, 1992, 418.

[19]Ibid., 37.

[20]Belousek, *Atonement*, 397.

[21]Ibid., 404.

[22]It is worth noting that in effect, both compromise the constancy of God, creating an untenable division between those things which God must be, and those which he can choose to be. Cf. Holmes, 'A Simple Salvation? Soteriology and the Perfections of God', 39.

Belousek prioritize one divine attribute over the others, arguing that God must act in accordance with one attribute, whereas he is free to act in keeping with another, should he choose to do so. God must be just, and he can be merciful; or he must be merciful, and he can choose to be just and exercise his wrath. What is behind this difference? Why can't he choose to be just and merciful, or what prevents us from affirming that he must be both just and merciful?

Theologians have long distinguished between different kinds of divine attributes: communicable and incommunicable, absolute and relative, external and internal (CD II/1, 345). Some distinctions originate in what we can or can't know about God, others distinguish between those attributes in which we can or cannot participate as creatures, while others work with essential attributes without which God simply would not be God, and others concerning which God, in his freedom, can enact or withhold. Such distinctions have a long history in theological reflection, and are not without their merits. At present, I will sketch an answer rooted in divine simplicity, though there are other ways of navigating this material.

According to Thomas, 'God is nowise composite, but is altogether simple' (ST, I.3.7), or as Holmes sums up his view, 'God's life is one, single and coherent; he is not divided into differing parts or pulled in different directions.' The various perfections refer to the same fundamental reality, the perfection of the triune God, but do so by capturing 'one or another aspect of that one simple perfection'.[23] That being the case, several implications ensue, including the impossibility of strongly distinguishing different attributes such as justice and mercy. Since both justice and mercy are different aspects of the perfection of the triune God, and they are not divided or pulled in different directions, we are wrong to speak as though one were more central or essential than the other. Any divine attribute of God simply is the one divine perfection of God viewed from a specific standpoint, and is therefore just as central to the divine life and economic activity of God as any other.

---

[23]Ibid., 38.

Working with a notion of divine simplicity, Barth honours the unity and diversity of the divine attributes by appealing to the pattern employed within the doctrine of the Trinity. '[God] is who He is and what He is in both unity and multiplicity. He is the One who is this many, and the many who are this One' (CD II/1, 323). Building upon this pattern of unity and multiplicity within the one God, Barth applies it to the divine attributes (or 'perfections', as he calls them):

> The multiplicity, individuality and diversity of the perfections of God are those of His simple being, which is not therefore divided and then put together again. In God multiplicity, individuality and diversity do not stand in any contradiction to unity. Rather the very unity of His being consists in the multiplicity, individuality and diversity of his perfections, which since they are His are not capable of any dissolution or separation or non-identity, and which again since they are His are capable of genuine multiplicity, individuality and diversity. (CD II/1, 332)

In other words, the Church can and should affirm the simplicity of God in the sense that there is a unity and multiplicity proper to God, both at the level of the triunity of God and that of the divine attributes. The latter are one just as God is one, and therefore cannot be divided against each other, and always mutually inform each other. Neither can they be reduced to a single attribute, for just as God in and of himself is Father, Son and Holy Spirit, so the divine character has a multiplicity proper to itself, in the form of a host of divine attributes.

And it is precisely these attributes that the triune God seeks to share with us in his mercy, by bringing us into the divine life (theōsis).

> Which of the attributes of God, in which as Creator, Reconciler and Redeemer He allows His creatures to share, is not, as His own, utterly incommunicable from the creaturely point of view, i.e., communicable only by the miracle of grace? And again, which of these incommunicable attributes has not God nevertheless communicated to the creature in that His Word was made flesh?

> Is not God's mercy completely unfathomable and inaccessible to us? And has He not implanted His eternity utterly in our hearts? In His Son God has opened up to us and given us all, His inmost self. (CD II/1, 345)[24]

This passage offers an indirect reaffirmation of divine simplicity, but does so by undercutting traditional distinctions between classes of attributes (alluded to earlier). This move is of great significance for several reasons. First, it pits an affirmation of divine simplicity against the usefulness of distinctions such as communicable and incommunicable attributes, undermining the latter. Second, it demands that we reinterpret the 'incommunicable' attributes in light of the work of Christ, wherein we see precisely those attributes being communicated to us. Third, we can extend Barth's thesis to chastise Belousek, Turretin and any other theologian who distinguishes between those attributes that God must exhibit in his interactions with humankind, and are therefore central to an account of the atonement, and attributes which God is free to enact, and therefore play a peripheral role within that doctrine.

God is one. There is no conflict within God between those elements of his character that are essential and those that are peripheral, between that which God can and cannot share, between that which is truly God and that which is partly, or somewhat God. God is who he is in the fullness of the divine life, a life in which there is no conflict, division or separation between Father, Son and Spirit. And God shares with us this life in Christ, and therefore shares with us the full and united life proper to himself, because anything less would be for God to share something other than himself. But because God shares himself in his fullness, in his oneness, we must do justice to this within the doctrine of the atonement, refusing to distinguish between essential and non-essential, central and peripheral, necessary or free attributes. Rather, we must delight in the ongoing task of appreciating the

---

[24]As Davidson puts it, '[I]f there is no straightforward insulation of divinity from the experience of the grave, there is also in this, at least as clearly, no suspension of God's infinite abundance, no differentiation of his properties into the essential versus the optional, the eternally absolute versus the temporarily dispensable. There is but the enactment of that which God's Goodness is, and thus is seen to be capable of being.' Ivor J. Davidson, 'Introduction: God of Salvation', ibid., 2.

role of each of God's attributes and their interrelations within the work of Christ, for it is by this that we come to appreciate the full extent of what God has given us in Christ, with all the attending implications for the vocation of the Church that finds its identity in God's self-giving.

Opera ad extra, and the doctrine of appropriations

Arguing for the unity of the divine attributes raises a pressing question for my thesis, which contends that every theory of the atonement derives its distinctive shape and character by emphasizing one (or a set of) divine attribute(s). If the multiplicity of divine attributes is not ultimately distinguishable into discrete, independent attributes, then isn't the necessarily one-dimensional emphasis of any theory of the atonement inherently opposed to the ultimate unity of the divine attributes? Where unity-in-diversity is the anthem, is there any potential for a solo beyond that of a clanging gong? To answer this question we return to the doctrine of the Trinity, which is the source of our commitment to and understanding of divine simplicity.

It is a theological commonplace that the external works of the Trinity are undivided (*opera trinitatis ad extra sunt indivisa*), for the triune God is one and undivided.[25] Augustine, for instance, writes that, 'with regard to this three [the triune God] the divine utterances have many ways of saying things about them individually which belong to them all, on account of the indivisible operation of their one and the same substance'.[26] That is to say, while Scripture says things about the individual persons of the Trinity, we understand these to apply to all three persons, because their common substance entails unified action. In explicit affirmation of Augustine's claim, Thomas interprets Gabriel's statement to Mary (Lk. 1:35), that the Holy Spirit would come upon her, as an action

---

[25]Cf. Richard A. Muller, *Dictionary of Latin and Greek Theological Terms: Drawn Principally from Protestant Scholastic Theology* (Grand Rapids, MI: Baker Academic, 2006), 213.

[26]Augustine, *The Trinity*, trans. Edmund Hill (Brooklyn, NY: New City Press, 1991), 84.

of the whole Trinity: 'the whole Trinity effected the conception of
Christ's body' (*ST* III, q. 32, a. 1). This much we would expect,
based on our previous reflection on divine simplicity. How, then,
do we account for the fact that Scripture does attribute different
actions to different persons of the Trinity, when we affirm that the
actions of the one God are undivided?

Continuing with Thomas, we find that he gives three reasons
for Gabriel's affirmation concerning the Holy Spirit, each revolving
around the fittingness of this attribution. For instance, Thomas
writes: 'This is befitting the term of the Incarnation. For the term
of the Incarnation was that that man, who was being conceived,
should be the Holy One and the Son of God. Now both of these are
attributed to the Holy Ghost. For by Him men are made to be sons
of God. . . . Again, He is the Spirit of sanctification' (*ST* III, q. 32,
a. 1). In conjunction with the affirmation that the external works
of the Trinity are undivided, the Church has traditionally posited
a doctrine of appropriations, in which we attribute to different
persons of the Trinity those acts or characteristics that seem to be
most fitting to them, as specified by the patterns of speech, action
and attribution throughout Scripture. We therefore speak of the
Father as Creator, for example, knowing full well that creation
was an act of the one God: Father, Son and Holy Spirit. These
appropriations, in keeping with Scripture, allow us to emphasize
the diversity proper to the Trinity, without allowing an ultimate
division that would belie the oneness of God.

Returning to the divine attributes, I would like to suggest that
the *opera ad extra* (undivided works of the Trinity) and doctrine of
appropriation could play a similar role to that which they play in
the doctrine of the Trinity. First, in keeping with the oneness of God
and the belief that the external works of the Trinity are undivided,
we affirm that that whole divine character is fully present in any
act of God. For instance, the justice, wisdom and patience of the
living God are always fully present in each of his acts. This rules
out any opposition or dichotomy between justice and mercy, wrath
and love, or any other grouping of attributes, and likewise eschews
assigning certain divine attributes to the Father, and others to the
Son and Spirit. Righteousness is just as proper to the Son as to the
Father, while mercy and love are true of the Father just as they are
of the Son. The question remains how theories of the atonement
are possible, given that they necessarily rely upon one (or a small

group of) divine attribute(s) to give character to a theory. Isn't this selection dismissive of the unity of God, and of the role that the *opera ad extra* ought to play in our thought regarding both the triunity of God and his divine character?

It is at this point that the doctrine of appropriations is of such service, for it provides warrant for us to relate certain divine attributes to a specific aspect of the work of the triune God in the death and resurrection of Jesus Christ, while keeping in mind the ultimate unity of the divine character. In other words, as long as such appropriations are chastened by an awareness of the ultimate unity of the divine attributes, we should avail ourselves of the opportunity to dwell upon the saving work of Christ from the standpoint of different attributes of God, as is fitting in different contexts and situations. Just as we can and should appropriate the work of atonement to the Son, or sanctification to the Spirit, we can and should emphasize the role of different attributes within the doctrine of the atonement.

Returning to our question: if the multiplicity of divine attributes is not ultimately distinguishable into discrete, independent attributes, then isn't the necessarily one-dimensional emphasis of any theory of the atonement inherently opposed to the ultimate unity of the divine attributes? In response, we can now say that affirming the oneness of the divine attributes (*opera ad extra*) is not in tension with developing individual attributes and their role in shaping the meaning of Christ's death and resurrection (doctrine of appropriations). The unity of the triune character is a rich and diverse unity, permitting and encouraging our dwelling upon individual aspects of this unity. In fact, the only way to honour the unity of the divine life and character is to honour it as a rich and diverse unity, both at the level of persons and character.

For this reason, the doctrine of the atonement must consistently work within the tension of unity and diversity, lest it fail to appropriately acknowledge one or the other. The danger is twofold. On the one hand, a false unity may dominate, in which a single theory of the atonement, rooted in a supposedly central or dominant attribute, leads to a permanent system that cuts off or undermines further exploration. On the other hand, a dangerous diversity may reign, in which different theories vie for attention, combating and contradicting each other, or take a more passive route of ignoring each other, operating without a common voice. Unfortunately, both of these dangers are amply evident in the history of the doctrine.

The doctrine of the atonement must integrate its commitment to the oneness and multiplicity of God into its account of the work of Christ, using the unity and diversity proper to the divine perfections as the foundation for its development and ordering of its complementary theories of Christ's saving work.[27] The result is a dynamic, rich and unified theological project, which honours the abundance of biblical and historical material. What we lose in rejecting the simplicity of a single sufficient orthodox position on this doctrine, we gain in affirming the abundance proper to the central act of the ever-rich God.

Atonement from and atonement for

Attention to the divine attributes in this fashion should heighten our awareness that these are the attributes of the living God, and as such, they are life-giving. While it is the case that the life-giving character of God can enact itself destructively in the presence of sin (e.g. holiness consuming the impure), this is not God's natural mode of activity. Because of this, we must be careful to construe Christ's work primarily as a constructive and life-giving reality: an atonement *for*. As Barth puts it:

> God Himself has said No in the sacrifice of His Son for us. . . .
> How can the divine Yes be rightly repeated if it does not include a repetition of this No? But it is distinguishable from the No of pessimism by the fact that like the divine No it is never addressed to creation as such but to the nothingness by which creation is surrounded and menaced . . . and especially by the fact that when it was originally spoken by God it was superseded by His Yes, so that it can only be a No surrounded by and concealed in a Yes, and therefore a retrospective and secondary No. (*CD* III/1, 386)

The 'yes' of God to his creation in Christ is the primal reality within which his 'no' also and temporarily finds its place. Accordingly, an account of the atonement must necessarily include that which we are redeemed *from* (the 'no' of God) – but the order or emphasis is

---

[27] Johnson, *God's Being*, 125.

vital. While in fact we are saved from sin, death and the devil, this is but one part of the good news, which by itself is no Gospel at all. Properly put, we are saved *for* abundant life with the triune God and his creation (the 'yes' of God).

The holy God sanctifies us that we might be holy (1 Pet. 1:16). The just God makes us just and righteous that these might roll on like a river and never-failing stream, watering the earth (Amos 5:24). The loving God showers his love upon us, that we might love in return. In him we are given freedom, unity and wisdom, for these too are proper to the divine life. Created by Christ Jesus, and saved in and through him, we were both made and saved 'for good works' (Eph. 2:10), for an abundant creaturely manifestation of the life of God. We are not prisoners released into a harsh and unwelcoming reality; rather, our release was from prison into an embracing, empowering and life-giving community, where we have freedom to work and serve with honour and dignity. We are not abused spouses and children, delivered from our tormentor but living on the street, looking for shelter and safety; rather, our delivery was from abuse into a loving, nurturing family where past fears and pains can be enfolded by joy, security and intimacy. We are not freed from our debts, penniless in a world of untrusting creditors; rather, freedom is of such a kind as to come with full restitution, full trust and complete resources for abundant life.

Why is this the case? Because the atonement is not primarily about overcoming sin – it is first and foremost about giving us life, and life abundantly (Jn 10:10). To put it differently, the atonement is not about death – it is about resurrection.[28] Where there is resurrection there has been death; but the latter is only the prerequisite for the former, and it is the former that is the goal of Christ's work.

> If Christ has not been raised, your faith is futile and you are still in your sins. . . . But in fact Christ has been raised from the dead, the first fruits of those who have fallen asleep. For as by a man came death, by a man has come also the resurrection of the dead. For as in Adam all die, so also in Christ shall all be made alive. (1 Cor. 15:17, 20-22)

---

[28] Cf. the role of the resurrection throughout the book of Acts, and the argument of Paul in 1 Corinthians 15.

The goal is not merely to have faith, not merely to undo the effects of sin and death – *the goal is the resurrection*, being made alive in Christ that we might be imitators of him, and in this way live out the divine life to the fulfilment of our creaturely existence. In short, the atonement is a fundamentally creative and life-giving reality. This is because God atones for our sin by means of himself, by means of his creative and life-giving character, by means of the same person and character that created us in the first place.[29] What does it mean to be reconciled to the God of Abraham, Isaac and Jacob, the God that became man in the person of Jesus Christ? It is to be swept up into the fullness of the divine life, while experiencing the overflow of this blessing at personal and social levels, and beyond that, in creation as a whole.

This constructive perspective on the meaning and significance of the death and resurrection of Jesus Christ calls for a primarily constructive use of the divine attributes. God comes to share with us his righteousness, justice, love and wisdom. While each of the divine attributes play a role in overcoming sin and its effects, we must not allow this necessarily destructive element of the atonement to overwhelm or minimize what is properly a creative, life-giving and constructive work of the triune God. Why did God become man? In order that he might share with us his honour, to make us wise, to carry us in his love and to fill us with his righteousness.

The shadow-side: Sin in the atonement

That Christ's death and resurrection is first and foremost a constructive act that re-establishes us in a creaturely partaking of the divine life does not mean that the atonement is only positive and life-giving. Resurrection presupposes death, and the restoration of our life with and in God presupposes our separation from him. While the order of our treatments allows the order and priority of the Gospel as good news to emerge clearly, it is vital that we not omit this secondary element: a proper understanding of that which Christ sought to overcome and destroy through his death and resurrection.

---

[29] '[God's] saving work, attested in Scripture, is the reiteration and opening up in creaturely time of his eternal character.' Davidson, 'Introduction: God of Salvation', 7.

We begin, once more, with the divine attributes. The attributes of the living God, we have recently noted, are life-giving; but this is not all they are. To those who are being saved, they are the nourishing power of God; but to those who reject God they take on an altogether different guise. In the presence of sin the divine character takes on a different mode of activity, a destructive mode, we might say. Luther develops this line of thought, suggesting that we think of the divine attributes in two different ways – (1) as lived within the immanent divine life and extended to us in a 'natural' mode and (2) in an 'alien' mode. The latter is an adaptation of God's natural character or way of relating to the circumstances of sin.[30] Within the triune life of God, the divine attributes are exclusively affirming, sustaining and glorifying. The justice of God cultivates the harmony and order of the divine life; his love forms the bonds of intimacy, while his holiness is the singular purity proper to himself. By enacting the divine character in creating, God opened up a range of new possibilities, including the primary goal of relationship with the creature. Included within this possibility, however, was a second and darker path, rejected by God: the rebellion of the creature, as it rejected the divine character and will.[31] Where God is wise, we sought to establish our own counterfeit wisdom, actively embracing foolishness. Where God is Lord, we fought for dominion, or relinquished our stewardship in various forms of slavish subservience. For every divine attribute there are a host of perversions, distortions, fragments and rejections, resulting in a diverse account of sin throughout the biblical narrative.[32]

---

[30]LW 51, 19. (Thanks to Robert Kolb for pointing out this distinction to me). Cf. Jeremy J. Wynne, Wrath among the Perfections of God's Life (New York: T & T Clark, 2010), 111. Also see von Balthasar's similar claim in TD, 192: 'If . . . we see a God who has founded [the world order] in love and thus accompanies it, it is not hard to understand that his love can appear in the mode of anger, punishing the disruption of his order by the imposition of suffering' (emphasis added). As I understand him, this concern is at the heart of Campbell's project as well – vindicating the natural mode of God's justice and holiness, in relation to the divine love. Campbell, The Nature of the Atonement, 51–2.

[31]In this context, I focus on rebellion against the divine character. The divine will is a concrete manifestation of the divine character, such that the two are in harmony. If we reverse this emphasis, our attention is drawn to matters of divine law and questions of obedience. While this has its place, I find it an overly narrow approach to understanding sin.

[32]Cole, God the Peacemaker, 68.

It is in this context, that of a creation groaning under creaturely rebellion against God's character, that atonement occurs. And while atonement is primarily a creative and life-giving work, it necessarily includes God's manifold reaction to sin in its multitude of forms. The key to properly understanding this reaction is, once again, the divine attributes. God does not save us by means of certain attributes, and deal with sin by means of others. Drawing on Luther, we might claim, for instance, that divine justice may be fundamentally about the order and harmony necessary for life; but in the presence of sin, it takes on an alien mode of activity which judges, punishes and ultimately destroys the sin or the sinner. But because this alien mode is ordered towards the natural mode of God's justice, the alien mode of activity does not have a life of its own, and is not at odds with the other divine attributes.

Shifting categories, we note that God is omnipresent. He is present to himself and to all that which he creates. His goal in creation is to share the divine life with the creature, that it too might have presence – a sphere of belonging and activity proper to the creature by means of which it can live, relate and extend itself through activity. But what happens when we sin against the omnipresent God? We reject the reality of divine presence, hiding from God, and abusing our creaturely presence by exiling some and forcing others to be near us, turning presence into a matter of power and efficiency rather than a gift necessary for free relationship. When God in Christ comes near us, that he might restore us to life with and in him, one aspect of this restoration is that of re-establishing our presence with God, in the Church, and in the world. But in the midst of this constructive project, the omnipresence of God takes on an alien mode of activity, destroying and casting down the tools and implements of false presence (2 Cor. 10:4), breaking bonds (Jer. 30:8), casting down walls, and removing the barriers which force or prevent the intimacy of free presence (Eph. 2:14). And because these barriers, bonds and tools, along with their disastrous effects, are bound up with our identity as sinners, Christ makes our sin his own. He bears in himself the full reality of our sinful opposition to divine omnipresence, bearing our exile and destruction (LW, 17, 223). But he does so that he might share with us the natural mode of his omnipresence: welcoming us into the kingdom and presence of the Father.

This reflection brings us two valuable insights. First, while Christ's death and resurrection is first and foremost a creative, life-giving work, it necessarily includes God's decisive response to and rejection of sin in all its forms. This response is the work of those same attributes that enliven us as we are swept up into the life of God, as they take on an alien mode of activity, destroying sin in its many forms. The central element of this divine response to sin is the death of Christ, in which the triune God brings the sin of humankind into himself in the person of the incarnate Son, where God fully enacts his response against sin.

Second, this understanding of sin enables us to better appropriate the biblical witness and the insights of different cultures and communities into the biblical testimony concerning sin. If we prioritize one of the divine attributes over the others, it follows that we will likely prioritize one aspect of sin. But this is as illegitimate concerning sin as it is with the divine character. Our vocation is to understand and oppose sin in all its forms, and the best way to do this is by taking up each aspect of sin into an account of the atonement that overcomes it. And we do this by attending to the divine attribute, which that particular sin opposes or perverts, exploring the natural *and* alien roles of that attribute within Christ's atoning work. This, in turn, gives us yet another entry into the riches of the biblical understanding of Christ's atoning work – through the back door of the biblical account of sin.

One way to accomplish this task is through careful study of the different ways the Bible speaks of sin, drawing upon the exegetical and theological sources which facilitate such work. A second, and ultimately complementary route, is to take a sociological approach, exploring the ways in which cultures think about sin, using this insight to overcome our biases and open our eyes to the ways that the Bible speaks of sin.[33]

A focused look: Wrath and penal substitution

Sustained reflection upon the divine attributes is the wellspring for a rich, creative and properly balanced account of Christ's saving work. But what happens when we explore Christ's death and

---

[33]This is path taken by Baker and Green in their work on shame within the Japanese culture. Baker and Green, *Recovering*, 153–70. This kind of work need not depend on natural theology or general revelation. Rather, it can use cultural engagement as an occasion for further and richer study of God's self-revelation in Scripture.

resurrection in light of God's retributive justice, or divine wrath, as penal substitution is wont to do? The mainstay of this approach is a strong affirmation of God's justice or righteousness, which holds that God must punish and pour out his wrath upon sin and the sinner, for in his love and goodness, neither for his own sake nor for that of the creature does he tolerate the perverting, consuming and depraving influence of sin.[34] In God's love, however, he chooses to take sin upon himself in the person of Jesus Christ, so as to fully exercise his righteous and wrathful response to sin, without utterly destroying the creature.[35] In this way Christ is our substitute, for he bears the wrath and penalty of God upon the sin that he truly bears, so as to save us from this destruction. In an act of supreme love and justice, he is our penal substitute.

This account has an established pedigree. Developing the insights of Anselm and Thomas,[36] it focuses on satisfying the divine justice/righteousness, by means of transferring or imputing our sin to Jesus Christ. Given prominence by John Calvin, it became for some Reformed theologians *the* explanation of Christ's work. For the most part, however, penal substitution was held as one of several elements in a full explanation of Christ's work, until in the late nineteenth and early twentieth centuries it calcified into a more stringent affirmation of penal substitution as 'the one and only correct way of talking about the atonement'.[37] The Scriptural support for this position is twofold. First, there is the witness so pervasive in Scripture to the reality of the divine judgement,

---

[34]For recent critical and defensive explorations of penal substitution, cf. Derek Tidball, David Hilborn, and Justin Thacker, eds, *The Atonement Debate: Papers from the London Symposium on the Theology of Atonement* (Grand Rapids, MI: Zondervan, 2008); Belousek, *Atonement*; Charles E. Hill and Frank A. James, eds, *The Glory of the Atonement: Biblical, Historical and Practical Perspectives* (Downers Grove, IL: InterVarsity Press, 2004); Stephen R. Holmes, *The Wondrous Cross: Atonement and Penal Substitution in the Bible and History* (London: Paternoster, 2007); Jersak and Hardin, *Stricken by God?*

[35]The heart of penal substitution is Christ bearing our sin – not the problem of who will be punished.

[36]Johnson, 'A Fuller Account: The Role of "Fittingness" in Thomas Aquinas' Development of the Doctrine of the Atonement', 310–17.

[37]Stephen R. Holmes, 'Ransomed, Healed, Restored, Forgiven: Evangelical Accounts of the Atonement', in *The Atonement Debate: Papers from the London Symposium on the Theology of Atonement*, ed. Derek Tidball, David Hilborn and Justin Thacker (Grand Rapids, MI: Zondervan, 2008), 276.

punishment and wrath against sin. Second, there are those passages which either anticipate (in the Old Testament) or speak of Christ bearing our sin and punishment, such that Christ is the means of the fulfilment of the divine judgement, punishment and wrath (Lev. 16; Isa. 53; Rom. 3; 2 Cor. 5). Together, these two lines of thought form the foundation for penal substitution.

The debate concerning this theory is extensive, so I will focus on the topic of divine wrath in the hope of furthering our thesis and bringing clarity to a crucial part of the argument concerning penal substitution.[38] The wrath of God is unlike his love or holiness, for it has no place as such within the life of the immanent Trinity. There was no wrath between Father, Son and Holy Spirit, which the triune God sought to share with us by means of his creative work. Wrath, we must say, is something new in the life of God – something new, due to the sin of the creature.[39] What, then, is it? Is wrath an attribute at all?

First, if wrath is an alien mode of God's divine life, then the focus should be first and foremost upon the natural mode of that same attribute, for it is this attribute, this aspect of the divine life, which God seeks to share with us through creation and redemption. Creation, as we have seen, is God's means of sharing the divine life with the creature, to the mutual joy of Creator and creature alike. Wrath, then, is preceded by, and must ultimately give way to, its dominant and natural mode of activity: the loving self-involvement of God.[40] This means that penal substitution, first and foremost, should focus on the love of God, witnessing to the reality of divine wrath only within this greater scheme. This would necessarily lead to substantial revisions in terms of how we express the necessity

---

[38] On the role of the doctrine of divine wrath throughout the history of the Church, cf. Stephen B. Murray, *Reclaiming Divine Wrath: A History of a Christian Doctrine and Its Interpretation* (New York: Peter Lang, 2011). See also the excellent chapter on the subject in: McCall, *Forsaken*, 49–92.

[39] For similar reasons (for where else is wrath so fully unleashed?) there is 'in the event of the cross . . . a "newness" . . . the enactment of unity in unprecedented form, the accommodation of death and its consequences within God's inextinguishable life'. Ivor Davidson, 'Salvation's Destiny: Heirs of God', in *God of Salvation*, ed. Ivor J. Davidson and Murray A. Rae (Burlington, VT: Ashgate, 2011), 165.

[40] As von Balthasar puts it, there is an 'inseparable unity of God's wrath and his love. . . . Wrath is the sign of God's involvement' (*TD*, 55). Cf. Tony Lane, 'The Wrath of God as an Aspect of the Love of God', in *Nothing Greater, Nothing Better: Theological Essays on the Love of God*, ed. Kevin J. Vanhoozer (Grand Rapids, MI: Eerdmans, 2001).

of Christ's death and resurrection, in which the constructive vision of Christ sharing the love of God with us is centre stage (Jn 3:16). Such a sharing includes an account of the attributes of God in their alien mode, but in that order, and with that emphasis. This, in itself, would go some small way towards assuaging current critiques of penal substitution.[41]

Second, this balance and proportion frees us to explore the role of the alien mode of the divine attributes within Christ's atonement. Does God sharing the divine life with us involve his attributes in an alien mode of activity (though one which is ordered towards a natural mode of relating)? We must answer this question with an unequivocal affirmation: 'No doctrine of atonement may ignore this reality [of the inseparable unity of God's wrath and his love], which is attested a thousand times in Scripture' (TD, 55). God's activity of blinding, hardening, crushing, destroying, punishing, exiling and forsaking, particularly evident throughout the Old Testament, but decisively present within the New Testament as well, leaves little room for us to affirm otherwise. The question is whether God, in Christ and through the latter's taking our sin upon himself, bears the fullness of God's alien mode of relating to sinful creation?[42] To take one example, Christ is forsaken by the Father (Mt. 27:46). But what is forsakenness, if not the alien mode of the divine presence? For the sake of God's presence with us, Christ bore our sin and the ensuing forsakenness of the Father, that in his resurrection and ascension to the Father we might in him enter the presence of God (Eph. 2:6).[43]

It is this point – the idea that in Christ God took upon himself the fullness of the alien mode of God's righteous response to

---

[41]I take it, for instance, that this would satisfy one of Belousek's central concerns in the early chapters of Belousek, *Atonement*.

[42]Penal substitution is a misnomer in one sense, in that the emphasis is not upon Christ's *being punished* in our place. Rather, the emphasis is upon him bearing our sin, and doing away with it through its destruction in the form of punishment. Cf. Luther's argument in his commentary on Galatians: *LW* 26, 277ff. Campbell's corrective in salutary, in his repudiation of a merely legal interpretation focused on punishment. In its place, Campbell offers a formulation more deeply relational, rooted in the fatherly love of God, but which still honours Christ's bearing our sin in a manner akin to the underlying logic of penal substitution. Campbell, *The Nature of the Atonement*, 118. For an exceptionally helpful interpretation of Campbell's work, see: T. F. Torrance, 'John Mcleod Campbell (1800-1872)', in *Scottish Theology: From John Knox to John Mcleod Campbell* (Edinburgh: T & T Clark, 1996).

[43]Cf. my argument in Johnson, 'A Temple Framework of the Atonement'.

sin – that penal substitution affirms so helpfully. While Scripture does not affirm penal substitution with all its central elements in a single passage, the above reflections encourage us to consolidate the Bible's teaching concerning justice/righteousness, wrath and Christ's substitution and vicarious bearing of our sin. Does this amount to a full statement of the atonement? Only if two criteria are met. First, it must include the role of the resurrection in establishing us in the love of God and in his justice and righteousness, equipping us in the Spirit to extend that love, justice and righteousness into the world around us. Second, it must acknowledge its completeness only to the extent that it offers a full account of Christ's saving work from the standpoint of divine justice/righteousness, and therefore one which must be accompanied by accounts rooted in other divine attributes. The net result is a (1) synthetic argument for penal substitution, while (2) demanding an overall constructive emphasis via the resurrection that focuses on the renewal of creation in justice/righteousness and (3) holding the door open for further complementary accounts of the work of Christ.

Was Jesus our penal substitute? Yes, but only inasmuch as there were bigger forces at play. In Christ, God showered his justice and righteousness upon, remaking us in his image that he might lead us in paths of righteousness (Ps. 23:3). But inasmuch as God, in his love, showers his justice upon us, he showers it upon us as sinners. And for justice to come into contact with sin is for it to renounce, reject and do away with it unequivocally. There is no place for injustice, for wrong and harm, within the nurturing and life-giving righteousness of God. But Christ, that we might be remade in the image of God, takes upon himself our sin that God might deal with this reality in the context of his own divine life. In this sense Christ is our penal substitute, within the larger dynamic of the triune God taking upon himself our plight, that we might share in his divine life, living lives in which 'justice roll[s] down like waters, and righteousness like an ever-flowing stream' (Amos 5:24).

Conclusion: A symphonic account

Our work on the role of the divine attributes within the doctrine of the atonement leads to the conclusion that whether or not one holds to penal substitution is a question of mixed significance. Some would have it be the authoritative explanation of the work of Christ – the standard or litmus test for orthodoxy within this doctrine. Others acknowledge it as one of many historical theories of the atonement, and quietly (or not so quietly) dismiss it in favour of other construals of the doctrine. On our view, both require some chastening.

First, while penal substitution develops the biblical witness to the justice and wrath of God, and in this does the Church a service, it should not hold any sort of pre-eminence within our theology for the simple reason that as a theory of the atonement, it necessarily stands alongside other equally valid, beneficial and biblical theories of the work of Christ. While elevation of penal substitution might be a polemically strategic move given various historical and contextual factors, the strengths of such moves must be weighed with their weaknesses, and held in proper awareness of the fact that such elevation is strictly chastened by the theological structure and shape of the doctrine. It is therefore both possible and beneficial to the Church that there be those whose emphasis upon other aspects of the work of Christ balances the emphasis on penal substitution found in other circles.[44]

Second, given that penal substitution (properly developed in a Trinitarian manner with regard to the biblical understanding of divine justice) is a valid theory of Christ's saving work which belongs in a full account of the doctrine, the reasons for which one might reject it are of considerable significance. If one does not hold to the doctrine simply because one is unfamiliar with it, being much more thoroughly acquainted with a sacrificial theory of the atonement, for instance, then that is a matter of little concern apart from our calling to seek a full knowledge of the triune God and the good news of Jesus Christ. However, an outright rejection of penal substitution raises different questions altogether, for the same arguments may very well compromise and undermine any biblical and traditional theory of Christ's saving work.

---

[44]This is only fair. If proponents of penal substitution elevate it artificially over other theories and aspects of Christ's saving work, they should expect that others will minimize it artificially.

The possibility exists that the theory of penal substitution in certain forms needs substantial revision.[45] Whether that is the case is not the burden of this chapter. Rather, our concern is with the theological foundation for developing theories of the atonement, and specifically the way in which the divine attributes shape these theories. The result of our inquiry is a vision for the doctrine yielding an ongoing project of developing new aspects and theories of the atonement. Because the work of Jesus is the work of God incarnate, it is a work involving the whole of the divine character, the fullness of the divine perfections. Each of the divine attributes therefore opens the door to new insights, new standpoints from which to reflect upon the work of Christ. Because this work is primarily constructive, we should first and foremost emphasize the natural mode of God's enacted character, the way in which he brings the character of the divine life to bear upon our plight, that we might share in that same life as his adopted children. But at the same time, because in this act God simultaneously confronts our sin, we must in this context develop the way that Christ bears our sin and therefore is the locus of the alien mode of God's enacted character. The result of such study will be the ongoing development and discovery of more and more aspects of that which Christ saves us for and from, to the benefit of our worship and service as the people of God.

---

[45]The strong affirmation of penal substitution, or any theological theory, for that matter, can and must go hand in hand with the confession that any theory as such may require substantial revision or even rejection on biblical grounds. Doctrine, like the Church, should always be reforming.

5

The Atoning Life of Christ

As we have seen, the atonement is a matter of God in Christ overcoming sin in such a way as to bring creation to its fulfilment. But because his work is so creative and life-giving, we must not confine our study of the atonement to the death of Christ: we must attend to far more than Good Friday as we meditate on Christ's re-creating, reconciling and restoring work. Though the cross is a constitutive element for this doctrine, and along with the resurrection is the hinge upon which all else turns, the work of reconciliation extends before and after that event, 'beginning at the sweet Incarnation and lasting until his blessed resurrection on Easter morning'.[1] In this chapter, we explore various periods or 'moments' of the life of Christ, considering the ways in which together they bring about atonement.[2]

Key to this exercise is attending to the scope of the atoning project:

Though Paul does not refer to the tree of life in Genesis 3, his controlling narrative is constantly pointing to the way in which the creator finally brings his human, image-bearing creatures, and indeed the entire cosmos, through the impasse of the fall, of the thorns and thistles and the whirling, flashing sword, to taste at last the gift of life in all its fullness, a new bodily life in a new world where the rule of heaven is brought at last to earth.[3]

---

[1] Norwich, *Showings*, 219.
[2] In this pursuit we will loosely follow the pattern of Calvin, who explores the saving significance of the various elements of the second article of the Apostles' Creed (*Inst*, 503–28).
[3] N. T. Wright, *The Resurrection of the Son of God* (Minneapolis, MN: Fortress, 2003), 373. Cf. Genesis 2:9 and the theme of life in the Gospel of John.

But how does Christ bring the cosmos, thorns and all, to the fullness of life? What does the life, death and resurrection of a man (albeit the God-man) have to do with matters of such a comprehensive scope? Recalling to mind Christ's identity as Creator and image of God will be of service at this point, giving us the resources for appreciating the saving aspect of every major period of Christ's life.

Jesus Christ is the one in whom the Father elected us before the foundation of the world (Eph. 1:4), and as such is prior to creation both in intention and execution.[4] All theological reflection on creation and its history must therefore take place within reflection upon Jesus, the one 'by [whom] all things were created, in heaven and on earth, visible and invisible, whether thrones or dominions or rulers or authorities – all things were created through him and for him (cf. John 1:1-3, 10). And he is before all things, and in him all things hold together.' (Col. 1:15-17). Not only is he the Creator of the world, he is also its inheritor (Heb. 1:2), simultaneously the one 'for whom and by whom all things exist' (Heb. 2:10). The events in the life of Jesus are events in the life of the one by and for whom all things were created, and in whom all things hold together. They are, accordingly, events of unparalleled cosmic significance, with ramifications for every created thing.

Though this is sufficient for our purposes, the Bible establishes an even closer connection between ourselves and Christ than that afforded by our creaturely relation to our Creator and the one in and for whom we exist. Jesus is 'the radiance of the glory of God and the exact imprint of his nature' (Heb. 1:3). That is to say, Jesus is the 'the image of the invisible God, the firstborn of all creation' (Col. 1:15; cf. 2 Cor. 4:4). Genesis begins the canonical development of our status as creatures made in the image of God (Gen. 1:26-7),[5] but the New Testament completes it, specifying that this image in which we were made is Jesus, the second Adam, or second image. Or rather, Jesus is the image to which we are predestined to conform (Rom. 8:29), of which Adam was the type (Rom. 5:14). In other

---

[4]As Julian puts it, '[B]y the endless intent and assent and the full accord of all the Trinity, the mediator wanted to be the foundation and the head of this fair nature, out of whom we have all come, in whom we are enclosed, into whom we shall go, finding in him our full heaven in everlasting joy by the prescient purpose of all the blessed Trinity from without beginning.' Norwich, *Showings*, 283.

[5]Ryan S. Peterson, 'Genesis 1', in *Theological Commentary: Evangelical Perspectives*, ed. R. Michael Allen (New York: T & T Clark, 2011), 15–19.

words, the events in the life of Jesus are all the more significant to humankind because he is the one in whose image we are made, his life is the life to which we conform, and it is our living from, in and for this image that constitutes our human flourishing within the purposes of God. 'There, in Christ, is, for the first time in the true sense, the One who stands, as such, for all others. He is also the Inaugurator, Representative, and Revealer of what through Him and with Him the many, *all* men shall also be, do, and receive.'[6]

This chapter explores the atoning significance of the life, death, resurrection and ascension of this man – the Creator of all things, the one in whom all things live and move and have their being, the one in whom all things hold together and, most importantly for ourselves, the one who, in this life, in this series of events, constitutes the image in which we are made, and to which we are predestined to conform. For these reasons, the events in the life and death of this God-man are of the utmost significance to those things and beings which have their being and purpose in him, in his life.

The life of Christ I

How does Christ's life, up to the point of his crucifixion, contribute to our reconciliation with God? If atonement were simply a matter of settling a debt by a payment of equal or great value, Christ could have died as an infant at the hands of the Herod (Mt. 2:16-18), rising three days later. What would be missing in such an account is the constructive aspect of Christ's work: the saving revelation of the Father, a life pleasing to God, a life into which we are brought, a life which is itself our at-*one*-ment with God. Calvin claims that 'from the time when he took on the form of a servant, he began to pay the price of liberation in order to redeem us', and proceeds to focus on the death of Christ. The only explanatory statement he offers in this context is that this redemption was achieved 'by the whole course of his obedience' (*Inst*, 507).[7] While Calvin points out a path, others must help us traverse it.

---

[6]Karl Barth, *Christ and Adam: Man and Humanity in Romans 5*, trans. Thomas Allan Smail (New York: Harper & Brothers, 1956), 31.

[7]Cf. the exceptionally strong role of Christ's life in: Friedrich Schleiermacher, *The Christian Faith* (Edinburgh: T & T Clark, 1968), 453.

Irenaeus' hermeneutic of recapitulation is of great assistance here, for his method equips us to explore the many ways in which the whole life of Christ takes up the history of sin, and fittingly reverses it.[8] 'God recapitulated in himself the ancient formation of man, that He might kill sin, deprive death of its power, and vivify man' (*AH*, 448). And on this basis of this recapitulated formation, God 'sum[med] up in Himself the whole human race from the beginning to the end' (*AH*, 551). Essentially this means that Christ took up human history (particularly that of Israel), and human experience, bringing these to fulfilment in the course of his life.

For one, this means that the history of Adam and Eve, Israel and indeed all of humankind is repeated and yet transformed in the course of the life of Christ.[9] Where we are tempted and fall, Christ was tempted and withstood. Where we (Jew and Gentile alike) break the law and/or covenants, Christ keeps them. Christ, under the same circumstances as our own, is obedient. The temptation of Christ is vital from this perspective, for where Adam and Eve, and later Israel, had failed, Christ withstood.[10] Not only does overcoming temptation qualify Jesus to be our saviour by his overcoming sin, both in terms of power (Mt. 28:18) and sympathy (Heb. 4:14-15) – it is itself atoning in that Christ, by being obedient where all of us fell, is redeeming human history by being obedient where we fell short, creating the new and decisive history into which we are brought or incorporated.

At the more individual level, Christ is simultaneously creating the pattern into which we are formed – a vital element of our salvation

---

[8]Irenaeus' thought is partly rooted in Ephesians 1:10 and the notion of 'summing up'.
[9]Michael F. Bird, *Jesus Is the Christ: The Messianic Testimony of the Gospels* (Downers Grove, IL: InterVarsity Press, 2012); Wright, *Victory*, ch. 11; Barth, *Christ and Adam: Man and Humanity in Romans 5*, 73.
[10]Wherever one locates Jesus' triumph over sin, the cross itself seems to be the least likely place, for it is 'an image of defilement, a gross manifestation of collective human sin. Jesus, then, does not conquer sin through death on a cross. Rather, Jesus conquers the sin of temptation in the wilderness by resistance.' Williams, 'Black Women's Surrogacy', 31. Milton, along these lines, locates the regaining of paradise not at the cross or resurrection (though he does not exclude these), but in the temptation of Christ. John Milton, 'Paradise Regained', in *John Milton: The Major Works* (New York: Oxford, 2008).

which is not merely a salvation *from*, but a salvation *into* the life and pattern of Christ.[11] As Torrance puts it:

> By living the life which Jesus Christ lived in our midst, the life of complete obedience to the Father and of perfect communion with him, the life of absolute holiness in the midst of our sin and corruption, and by living it through the whole course of our human existence from birth to death, he achieved within our creaturely being the very union between God and man that constitutes the heart of atonement, effecting man's salvation and restoration to communion with God the Father.[12]

And this communion is important not merely as the first of many, not merely as an example to inspire us, but as the reality into which we are swept. It is this 'original activity of the Redeemer . . . which belongs to Him alone, and which precedes all activity of our own' into which 'He assumes us into this fellowship of His activity and His life'.[13] Jesus had to live this life for it is our incorporation or assumption into this life by the Spirit which is our at-one-ment with God, which constitutes our salvation.

This emphasis on the saving life of Christ as recapitulation includes his *bodily* life, his struggle against the temptations and passions interwoven with the threat of death such as they are. Given that the mystery of Christ is the 'preconceived goal for which everything exists', in himself he is 'the recapitulation of the things he has created' by bringing them to fulfilment from within their fallen state in himself.[14] In this way Christ became, 'not only the beginning of redemption in time, but also the eternally inexhaustible source, adequate for every further development, of a spiritual and blessed life'.[15] Picking the fruit in the Garden of

---

[11]McKnight, *Community*, 56–8; Lane, 'Bernard of Clairvaux: Theologian of the Cross', 250.

[12]Thomas F. Torrance, *Space, Time, and Resurrection* (Grand Rapids, MI: Eerdmans, 1976), 47.

[13]Schleiermacher, *The Christian Faith*, 425.

[14]Maximus the Confessor, *On the Cosmic Mystery of Jesus Christ: Selected Writings from St. Maximus the Confessor*, trans. Paul M. Blowers and Robert Louis Wilken (Crestwood, NY: St. Vladimir's Seminary Press, 2003), 124.

[15]Schleiermacher, *The Christian Faith*, 461.

Eden, we reaped 'bodily corruption and death, and the liability and propensity to every passion'.[16] Christ came to undo this work, binding to himself a fallen human nature that he might 'cleanse it of the taints of ignorance . . . , render its natural operation steadfast by the Spirit . . . , and cleanse it of the decay of the passions'.[17] In significant measure Jesus accomplished this by means of what have become known as the spiritual disciplines, exercises such as fasting, prayer and study by means of which he brought his body and soul into the pattern of Spirit-filled life intended by God. These disciplines are therefore saving in the sense that through them Christ achieved the life which is itself our salvation.[18] The life of Christ is that into which we are saved: a life of spiritual discipline. Our participation in this life is therefore saving in the sense that it is our participation in salvation, our participation in the life of Christ.[19]

In the next section, we will focus on the negative dimension of this assumption, but at present, we are dwelling on the life-giving fact that in assuming what we are, Christ takes up human nature so as to live the reality into which we are saved: the eternal communion of interpersonal love in creaturely form. For as Schleiermacher says, the 'total effective influence of Christ is only the continuation of the creative divine activity out of which the Person of Christ arose'.[20] Or, locating this same point within a broader framework, McKnight writes that 'the atonement begins in the *perichoresis* of God', which 'becomes incarnate in the Son of God . . . in order to draw us into that *perichoresis*'.[21] As we learn from Brontë's *Wuthering Heights*, removing a child from abandonment is only one small part of the problem, for that 'bringing out' is only as helpful as the reality into which the child is 'brought in'. The truly saving reality is that of the family adopting the child, or in this case, the reality of the life

---

[16]Maximus the Confessor, *Cosmic Mystery*, 76.

[17]Ibid., 85.

[18]This, in brief, is my attempt to correct the oversight typical of theologies of the atonement lamented in: Dallas Willard, *Spirit of the Disciplines* (New York: Harper Collins, 1991), 33.

[19]To be clear, this is no salvation by works in the sense that our own works save us. Rather, it is a salvation by works in the sense that through these disciplines we are participating in the work of Christ. It is his work, and not ours, which is saving.

[20]Schleiermacher, *The Christian Faith*, 427.

[21]McKnight, *Community*, 60.

of Christ into which we are saved. Salvation from sin through the death of Christ is nothing apart from our salvation into his life, and for this reason, his life prior to the cross is atoning, as the reality in which our salvation consists.

The cross

'To define the way of salvation more exactly, Scripture ascribes [the payment of the price of our liberation] as peculiar and proper to Christ's death. He declares that "he gave his life to redeem many" [Matt. 20:28]' (*Inst*, 507). While the life of Christ is his obedience in our stead and the reality into which he brings us, it is simultaneously his entry into a fully human life, a life which, because lived in a fallen world, moves irreversibly towards death. This death, according to the Gospels, was a necessary event willed in a complex manner by God, for us and for our salvation. Though Christ's death is not itself the atonement, for in and of itself it is not saving, it is an essential component of Christ's work, fulfilling God's response to sin.

'My Father, if possible, let this cup pass from me; nevertheless, not as I will, but as you will' (Mt. 26:39). Jesus understands this cup, the cup of God's wrath in the form of his death on the cross, to be willed by God.[22] But why would God will such a thing? Much of our work in this book has emphasized the life-giving creative nature of Christ's atonement. But this cannot be at the expense of the destruction, judgement, wrath and death included within this same event – for while in the work of Christ God says 'YES' to humankind in Christ, he simultaneously says 'NO' to sin, evil and death. The Old Testament consistently holds the compassion of God for his people and his creatures in tension with his righteous anger against them, though ultimately prioritizing the former. Deuteronomy holds

---

[22]Cf. Cousar, *A Theology of the Cross: The Death of Jesus in the Pauline Letters*, 26–7; Dillistone, *Jesus Christ and His Cross: Studies on the Saving Work of Christ*, 57–8. However, see the arguments by Borg and Alison to the contrary. Marcus Borg, 'Executed by Rome, Vindicated by God', in *Stricken by God? Nonviolent Identification and the Victory of Christ*, ed. Brad Jersak and Michael Hardin (Grand Rapids, MI: Eerdmans, 2007), 159–61; James Alison, 'God's Self-Substitution and Sacrificial Inversion', ibid., 178.

blessings and curses in the balance (Deut. 28), hinging on the choice of Israel (Deut. 30). In this vein the prophets shift from one to the other, now speaking of God's wrath, judgement and destruction, and then shifting to his love and grace. The cross was necessary for God's purposes as the fulfilment of his rejection and destruction of sin, of his consistent warnings, commands and promises regarding human sin. Christ's work on the cross is the great fulfilment of God's rejecting, cleansing, cursing, purging, exiling, punishing, shaming and destroying of our sin.

The threat of death to Adam and Eve (Gen. 2:17), the threat of exile to the Jews, should they violate the covenant (Lev. 26:14-33), the threat against the Ninevites, just barely avoided (Jon. 3:4) . . . God had passed over the sins of humankind, but not so as to overlook them – he passed over these sins so as to deal with them at the right time and the right way.[23] 'God put forward [Christ] as a [propitiation/expiation] by his blood . . . to show God's righteousness, because in his divine forbearance he had passed over former sins' (Rom. 3:25-26). This was necessary for God's forbearance is his patience – a patience ordered towards the fruition of God and his creatures, an act in which 'space and time are given with a definite intention, where freedom is allowed in expectation of a response' (CD II/1, 408). God was patient, he gave us freedom and time, so as to deal with our sin in the right way and right time. In other words, it is a patience that is in full harmony with God's utter opposition to sin in all its forms; but because God is not a slave to this opposition to sin, he is free to be patient in his dealing with it. And this patience finds its fulfilment in Gethsemane – the determined time and place for dealing with the reality of sin once and for all.

With the silence of God for an answer (Lk. 22:39-46), Christ resolutely moves towards his crucifixion on Golgotha, a death that we must understand on a variety of levels in order to do justice to the conjunction of forces and wills operative therein. Physically, the

---

[23]To be sure, he did not pass over these sins completely. Adam and Eve were sent from the garden, Israel was exiled, and many sins were punished – but God's response was always mingled with grace and patience, always giving room and making space for his sinful creatures, always seeking to bring them back to himself. The judgement, the punishment and the wrath were always muted, always a witness and testimony to that which would one day be fully unleashed without restraint.

death of Christ was a painful and shameful crucifixion.[24] In this, Christ took upon himself the sin, pain, suffering and death resulting from the Fall, suffering at religious, social, political and theological levels. Relationally, Christ experienced sin in the form of betrayal and denial, taking upon himself the broken relationships between neighbours in a corrupt world, including the ruptures with family (Mt. 12:48; Jn 19:25-27), friends (Jn 18:15-18, 25-7), race (Lk. 23:18) and, in certain respects, his own relationship with the Father (Mt. 27:46). Socially, Jew (Mt. 27:24-5) and Gentile (Mt. 27:27-38) alike rejected Jesus. Outcast by his people and the dominant power, Jesus was crucified for a complex set of politically charged reasons, taking upon himself the social and systemic consequences of sin in a world meant for a communal relationship.[25] Cosmically, the earth revolted at the crucifixion of its maker, with darkness and an earthquake (Mt. 27:51; Lk. 23:44-45) – witnesses to the cosmic nature of the suffering and death of Christ, bearing the crown of thorns and thereby the earth's great curse.[26] Theologically – but this is the key! What did the death of Christ entail in terms of his relationship with the Father?

NT Wright tells us: '[T]he way of the shepherd-king was to share the suffering of the sheep. The way of the servant was to take upon himself the exile of the nation as a whole. As a would-be Messiah, Jesus identified with Israel; he would therefore go ahead of her, and take upon himself precisely that fate, actual and symbolic, which he had announced for nation, city, and Temple.'[27] On the one hand, Jesus taking this fate upon himself is a political event, for this exile is at the hands of an opposing power. But there is more to

---

[24]Hengel, *Crucifixion*; Wright, *Victory*, 543-4.

[25]*Victory*, 543-52.

[26]Herbert, *The Complete English Poems*, 28. In 'The Sacrifice', Herbert writes:

> Then on my head a crown of thorns I wear:
> For these are all the grapes *Sion* doth bear,
> Though I my vine planted and wat'red there:
> Was ever grief like mine?

> So sits the earth's great curse in *Adam's* fall
> Upon my head: so I remove it all
> From th' earth unto my brows, and bear the thrall
> Was ever grief like mine?

[27]Wright, *Victory*, 608.

it than that, for the people of Israel was God's chosen people, such that its blessings were by the hand of God, as were its sufferings (cf. Deut. 28). To suffer exile (being killed outside the city walls at the hands of the Romans) was to suffer the punishment of God at the hands of foreign powers, but foreign powers *in the hands of God*. 'The Lord will bring you and your king . . . to a nation that neither you nor your fathers have known' (Deut. 28:36), '[Y]ou shall serve your enemies whom the Lord will send against you' (Deut. 28:48), and 'The Lord will bring a nation against you from far away' (Deut. 28:49). Jesus, that is, suffered *God's* exiling of Israel, rather than mere political or social oppression distinct and separate from the unique judgement of God. It was the Lord that laid on him our iniquity as the representative of Israel (Isa. 53:6); it is the theological dimension of the event which gives the whole its meaning.[28]

What then is the cross of Christ? What does his death mean for us? Christ's death is the great undoing; the great pruning (Jn 15:2), clearing and burning of God's garden (Rom. 11:17-24); the slaughtering of the sacrifice (Ex. 24:3-8) and accompanying use of its blood to cleanse the altar and its implements (Heb. 9:21-22); the bearing of the curse (Gal. 3:13-14), the shame and the judgement; the punishment (Isa. 53:9), exile (Isa. 53:8) and rout (Num. 14) of God's chosen people Israel; the cataclysmic overwhelming and destruction of God's creation in the death of the incarnate maker, retelling of the stories of Noah (Gen. 5–10), and Sodom and Gomorrah (Gen. 18–19) in which not a single righteous man was found. It is the making good of God's promise of death (Gen. 3:3), made so long ago to our first parents' sin, the final work of the tree of knowledge of good and evil in bearing its maker who was made to be a curse (Gal. 3:13). In short, it is the great response of God to sin, evil and death, which ultimately can have no place within the will of God, and though granted a temporary place in the patience of God, must ultimately give way utterly and without a trace before the grace, holiness, love and righteousness of God.

---

[28]Keep in mind the work of Chapter 3, which establishes this as a fully Trinitarian event in which as Father, Son and Holy Spirit, God brings sin into his own life through the incarnation of the Son, so as to deal with our sin by means of properly Trinitarian resources of the divine life.

Being dead: Holy Saturday

To our reflection on the dying of Christ, we must add a reflection on his being dead. Calvin writes that 'death held us captive under its yoke; Christ, in our stead, gave himself over to its power to deliver us from it' (*Inst*, 511), explaining this by building on the creedal affirmation of Christ's descent into hell. This he specifies as 'undergo[ing] the severity of God's vengeance, to appease his wrath and satisfy his just judgement. For this reason, he must also grapple hand to hand with the armies of hell and the dread of everlasting death' (*Inst*, 515). In the present section we explore the meaning of Christ being dead, or put differently, the significance of Holy Saturday – the day between the death and resurrection in Christ.

One well-attested possibility emphasizes the harrowing of hell, in which Christ, 'being put to death in the flesh but made alive in the spirit', went and 'proclaimed to the spirits in prison, because they formerly did not obey, when God's patience waited in the days of Noah' (1 Pet. 3:19). This is the path taken by John of Damascus, who writes:

> The soul when it was deified descended into Hades, in order that . . . He might bring light to those who sit under the earth in darkness and shadow of death: in order that just as He brought the message of peace to those upon the earth . . . so He might become the same to those in Hades.[29]

Just as Christ's work is effective for those living during and after his ministry and ascension, so it was effective for those who died before him. One thing Christ appears to have done on Holy Saturday was proclaim the good news to those in Hades (*not* hell), that they might rise with him.

Thomas notes the same point, but in typical Thomistic fashion notes other reasons for Christ's descent into hell. 'It was fitting,' he writes,

> for Christ to descend into hell. First of all, because He came to bear our penalty in order to free us from penalty, according to

---

[29]Damascus, *Orthodox Faith*, 72–3.

Isa. liii. 4: *Surely He hath borne our infirmities and carried our sorrows.* But through sin man had incurred not only death of the body, but also descent into hell. Consequently . . . it was fitting for Him to descend into hell in order to deliver us also from going down to hell. (*ST*, 3.52.1)

While death of the body is certainly one consequence of our rejection of God and his good gifts, it is not the only one. In this regard, Acts 2:24 is a better place from which to consider Christ's descent into hell than 1 Peter, regarding its affirmation that 'God raised [Jesus] up, loosing the pangs of death, because it was not possible for him to be held by it', following with a reference to Psalm 16:10: 'For you will not abandon my soul to Sheol, or let your holy one see corruption.'[30] What does it mean for Christ to be loosed from the pangs of death, for him to experience but not be abandoned to Sheol?

Drawing on a host of sources, von Balthasar argues against an active 'descent' and combat with the demonic forces, arguing instead for a culmination of the logic of the incarnation (as seen in Irenaeus, Athanasius and others), in which the Son takes what is ours, that he might save it. Citing Thomas (*ST*, III.52), he contends that because the 'penalty which the sin of man brought on was not only the death of the body . . . [but] also a penalty [which] affected the soul . . . the soul paid the price in being deprived of the vision of God'. Accordingly, 'in order to assume the entire penalty imposed upon sinners, Christ willed not only to die, but to go down, in his soul, *ad infernum* [to hell].'[31] Concerning the nature of this experience, von Balthasar suggests that it was a vision of death, of sin in itself, an experience in which 'Christ takes the existential measure of everything that is sheerly contrary to

---

[30] On the biblical material relevant to the descent into hell, or Holy Saturday, cf. David Lauber, *Barth on the Descent into Hell: God, Atonement and the Christian Life* (Burlington, VT: Ashgate, 2004), 76–112. Against von Balthasar's interpretation, see: Alyssa Lyra Pitstick, *Light in Darkness: Hans Urs von Balthasar and the Catholic Doctrine of Christ's Descent into Hell* (Grand Rapids, MI: W.B. Eerdmans, 2007).

[31] Hans Urs von Balthasar, *Mysterium Paschale: The Mystery of Easter*, trans. Aidan Nichols (San Francisco: Ignatius Press, 1990), 164. For a quite different approach to Holy Saturday, much more closely aligned to Moltmann than to Barth, Cf. Alan E. Lewis, *Between Cross and Resurrection: A Theology of Holy Saturday* (Grand Rapids, MI: Eerdmans, 2001).

God, of the entire object of the divine eschatological judgment.'[32]
This was, in other words, an utterly passive experience in which
Christ suffers the reality of hell for us.[33] And if, 'contemplating
the Cross, we read the terrible warnings that Yahweh addresses
to his people if it breaks the covenant (Lev. 26; Deut. 28:15-68) –
and the covenant is broken more radically than ever before in
the rejection of the Messiah – we get some idea of what it means
for Jesus to be under the "curse" of the Law and to be "made to
be sin"' (TD, 336). That is to say, 'the Son of God bears sinners
within himself, together with the hopeless impenetrability of their
sin, which prevents the divine light of love from registering in
them. In himself, therefore, he experiences . . . the hopelessness of
their resistance to God and the graceless No of divine grace to this
resistance' (TD, 349).

Trinitarian questions abound at this point, for the descent into
hell would seem to posit a rupture between the Father and the
incarnate Son.[34] Moltmann (speaking of the cross rather than
the descent into hell) goes so far as to posit that 'the cross of the
Son divides God from God to the utmost degree of enmity and
distinction. The resurrection of the Son abandoned by God unites
God with God in the most intimate fellowship.'[35] The danger with
such a claim is that we posit a rupture in the being and life of God
so complete that the atoning work of Christ ceases to be God
saving us by means of sharing himself with us. Far better to take
the path of Barth, von Balthasar and others who explore the reality
of God's triune life as containing within itself those resources for
Christ's experience of hell. Barth, for instance, writes that 'distance
and confrontation, encounter and partnership, are to be found in
Himself. In Himself, therefore, there is to be found . . . the eternal
form of the answer and solution' (CD IV/2, 343). By this, Barth
means to say that there are resources within the triune life of God
for the reality experienced by Christ in his separation (but not

---

[32]von Balthasar, *Mysterium Paschale*, 174.
[33]Edward T. Oakes, 'The Internal Logic of Holy Saturday in the Theology of Hans
Urs von Balthasar', *International Journal of Systematic Theology* 9, no. 2 (2007):
192. von Balthasar goes to some length to distinguish Sheol and hell, giving a
Christological account of the latter.
[34]For an introduction to this topic, cf. McCall, *Forsaken*, 13–47.
[35]Moltmann, *The Crucified God*, 152.

rupture!) from the Father under the condition of his bearing our sin.[36] In short, the descent into hell is the enactment of separation and distance within the Trinity for our sake and for our salvation, so that Christ can bear and exhaust the full implications of our sins in the form of suffering the reality of hell for us.[37]

What then is the significance of Christ's descent into hell? In this event, Christ suffered the utmost consequences of our sin. But this need not preclude his consequent preaching to those in hell, leading the faithful from its depths (1 Pet. 3:18-20). Neither need it preclude Thomas' third point, namely, his triumphing over hell through his display of power (*ST*, 3.52.1). The descent into hell is the final, deepest and most extreme form of the trajectory established in our reflection upon the death of Christ, which simultaneously raises to a fervent pitch the urgent need for an equally strong affirmation of the doctrine of the resurrection – for as we will see in the next section, the full and proper meaning of Christ's death and descent into hell become evident only from the morning light of Easter Sunday and the resurrection of Christ.

Resurrection

One of the more unfortunate events in the history of the doctrine of the atonement was Anselm's failure to sufficiently develop the role of the resurrection within his construal of Christ's satisfying work. Repeating Athanasius' argument that it would be unfitting of the Creator to allow his rational creatures to utterly perish, and that God must bring them to their intended purpose of rejoicing in him (*De inc*, 63), Anselm argues that 'this cannot be done . . . except through the paying of complete recompense for sin' (*CDH*, 317), without any reference to the resurrection of Christ. In doing so, Anselm bequeathed to those following him the notion that we could speak of satisfaction without resurrection, or the more subtle tendency to overemphasize Christ's death while minimizing his

---

[36]Cf. Johnson, *God's Being*, 73–8. von Balthasar's notion of *primal kenosis* plays much the same role as Barth's account of separation and distance within the triune life.

[37]One might portray this separation or distance in terms of the separation of a married couple, as opposed to divorce, to capture the simultaneous distance and unity, while rejecting a final rupture.

resurrection.[38] This, according to Robert Jenson, is one of the two disastrous errors of early Christian theology of the atonement[39] – but what is the resurrection, that its omission is so disastrous?

Anselm claimed that we needed to pay 'complete recompense', or offer full satisfaction, 'for sin'. But what does it mean to offer satisfaction to God? And precisely what are we satisfying? The meaning of the Latin (satis-facere) is 'to make full', suggesting the bringing to completion of a purpose, providing for a need, or paying a debt. In Anselm's case, we were to satisfy the honour of God, giving him the honour due to him as the Creator, by means of our creaturely flourishing. Unfortunately, Anselm locates this satisfaction in the death of Christ, or, as he sometimes puts it, the life of Christ offered on the cross (CDH, 2.18). But we must be careful how we use the notion of satisfaction, for what, precisely, is being satisfied, is a question of great significance.[40] Anselm's regard for compensating God's lost honour is but a small part of the problem of satisfaction, accounting for significant imbalances in his thought.[41]

---

[38]This is only a tendency – as we will see, many theologians still made significant use of the resurrection. It could perhaps be said, unfortunately, that this tendency is still to be found today.

[39]Robert Jenson, 'On the Doctrine of the Atonement', *The Princeton Seminary Bulletin* 27, no. 2 (2006): 102. The other error is the severing of the doctrine from its roots in the history of Israel, an error I plan to address in greater depth in a future volume.

[40]Barth, for instance, warns against the idea that Christ offers satisfaction to the wrath of God (CD IV/1, 253), in part because wrath itself is not a divine attribute in the same way that love and justice are (cf. our earlier treatment of modes of divine attributes).

[41]'Apart from God's No, in judgement and crucifixion, the resurrection would be only an empty show of wonderful power – it would not have any saving content to it, it would contain no forgiveness. By itself the expiatory death of Christ would mean only judgement, not life, only rejection of guilt. ... The vast significance of the crucifixion and resurrection emerges only as we see that here *redemption and creation come completely together*, in such a way that they gather up all the past and proleptically include the consummation of all things at the end.' Torrance, *Space, Time, and Resurrection*, 58. The resurrection of the suffering Messiah is not merely a display of a power foreign and inaccessible to us, for as the resurrection of the one who made our sufferings his own, it is the display of a power for and in us, a power which contains a verdict on our present plight: the full assertion and reality of God's good pleasure with the person and work of the Son, in whom the plight of creation has been addressed; the judgement which contains both the denouncement of sin and the creation of righteousness, first for Jesus himself, and then, in him, for those who are in Christ. Ibid., 51.

Filling out Anselm's project, Christ's work is indeed a work of satisfaction, but one that brings to fullness and completion the plan of God for his creatures: his intention to share with us the divine life.[42] For this reason Christ's work must first and foremost be a creative and life-giving sharing of the divine life, and we must adhere to Cyril's emphasis that Christ 'descended so that he might restore the resurrection to those on earth, something he alone had formed afresh for human nature since he became "the first-born from the dead"'.[43] While this includes the death of Christ and can readily acknowledge the satisfaction of the divine honour in its redemptive mode (i.e. satisfying for the ways we have dishonoured God), this 'No' to our sin in all its forms and consequences is strictly secondary in importance when it comes to God's purpose and the necessity of the atonement.[44] First and foremost is the satisfaction offered by the bodily resurrection of Jesus: the decisive and victorious sharing of the divine life with the redeemed and resurrected creature.[45] As McKnight puts it, '[F]or Paul the atonement is a comprehensive work of not only wiping the slate clean of sins but also of restoring cracked Eikons [humankind] by gifting them with the life of God so they participate in God's life.'[46] Or as Calvin puts it, 'We divide the substance of our salvation as follows: through his death, sin was wiped out and death extinguished; through his resurrection,

---

[42]Julian of Norwich writes beautifully of the resurrection as birth and satisfaction of the divine love: 'But our true Mother Jesus, he alone bears us for joy and for endless life, blessed may he be. So he carries us within him in love and travail, until the full time when he wanted to suffer the sharpest thorns and cruel pains that ever were or will be, and at last he died. And when he had finished, and had borne us so for bliss, still all this could not satisfy his wonderful love.' Norwich, *Showings*, 298; cf. 304.

[43]Cyril, *On the Unity of Christ*, trans. John Anthony McGuckin (Crestwood, NY: St. Vladimir's Seminary Press, 1995), 126. One might say, along these lines, that Jesus died that he might rise again. The goal of Christ's work was the resurrection; death was the necessary step towards that goal, without which it would have been impossible. Cf. Moltmann, *The Crucified God*, 186. Luther, in a similar train of thought, writes that just as Christ died for us, so also he rose for us. *LW* 58, 104.

[44]For those inclined to think of the death of Christ as the basis of our justification, cf. Romans 4:25, and Paul's claim that Christ was 'raised for our justification'.

[45]This is a matter of bodily life. The reduction of resurrection to 'resurrection faith' and 'extraordinary impact of his personality' will not suffice. Troeltsch, *The Christian Faith: Based on Lectures Delivered at the University of Heidelberg in 1912 and 1913*, 88.

[46]McKnight, *Community*, 71. Isaiah 53:11 locates God's satisfaction in the fruit of Christ's work, rather than his suffering.

righteousness was restored and life raised up, so that – thanks to his resurrection – his death manifested its power and efficacy in us' (*Inst*, 521). How then is the resurrection God's work of satisfaction?

The death of Christ, in which he takes upon himself all that resists and keeps us from the character and purposes of God, is an essential component of Christ's work; but it is not the whole work. Paul goes so far as to say that 'if Christ has not been raised, your faith is futile and you are still in your sins' (1 Cor. 15:17), for the goal is not to be freed from our sins so much as it is to be made alive in Christ (1 Cor. 15:22), a reality which includes and transcends freedom from sin.[47] What then is the resurrection? The resurrection is the satisfaction of God, for it is the point at which the Father 'brings his work to completion; the Father, in exalting his Son, also brings the Son's mission to its conclusion, and makes the Son visible to the world, spreading abroad there the Spirit which is common to them both' (*MP*, 189; cf. 205). The resurrection is the exaltation and revelation of the Son in God's determinative and irrevocable act of re-creation, 'salvific because they restore the covenant and promises of God' and renew 'all of creation'.[48] Along the way, it is the 'mighty act of God within our humanity and its sin, corruption and death, shattering the powers

---

[47]Cf. the argument of Romans 6, which speaks of dying to sin, while emphasizing being 'alive to God in Christ Jesus'. Thomas notes the argument that the resurrection was not necessary since 'Christ's Passion sufficed for our salvation, since by it we were loosed from guilt and punishment' (*ST*, 3.53.1arg.3). In response, he writes that Christ's resurrection was necessary 'in order to complete the work of our salvation: because, just as for this reason did He endure evil things in dying that He might deliver us from evil, so was He glorified in rising again in order to advance us toward good things; according to Rom. iv.25: *He was delivered up for our sins, and rose again for our justification*' (*ST*, 3.53.1). Along these lines, Pseudo-Dionysius weaves together redemption and resurrection, arguing: 'Redemption . . . raises a thing up from an evil condition and sets it firmly where it ought to be, adding on lost virtue, bringing back order and arrangement where there was disorder and derangement, making it perfect and liberating it from defects.' Pseudo-Dionysius, *Pseudo-Dionysius: The Complete Works*, 114.

For Paul, the resurrection goes hand in hand with the crucifixion, so much so that 'there is a presumption in the text that when the one is mentioned or discussed the other is implied'. Cousar, *A Theology of the Cross: The Death of Jesus in the Pauline Letters*, 103.

[48]Trelstad, 'Cross Examinations', 112.

of evil in an utterly decisive way', but it is this within the bigger picture of the achievement or satisfaction of his manifold creative purposes.[49]

But to speak of fulfilment is to harken back to origins and purposes, and the event of creation, for the resurrection 'is akin to the creation in the beginning; and the Gospel is the good news that God is creating a new world'.[50] The resurrection disdains comparison to mere coming-back-to-life or resuscitation. Rather, it is a fundamentally different mode of human existence – the establishment of the creature in the life of God on the far side of death. But the fact that it is a fundamentally new event in no way undermines our present existence and history. To the contrary, it fulfils it:

> History matters because human beings matter; human beings matter because creation matters; creation matters because the creator matters. And the creator, according to some of the most ancient Jewish beliefs, grieved so much over creation gone wrong, over humankind in rebellion, over thorns and thistles and dust and death, that he planned from the beginning the way by which he would rescue his world, his creation, his history, from its tragic corruption and decay; the muddled and rebellious human beings, from their doubly tragic fate; the way, therefore, by which he would most truly be himself, would *become* most truly himself. The story of Jesus of Nazareth which we find in the New Testament offers itself, as Jesus himself had offered his public work and words, his body and blood, as the answer to this multiple problem: the arrival of God's kingdom precisely in the world of space, time and matter, the world of injustice and tyranny, of empire and crucifixions. This world is where the kingdom must come, on earth as it is in heaven.[51]

---

[49]Torrance, *Space, Time, and Resurrection*, 31. As Denny Weaver puts it, '[T]he resurrection of Jesus is the definitive victory of the reign of God over the reign of evil, whether or not any individual sinner perceives the resurrection.' J. Denny Weaver, *The Nonviolent Atonement* (Grand Rapids, MI: Eerdmans, 2001), 219.

[50]Torrance, *Space, Time, and Resurrection*, 31.

[51]Wright, *The Resurrection of the Son of God*, 737. Along these lines, Luther correlates the resurrection and the beginning of Christ's reign in his commentary on Isaiah 52:13. *LW* 17, 215.

What is the resurrection? It is the fulfilment of the Creator's work, not by means of an altogether new and different work alongside or after the present creation, not by means of doing away with the present creation, but *within* the present creation, so that the present tragedy is both honoured in its reality and integrity, while simultaneously rescued, renewed and fulfilled.[52] Resurrection takes the present creature in its state of death, rebellion and decay, and brings it to life, completion and glory. Resurrection thus honours the identity and plight of creation, while freeing it from those realities, both internal and external to itself, which keep it from achieving its full fruition in the fellowship of the Creator.

How can this be? We have as little recourse to explain this re-creation as we do to explain the original creation, for this is a fundamentally new mode of creaturely existence. But we can witness to the reality of the resurrection, and rejoice in the way that it both honours the integrity and history of the creature, while simultaneously bringing it to a completion which was utterly inaccessible to it of its own recourse. Paul works with precisely this interconnection of creation, continuity and discontinuity in 1 Corinthians 15. Relying on creation language in the preceding verses, he explores the continuity by means of discontinuity: the same creaturely entity was sown as perishable, but raised imperishable, sown in dishonour, raised in glory, sown in weakness, raised in power (vv. 42–3). The transformation implies the continuity, but the emphasis is on the change, as we 'bear the image of the man of heaven' (v. 49), thereby fulfilling the teleology behind the Genesis creation narrative with regard to the image of God[53] – an existence oriented towards abundant life in, through and for the one in whose image we are made, Jesus Christ (Col. 1:15), an existence yielding the full satisfaction of our creaturely longings.[54]

---

[52]As Girard puts it, '[T]he resurrection is not only a miracle, a prodigious transgression of natural laws. It is the spectacular sign of the entrance into the world of a power superior to violent contagion.' René Girard, *I See Satan Fall Like Lightning* (Maryknoll, NY: Orbis, 2001), 189. This, in strong contrast to Borg, who greatly limits the meaning of the resurrection. Borg, 'Executed by Rome', 162–3.

[53]That the *imago Dei* is more of a teleology than an ontology cf. Tanner, *Christ the Key*, 1–57.

[54]Just as with glory, the satisfaction of God goes hand in hand with the satisfaction of the creature. The glory of God is the glory of the creature, because God is a gracious and sharing God, who has made his good to be our own.

The key to this satisfaction and the sphere within which it takes place, is the fulfilment of the election of Jesus Christ: the completion of God's purposes for him as the Messiah of Israel, the head of the Church and the Lord of heaven and earth, the fate of the whole cosmos is bound up with him. As Romans 1:4 puts it, Christ Jesus 'was declared to be the Son of God in power according to the Spirit of holiness by his resurrection from the dead', an act in which the Father highly exalts him, and 'bestows on him the name that is above every name, so that at the name of Jesus every knee should bow, in heaven and on earth and under the earth' (Phil. 2:9-10) – an exaltation which brings order to creation and reconciles all things to himself (Col. 1:15-20).

And because the resurrection of Jesus Christ is a cosmic event of re-creation it is likewise an individual and corporate event of unparalleled significance for the Church, for as Romans 6:8 tells us, 'if we have died with Christ, we believe that we will also live with him', and Ephesians and Colossians make the even bolder claim that we have been raised with Christ, and are seated with him in the heavenly places (Col. 3:1; Eph. 2:6).[55] According to Torrance, 'The seed that is raised up is not only Jesus the Messiah as an individual but the body of all those who are involved with him in his anointed humanity. In Christ the whole resurrection is already included in a decisive way. The New Humanity is already raised up in Christ,' though the full revelation of this reality is pending.[56] To be a Christian is to be raised up in Christ – the Church is the people of the resurrection.

While the nature of resurrected life is ambiguous this side of Christ's second coming, one thing is clear: resurrection satisfies our deepest longings, giving us 'fullness of indestructible life' in which 'an ontological leap occur[s], one that touches being as such, opening up a new dimension that affects us all, creating for all of us a new space of life, a new space of being in union with God'.[57] The key to this statement is its conclusion, for it is union with God that

---

[55]'The resurrection, in the full Jewish and early Christian sense, is the ultimate affirmation that creation matters, that embodied human beings matter. That is why resurrection has always had an inescapable political meaning.' Wright, *The Resurrection of the Son of God*, 730.

[56]Torrance, *Space, Time, and Resurrection*, 34.

[57]Joseph Ratzinger, *Jesus of Nazareth. Part Two, Holy Week: From the Entrance into Jerusalem to the Resurrection* (San Francisco: Ignatius, 2011), 274.

gives shape and meaning to this life. The resurrection is no matter of a generic or unspecified 'eternal life', but rather the specific form of creaturely life in and with the triune God. As Torrance puts it, '[T]he risen Jesus Christ is the living Atonement, atonement in its glorious achievement not only in overcoming the separation of sin, guilt and death, but in consummating union and communion with God in such a way that the divine life overflows freely through him into mankind.'[58] This, more than anything else, is what the doctrine of satisfaction is truly about: satisfying God's desire for union with humankind in and through the incarnate Son, Jesus Christ. 'Atonement without resurrection would not be reconciliation and without reconciliation atonement had not reached its proper end in union with the Father, in peace. It is thus the resurrection of our human nature in Christ into communion with the life of God that is the end and goal of atonement.'[59]

An implication of this line of thought is that must follow Calvin's rule that 'whenever mention is made of his death alone, we are to understand at the same time what belongs to his resurrection [and vice versa]' (*Inst*, 521). Beyond this, we must strive to pair the death and resurrection of Christ in thought, word and deed. And I know of no better example of this than the painting of Christ crucified upon an Easter lily, painted on a panel in St Helen's Church, Abingdon. The violence and horror of the cross bound up with the life, joy and beauty of the lily binds together heart and soul of both sides of this event, in an image that bears sustained meditation.[60]

The life of Christ II (Ascension, Pentecost and second coming)

But to speak of the resurrection is to speak of the ascension of Jesus into heaven, where he is seated at the right hand of the Father, for the two are inextricably bound in Scripture. And because the resurrection is the fulfilment of human existence, it cannot be separated from the biblical promises and covenants brought to

---

[58]Torrance, *Space, Time, and Resurrection*, 55; cf. p. 67.
[59]Ibid., 67.
[60]John Edwards, 'Lily-Crucifixions in the Oxford District', *Oxford Art Journal* 2(April 1979): 43–5.

completion not simply in Jesus' rising from the dead, but his rising to the right hand of the Father (Heb. 2:29-36). The ascension, in other words, is atoning, or salvific (*ST*, III.56.6), for it is the 'goal of Jesus Christ's work', the point at which that which has occurred shifts suddenly to the present: '"He *sitteth* on the right hand of God. . . ." It is as if we had made the ascent of a mountain and had now reached the summit.'[61] It is here that the kingdom is truly inaugurated (*Inst*, 522), whence Christ rules in the power and glory of God, 'that he might fill all things' (Eph. 4:10), bringing order and justice to his creation, from here that we are lavished with the spiritual riches of Christ, from here that Christ 'quicken[s] us to spiritual life, sanctif[ies] us by his Spirit, adorn[s] his church with divers gifts of his grace', and in short showers upon us the blessings of at-one-ness with God (*Inst*, 525; Eph. 4:11).

The ascension, in other words, is the most fitting place to speak of the doctrine of satisfaction touched on elsewhere – the place where God's desires and promises are fulfilled.[62] As Farrow puts it:

> The ascension of Jesus Christ is also an act of perfecting grace, completing what was begun when the Spirit . . . hovered over Mary, who brought forth a son. Not only does it fully erase the alienation between God and man introduced in the fall, it fully establishes the communion between God and man at which God was already aiming in creation itself.[63]

Here we have the culmination, the communion between God and ourselves through the installation of our Mediator at the Father's right hand. It is his offering of himself, his life, in the complete and irreversible finality of a graced task brought to completion in the verdict of the Father, that more than anything seals the work of Christ as being completed once and for all.[64] And it is our inclusion

---

[61]Barth, *Dogmatics in Outline*, 124.

[62]In this line of thought, Christ's death initiates the new covenant, and is integral to it, but it is the high-priestly ministry of Christ in the resurrection and ascension that constitutes the end or goal of this covenantal act. Cf. David M. Moffitt, *Atonement and the Logic of Resurrection in the Epistle to the Hebrews* (Boston: Brill, 2011). 285.

[63]Douglas Farrow, *Ascension Theology* (London: T & T Clark, 2011), 122.

[64]Cf. Moffitt, *Atonement and the Logic of Resurrection in the Epistle to the Hebrews*. Our project develops a greater role for the death of Christ than does Moffitt's, partly due to Moffitt's focus upon the book of Hebrews, though it should be clear that I am quite sympathetic with Moffitt's constructive project.

in this installation through our union with the Mediator (Eph. 2:6)[65] that opens 'up for us the true destiny of man', the 'setting of man, once and for all, within the open horizons of the trinitarian life and love, where he may flourish and be fruitful in perpetuity'.[66]

Lest we wander too far from the biblical framework for understanding this point, we do well to attend to Peter's sermon at Pentecost. Towards the conclusion of his argument, he says to the Jews:

> This Jesus God raised up, and of that we are all witnesses. Being therefore exalted at the right hand of God, and having received from the Father the promise of the Holy Spirit, he has poured out this that you yourselves are seeing and hearing. (Acts 2:32-33)

Two points in this passage merit careful attention. First, Peter connects resurrection and ascension as though the latter naturally and necessarily flows from the former, justifying our earlier connection of these two events. Second, this is one part of a larger argument concerning Christ fulfilling ancient prophesies, including his enthronement on the seat of David and his reception of the promised Holy Spirit (Joel 2:28-32).[67] The work of Christ was aimed above all at bringing to completion God's creative purposes as reaffirmed in the history of the covenants and promises God made to his people Israel.[68] And at the heart of these promises was God's gift of his Spirit to his people. Ascension and Pentecost go hand in hand, for what Christ received through his ascension he shares with us at Pentecost.

---

[65] Thomas and Calvin make this point in terms of the relation between the head and members of the body (*ST*, III.57.6; *Inst*, 524). Cf. Barth, *Dogmatics in Outline*, 125.

[66] Farrow, *Ascension Theology*, 22, 36. Boff, interweaving resurrection and ascension in a biblically warranted manner, writes: 'Resurrection means the complete and definitive enthronement of human reality, spirit and body together, in the atmosphere of the divine. In other words, resurrection is complete hominization and liberation.' Boff, *Passion*, 66. Cf. Thomas F. Torrance, *Atonement: The Person and Work of Christ* (Downers Grove, IL: InterVarsity Press, 2009), 294.

[67] Cf. Isa. 44, Ez. 36 and Zech. 12. A second and related prophecy is the writing of the law upon the heart.

[68] This conjunction of promise and Holy Spirit is precisely what Farrow means when he writes about the ascension being our 'deification' within the 'horizons of the trinitarian life'. Farrow, *Ascension Theology*, 22, 36.

So why did Jesus need to ascend? Why did he need to leave so as to send us the Spirit (Jn 16:7)? Jesus needed to ascend so as to receive the promised Spirit from the Father (Acts 2:32), in order to then send his Spirit to us (Acts 2:33).[69] Only by receiving the covenantal promise as the pure and faithful man who had endured suffering and temptation in our place – only as the one who took upon himself our filth, was cleansed by his death, and cleansed us and the heavenly places (Heb. 9), could he receive and send this Spirit, his Spirit, to accomplish his work in us.[70] Ascension was necessary to bring the work of Christ to completion so that the Spirit of Christ could carry on his work, fulfilling the plan of God by bringing us into creaturely union with himself and all that the presence of the Spirit entails.[71]

And it is for this risen and ascended Lord in the power of the Spirit at the right hand of God that we wait, for his second coming in glory when his already completed work will be made manifest and final. For though the ascension is the culmination, it is simultaneously a hiatus, 'an eschatological pause or interval in the heart of the parousia' during which time we wait for this kingdom to be 'openly manifested at the time when the veil will be taken away'.[72]

Conclusion

The temptation to reduce the work of Christ to that of the cross is a powerful one. As Paul says, he resolved to know nothing except Christ crucified (1 Cor. 2:2), and the Bible regularly sums up the work of Christ in this way. Even a casual glance at the resurrection

---

[69]As Burgess reminds us, '[T]he Spirit is Jesus' Spirit, and the Spirit's work is Jesus' work. . . . It is essential to understand at the outset that in the person of the Spirit we have to do with the mediated agency of the ascended Son, and thus pneumatology bears close relation to ascension theology.' Andrew R. Burgess, *The Ascension in Karl Barth* (Burlington, VT: Ashgate, 2004), 43–4.

[70]Hebrews supports Peter's assertions in Acts that 'Jesus was only qualified to become high priest *after* his resurrection. Only after this event was he further able to enter into God's presence in heaven to offer his atoning sacrifice there.' Moffitt, *Atonement and the Logic of Resurrection in the Epistle to the Hebrews*, 228.

[71]Cf. Farrow, *Ascension Theology*, 48.

[72]Torrance, *Atonement: The Person and Work of Christ*, 303; cf. 309.

awakens us from this reductionist haze – but we cannot stop there. Moving outward, attention to the goal of Christ's atoning work as bringing us into the fellowship of the divine life loads the life of Christ with significance, which of course spills over into his resurrected life, with all that Scripture has to say about the saving significance of the ascension and Christ's receiving and sharing of the promised Holy Spirit. In short, once we begin to see the atonement as a work including but not limited to Jesus' death on the cross, we quickly expand to include the whole life of Christ.

This need not flatten the life of Christ into a homogenized mass of equally salvific or atoning events, however. Balance and proportion are as vital here as they are to every other Christian doctrine, and our emphasis must always be on the crucified and risen Lord, for these two events, the end of the old creation and the beginning of the new one in Christ, form the core around which the other moments of Christ's life have their role to play in expanding our understanding of the way in which the whole life of Christ is for us and for our salvation.

6

Atonement and the Created Spectrum

The Apostle's Creed tells us that in Christ God became man and suffered 'for us and for our salvation', and to this point in the book we have adhered to this statement, dwelling on various implications of the fact that it was this God that became man for us. But in our commitment to exploring the riches and diversity of the atonement, we now venture to push beyond this constraint, considering anew 'for whom' or 'for what' Christ become man. Certainly 'for us' – but for whom else, and what else? Most treatments of the atonement are largely anthropocentric, focusing principally or exclusively on the nature, plight and salvation of humankind. But the Bible and history of doctrine affirm that God became man for reasons including but also transcending our plight. In this chapter, we consider for whom or for what God become man, and our answer will range from God himself to the earth he created, and everything in between. For as McKnight writes, 'the atonement – from beginning to end – is designed to resolve the macroscopic problem of evil and sin' – a problem extending far beyond our own sin and evil, impacting every aspect of the created order in some fashion.[1] Given the nature of the problem, the solution must be nothing short of cosmic in scope.[2]

The key to this line of thought is Pseudo-Dionysius' thesis that 'this Salvation, benevolently operating for the preservation of the world, redeems everything in accordance with the capacity of things

---

[1] McKnight, *Community*, 61.
[2] Gunton, *Actuality*, 168–9.

to be saved and it works so that everything may keep within its appropriate virtue'.[3] John Wesley similarly claims that 'the Creator and Father of every living thing is rich in mercy towards all; . . . he does not overlook or despise any of the works of his own hands; . . . he wills even the meanest of them to be happy, according to their degree', a matter which he later specifies in terms of the 'proportion to that measure of his own image which he has stamped upon [each creature]'.[4] Christ's atonement was not 'for' all things in the same way, because all things are not the same. As Creator, God endowed his creatures and creations with different capacities and natures, or, as Wesley puts it, he has provided them with varying degrees of potential to partake of the divine image. The purpose behind this was that 'the universe might be perfect', through God's instituting 'the various degrees of things' throughout his creation (ST, 1.2.112.4). And because he loves his creation and longs for its perfection, God in his wisdom designed the work of Christ in such a way as to bring a salvation to each of his creatures in a manner appropriate to their respective natures, appropriate to the degree or manner of their partaking of the divine image. And as sin and evil threw all of creation into disarray, all of creation is restored by the work of the God-man.

In this chapter we explore the spectrum of the created order, loosely following a medieval cosmology, ranging from the angels in heaven to those creatures and creations that fill the earth (including animals, inanimate creation and the earth itself), concluding with the lowest creatures: the demons. In each case, we consider the ways in which the work of Christ could impact both their experience of sin and the fulfilment of their being, in accordance with their respective natures. While this task may seem to be a distraction from the core concerns of the biblical witness, the benefits of such work are extensive. As we will see, such an effort simultaneously broadens and balances our account of Christ's work, making sense of the many ways in which Scripture speaks of the relevance of this work for things beyond humankind, while simultaneously preventing the anthropological effects of Christ's work from gaining a false supremacy. Ultimately, this chapter offers a delightfully

---

[3] Pseudo-Dionysius, *Pseudo-Dionysius: The Complete Works*, 114.
[4] John Wesley Sermon 60, The General Deliverance, Romans 8:19-22, paragraphs 2 and 5.

FOR HIMSELF

ironic support for the human implications of the atonement, for as we will see, the best way to appreciate the implications of Christ's death and resurrection for us is to understand how the same work impacts the whole cosmos, of which we are a small part.

God became man for God

This chapter moves from the highest and noblest of God's creatures (the angels) to the lowest and most repulsive (the demons). It begins, however, with the Creator himself: a line of thought as surprising as it is beautiful, for God became man not only for his creation, but *for himself*. Of course God did not sin, and was under no obligation to repent or atone for himself – but Christ's atonement is not irrelevant to God, who is affected by sin through the bonds he establishes and upholds with his creatures.[5] We find in Romans 3:25-26 the curious statement:

> This [putting forth of Christ as a propitiation/expiation] was to show God's righteousness, because in his divine forbearance he had passed over former sins. It was to show his righteousness at the present time, so that he might be just and the justifier of the one who has faith in Jesus.

Of interest to us is the goal that God *might be just*. While acknowledging that God intends to demonstrate or reveal his righteousness, as well as make his people righteous and just in the process, Paul includes a surprising divine motive for the incarnation: that *God might be just*. According to Paul, the divine patience with sin was throwing into question not only our appreciation of God's

---

[5] I agree in a qualified way with Holmes that '"If God is simple and *a se*, then nothing outside of God, which is to say nothing in creation, affects God's life in any way,' since in this argument it is only God's prior will to be affected which enable creatures to affect him. In other words, creatures do not affect God – God's will to be affected, together with the works of his creatures, affects God. In other words, I affirm God's *aseity* in a manner qualified by God's election to be in fellowship and therefore to be affected by his creatures. *Aseity* always remains the foundation for any interactions, guaranteeing that God does not change because his interactions are out of his own limits, the resources of his own life. Holmes, 'A Simple Salvation? Soteriology and the Perfections of God', 43.

justice, but the thing itself – to the point that God became man in Christ to be just; to reaffirm his own proper justice which he had put at stake in his dealings with humankind.[6]

Being one, God's patience is not contrary or opposed to his justice. God's justice is a patient justice, and his patience is just. What then accounts for the waiting, for the dilemma God seemed to be putting himself in? In what sense can God be caught in a dilemma and, in that limited but real sense, suffer the effects of sin? At this point it is helpful to draw on Irenaeus' insight that 'the Lord, coming to the lost sheep, and making recapitulation of so comprehensive a dispensation . . . [was necessary,] inasmuch as the whole economy of salvation regarding man came to pass according to the good pleasure of the Father, in order that God might not be conquered, nor His wisdom lessened, [in the estimation of His creatures]' (AH, 455).[7] The justice and patience of God are enacted within a specific dispensation or economy – a plan or purpose of God rooted in his good pleasure – and it is this plan or economy which provides the framework for understanding God's dilemma.[8]

The atonement was necessary for God inasmuch as God freely bound himself to the purposes or good pleasure he had for his creatures, to this 'dispensation', as Irenaeus calls it. By setting about to create rational creatures in his image (AH, 455), giving them natures and purposes, promises and covenants, God bound the fate of these creatures to himself. As their Creator, their success or failure would be his own, for their success or failure would be the success or failure of God's project; God's intentions. The key premise is that purposes, promises and creative acts constitute a form of union between the one making them and the objects that they concern. The failure of a specified purpose, such as that of building a house, is not simply a failure with regards to the abandoned half-built

---

[6]Kotsko, Politics, 193.

[7]Cf. De inc, §13 and CDH, 315–19.

[8]Borg asks: 'Is God limited in any way? Is God limited by the requirements of law?' Borg, 'Executed by Rome', 158. It is vital to the Christian faith that we answer in the affirmative. Of course God is not limited by anything outside of himself, by his creation. But his love is a lawful love – a love that makes and keeps agreements, promises and laws. Is God limited in any way? Yes – many ways! And all of them self-imposed acts, deeply reflective of his loving character. In this way, we can affirm with Kotsko, that 'God in turn is determined by God's relationship to the world'. Kotsko, Politics, 193.

house; it is a failure on the part of the owner who ventured on the project only to run out of capital, resulting in shame and loss.

Irenaeus helps us see how God's wisdom was at stake in binding himself to his creatures, and how God, through his creatures, could in some sense 'be conquered'. God had put himself forward, binding himself to his creatures through his purposes and covenants, so that in a very real (though limited) sense, he had put himself at stake, and given himself over to their power.[9] God freely bestowed upon his creation the power of compromising his purposes, tainting his wisdom and goodness. This power, never one that the creature imposes upon God, but continually granted and upheld by the Creator, is nonetheless a real and binding power.[10] As von Balthasar puts it:

> In creation, God fashions a genuine creaturely freedom and sets it over against his own, thus in some sense binding himself. It is possible to call this creation, together with the covenant associated with it . . . a new 'kenosis' on God's part, since he is thereby restricted, implicitly by creaturely freedom and explicitly by the covenant with its stated terms. (*TD*, 328)

And it is this self-restriction, or purposing of God, which makes sin a problem for God, for the failure of the creative project is a failure on the part of the Creator.

What is the nature of this constraint? That of being the God he is, as the God of this creation; of being the living, glorious, loving, wise and just God, not only in and for himself, but with and for his creation: 'that it is He who is with [us] as God' (*CD* IV/1, 4). And how is this a constraint? God takes this sharing of himself with his creation to be a matter of identity.[11] God names himself by means of his relationship with us (Ex. 3.14-15). He takes upon himself our flesh (Jn 1). He cares deeply about what we think of

---

[9]The tension of whether and to what extent God has bound his honour to his creation is one of the significant tensions within Anselm's thought (*CDH*, 288–9).

[10]As Thomas puts it, God does not become a debtor to anyone simply; rather, he becomes a debtor to himself, through previous divine ordination, and in this sense only becomes our debtor. *ST*, I-II.114.1.

[11]Kevin W. Hector, 'Immutability, Necessity, and Triunity: Towards a Resolution of the Trinity and Election Controversy', *Scottish Journal of Theology* 65, no. 01 (2009): 64–81.

him (Ex. 32.11-14) – far more than we care to acknowledge.[12] God is deeply affected by our sin, for the plight of the creature, without ceasing to be the real and deadly concern of the creature, is simultaneously the plight of the Creator – just as the plight of a rebellious child is simultaneously the plight of the parents that love her. In the act of creating, God puts his honour, power and wisdom on the line, both to be glorified and tested. Sin brought into question not only God's justice, but his wisdom and patience . . . in fact, the whole character of God – for God's goal was to share the fullness of his character with us in such a way that we might know and rejoice in it. To fail to share himself in this way, would be for God to fail in terms of his freely expanded identity – the identity he took on as our Creator, as the God who covenanted with us, and as the God who names himself by his actions with and towards us. But as Thomas reminds us, God's purpose cannot fail (*ST*, I-II.112.3)!

Why then did God become man? That God might fulfil the purposes he bound to his identity, and the promises and covenants he made to his creatures, thereby saving himself from the effects of sin by ensuring the fulfilment of the purposes he so firmly bound to his heart, disdaining to hold them at arm's length. Given the indirect power sin has over God through its power over God's creation, given the indirect power it has over God through the creative and covenantal bonds by means of which God unites himself to his creation, God became man to vindicate himself by vindicating his creation, bringing it to its proper goal. The atonement is God's work for God just as much as it is for us, because being the God that He is, and being God for us, are one and the same for the God who created, sustains and binds himself to us. God became man for the Creator God: for himself.

---

[12] As John of the Cross puts it: 'The tenderness and truth of love by which the immense Father favors and exalts this humble and loving soul reaches such a degree . . . that the Father himself becomes subject to her for her exaltation, as though he were her servant and she his lord. And he is as solicitous in favoring her as he would be if he were her slave and she his god. So profound is the humility and sweetness of God.' John of the Cross, 'The Spiritual Canticle', in *The Collected Works of St. John of the Cross* (Washington, DC: Institute of Carmelite Studies, 1979), 581. Cf. Adam Johnson, 'The Crucified Bridegroom: Christ's Atoning Death in St. John of the Cross and Spiritual Formation Today', *Pro Ecclesia* XXI, no. 4 (2012): 399–402.

God became man for the Angels

From this consideration of God himself, we move to his throne-room and its denizens, for while Adolf von Harnack claimed that '[the kingdom] is not a question of angels and devils, thrones and principalities, but of God and the soul, the soul and its God',[13] Charles Hodge reminds us that 'so much is said in the Scriptures of good and evil angels . . . that the doctrine of the Bible concerning them should not be overlooked'.[14] Relevant to our interests, Colossians 1:19-20 says that 'in [Jesus Christ] all the fullness of God was pleased to dwell, and through him to reconcile to himself all things, whether on earth or in heaven, making peace by the blood of his cross'. What does it mean to affirm that Christ's death and resurrection reconciled the things *in heaven* to himself?[15]

The most familiar view regarding the impact of Christ's work on the angels is that of repopulating the heavenly city emptied by the fall of the angels.[16] But the work of Christ affected the angels in other ways as well, for it changed their song – no small matter for a being whose primary end is to worship![17] Foundational to this change, the work of Christ revealed the character of God to the angels in an unprecedented way, leading to a corresponding change and development in the knowledge of the angels. As Jonathan Edwards argues, '[T]he perfections of God are manifested to all creatures, both men and angels, *by the fruits of those perfections, or God's works* . . . so the glorious angels have the greatest manifestations of

---

[13]Harnack, *What Is Christianity*, 56.

[14]Charles Hodge, *Systematic Theology*, vol. 1 (Grand Rapids, MI: Eerdmans, 1986), 637.

[15]Adam Johnson, 'Where Demons Fear to Tread: Venturing into an Obscure Corner of the Doctrine of the Atonement Concerning the Un-Fallen Angels', *Journal of Reformed Theology* (Forthcoming).

[16]Origen, 'De Principiis', in *Ante Nicene Fathers of the Christian Church*, ed. Alexander Roberts and James Donaldson (Peabody: Hendrickson Publishers, 2004), 289. Augustine, *The Augustine Catechism: The Enchiridion on Faith, Hope, and Love*, ed. Boniface Ramsey, trans. Bruce Harbert (Hyde Park: New City Press, 1999), 61. Augustine supports this last point with Luke's claim that we will be equal to the angels (20:36). Anselm, 'Why God Became Man', in *The Major Works*, ed. Brian Davies and G. R. Evans (New York: Oxford University Press, 1998), 289–300.

[17]Compare the songs of Isa. 6 and Rev. 5.

the glory of God by what they see . . . in the death and sufferings of Christ.'[18] Reinforcing his point, he writes: '[W]hat they beheld of the glory of God in the face of Christ as man's Redeemer, and especially in Christ's humiliation, greatly increased their holiness and their obedience.'[19] Such spiritual growth unfettered by sin naturally overflows into worship. At the sight of Christ the angels are 'filled with admirations of God, ascribing praise, honour, and glory unto him for evermore; for the beholding of the mystery of the wisdom of God in Christ . . . is the principal part of the blessedness of the angels in heaven'.[20] Prior to the work of Christ, the angels praised God because he was the Creator. But Hilary of Poitiers tells of how, upon his resurrection, they praised him because 'He conquered death, broke the gates of hell, won for Himself a people to be His fellow-heirs, [and] lifted flesh from corruption up to the glory of eternity.'[21]

But if the worship of angels can change, are there limits upon the extent to which they can change in other regards? Can they change for the worse, and fall from grace? The Church typically asks this question under the category of the 'confirmation' of the angels. Some Protestant theologians departed from the traditional Augustinian view that rooted confirmation in the angels' choice not to fall, tying the confirmation of the angels to the atoning work of Christ. Of Colossians 1:20 Calvin writes that it was 'necessary that angels, also, should be made to be at peace with God, for, being creatures, they were not beyond the risk of falling, had they not been confirmed by the grace of Christ'.[22] John Donne offers a similar exploration of this theme:

How have [the angels] any reconciliation (Col. 1:19-20)? . . . They needed a confirmation; for the Angels were created in blessednesse, but not in perfect blessednesse. . . . But to the Angels

---

[18]Jonathan Edwards, *The Works of Jonathan Edwards*, vol. 20 (Yale, CT: Yale University Press, 2002), 197.

[19]Jonathan Edwards, *The Works of Jonathan Edwards*, vol. 20, p. 199.

[20]John Owen, *The works of John Owen*, vol. 1, p. 265.

[21]Hilary of Potiers, *On the Trinity*, trans. S. D. F. Salmond (Grand Rapids, MI: Eerdmans, 1983), 63.

[22]John Calvin, *The Epistle of Paul the Apostle to the Galatians, Ephesians, Philippians Colossians, Thessalonians, Timothy, Titus and Philemon*, trans. William Pringle (Grand Rapids, MI: Baker, 1979), 156.

that stood, their standing being of grace, and their confirmation being not one transient act in God done at once, but a continual succession, and emanation of daily grace, belongs to this reconciliation by Christ, because all manner of grace, and where any deficiency is to be supplyed . . . proceeds from the Crosse, from the Merits of Christ.[23]

While the need for confirmation provides one avenue for exploring this topic, the mystery of the incarnation provides a second. Edwards writes that:

It was fit that the angels should be confirmed after they had seen Christ in the flesh, for this was the greatest trial of the angels' obedience that ever was. If the other angels rebelled only at its being foretold that such an one in man's nature should rule over them . . . how great a trial was [it] when they saw a poor, obscure, despised, afflicted man, and when they had just seen [him] so mocked and spit upon, and crucified and put to death, like a vile malefactor! This was a great trial to those thrones, dominions, principalities, and powers, those mighty glorious and exalted spirits, whether or no they would submit to such an one for their sovereign Lord and King.[24]

Given this ignorance and the ensuing 'trial' of the angels as they witnessed the events of the incarnation, life and passion of Jesus Christ, it was the fulfilment of God's plan through the resurrection of Christ that confirmed the angels through their witness of the unsearchable wisdom of God. The work of Christ was for the angels in that it confirmed, or decisively established them in their creaturely perfection with God, with ensuing effects in their understanding and worship.

Our final line of inquiry considers the impact of Christ's atonement upon the unfallen angels as he becomes their 'head', bringing order to the angelic ranks (and the whole of creation). The *Catholic Catechism* states: 'Christ is the center of the angelic world.

---

[23] John Donne, *The Sermons of John Donne*, ed. George R. Potter and Evelyn M. Simpson, vol. 4 (Los Angeles: University of California Press, 1959), 298–9.

[24] Jonathan Edwards, *The Works of Jonathan Edwards*, vol. 18, p. 59. Cf. Owen, *The Glory of Christ*, in The Works of John Owen, vol. 1, p. 374.

They are *his* angels. . . . They belong to him because they were created *through* and *for* him.'[25] While they were clearly created through and for Christ, he has not always been the centre of their world in the same way. Calvin inquires: 'But who might reach [fallen man]? . . . One of the angels? They also had need of a head, through whose bond they might cleave firmly and undividedly to their God [cf. Eph. 1:22; Col. 2:10]' (*Inst*, 464). It seems that the way in which the triune God elected himself to be head of the angels was as the incarnate Son, Jesus Christ – and therefore the angels awaited their rightful head from the time of their creation until the incarnation, passion and ascension of Jesus.

But what changed for the angels, upon the installation of Jesus Christ as their head? Their role on earth was at least partly political: 'The ancient notion of the angels of the nations (e.g., Deut. 32:8-9 [LXX]; Dan. 10:13; 10:20–11:1; 12:1) suggests that they were regarded as the guardians of social order.'[26] Working with the connection between human and angelic justice, Barth notes, '[W]hat seems to be meant here [Eph 1:10 and Col 1:20] is that in Christ the angelic powers are called to order and, so far as they need it, they are restored to their original order'.[27] In other words, the angels are involved in the political or social order, and the work of Christ involves restoring justice at this level of reality.[28] In being crowned king, and putting his kingdom into order, Jesus brought order to the angelic realm as well. While the angels need not be justified for their sin, they needed the benefits of justification in the sense of a restoration of cosmic justice and order.

Blaise Pascal warns: 'Man must not think he is on a level with either beasts or angels, and he must not be ignorant of those levels, but should know both.'[29] This is just as true of soteriology as it is of cosmology, for attending to the relationship between the angels

---

[25] *Catechism of the Catholic Church* (Mahwah: Paulist Press, 1994), 86.

[26] Lawrence Osborn, 'Entertaining Angels: Their Place in Contemporary Theology', *Tyndale Bulletin* 45, no. 2 (1994): 286.

[27] Karl Barth, *Community, State, and Church: Three Essays*, trans. H. M. Hall, G. Ronald Howe and Ronald Gregor Smith (Garden City: Doubleday, 1960), 117.

[28] This seems to be at the heart of C. S. Lewis' cosmic understanding of the atonement in his *Space Trilogy*.

[29] Blaise Pascal, *Pensées and Other Writings*, ed. Anthony Levi, trans. Honor Levi (New York: Oxford University Press, 1995), 38.

and Christ's atonement opens our eyes to the variety of ways which Christ reconciles things to himself which were never actually fallen, by bringing fullness, wisdom, confirmation and order to his creation. The death and resurrection of Christ is a cosmic event, and though it affects us differently than it does the angels, it is no less relevant to them than it is to us. Our salvation in Christ is but a key part of far greater work as God reconciles all things to himself in the work of Christ (Col. 1:20).

God became man for humankind

Works on the atonement tend to err on the side of anthropocentrism – an error we are correcting in the present chapter. Nevertheless, humankind was the object (if not exclusively so) of the incarnation, and we must always remember that God became man so as to atone for the sins of individual men and women, bringing them to creaturely fulfilment in and through fellowship with the triune God. The atonement is about the love of God for each one of us – a self-sacrificial love which has done, is doing and will do everything possible to bring us out of our sin and death into a relationship with him and the happiness this entails at every level of our being. In keeping with the cosmic emphasis of this chapter, and our attention to the ways in which Christ's work was effective for humankind, we here develop two aspects of the anthropological implications of Christ's death and resurrection: for society on the one hand, and the body on the other, both of which complement the typical emphasis on matters of the soul.[30]

Augustine writes: 'God chose to create the human race from one single man. His purpose in doing this was not only that the human race should be united in fellowship by a natural likeness, but also that men should be bound together by kinship in the unity of concord, linked by the bond of peace.'[31] It is the human

---

[30] Along these lines, I recommend the work of Adam Kotsko for his consistently social-relational emphasis. Kotsko, *Politics*, 187–206. It is worth noting, though, he does so from a distinctly religionless standpoint which contrasts starkly with the approach adopted here. Ibid., 184–6.

[31] Augustine, *The City of God against the Pagans*, trans. R. W. Dyson (New York: Cambridge University Press, 1998), 581.

at the heart of Gospel / Biblical story

not me — WE — a people

race, united in fellowship through communion with God, which is at the heart of God's creative and covenantal purposes. Paul recalls a time when the Gentiles were 'separated from Christ, alienated from the commonwealth of Israel, and strangers to the covenants of promise, having no hope and without God in the world' (Eph. 2:12). The work of Jesus Christ, he explains, is a matter of stepping between these two alienated groups, bringing them near to each other 'by the blood of Christ. For he himself is our peace, who has made us both one and has broken down in his flesh the dividing wall of hostility . . . [that he] might reconcile us both to God in one body through the cross, thereby killing the hostility' (Eph. 2:13-16).

While we could perhaps argue that this is simply an application of salvation to the social sphere of Jew/Gentile relations, the text pushes us deeper. This is a matter of the covenants, of God's purposes for the people of Israel – this is the 'mystery of Christ' – namely, that Gentiles are fellow heirs alongside the Jews (Eph. 3:1-6). Of course this mystery and good news includes the salvation of individuals, but it is more than that, for God's primary purpose is collective: 'Go from your country . . . to the land that I will show you. And I will make of you a great nation' (Gen. 12:1-3). Never at the expense of the individual, at the heart of God's purposes lies a people. As N. T. Wright puts it, the Christian emphasis on mission 'can only be explained in terms of the belief that Israel had now been redeemed, and that the time for the Gentiles had therefore come'. In other words, 'Israel's god had finally vindicated his people,' such that Jesus 'really did constitute the fulfillment of Israel's covenant expectations', leading into a new and transformed family or people.[32]

The death of Jesus is the death of a single man. But as the one in whom we have died and risen (Rom. 6:4; Col. 3:6; Eph. 2:6), his death and resurrection was an irreducibly social and therefore political event: the reconstitution of humankind in himself, and therefore the reconstitution of every social and ethnic group.

---

[32]N. T. Wright, *The New Testament and the People of God* (London: Fortress, 1992), 445–7. Few theologians have done a better job of capturing the social nature of God's purposes for a people than Karl Barth, who locates his treatment of Israel and the Church prior to his consideration of the election of the individual in his account of predestination/election (*CD*, II/2).

In taking upon himself 'all the racial hatred and division in the world . . . *he killed it*', restoring 'humanity to its true state'.[33] The atonement of Jesus Christ, in thorough keeping with the biblical narrative, is an intrinsically social event, ordered towards the formation of the people of God, in fulfilment of the covenants God made with Israel to the benefit of the nations,[34] in which the benefits of the atonement shower down not merely upon every individual, but every family, group, race and people.

But this social emphasis, stressing the people of Israel, grants us a new perspective on the reality of sin. 'What good will it do to eliminate the individual oppressor when the oppressive structure of which the individual is but an agent continues to guarantee oppression? . . . The more profound drama is social reality itself. It is the very structure of the system that is wicked.'[35] Sin is not merely an individual matter between the soul and its God; while it includes this, it is simultaneously an irreducibly social matter because we are irreducibly social beings who derive their existence and purpose from an irreducibly social God: Father, Son and Holy Spirit. Financial systems, trade systems, political actions at the local and national level – these are just as much the sphere of the Gospel as our guilty consciences, for the work of Christ, cosmic in scope, brings the character of God to bear upon these aspects of reality no less and no more than others. The thanksgiving owed by Christians to the grace of God received in Christ must therefore be a sociopolitical matter of local, national and international big-picture witnessing, just as it is necessarily a matter of personal evangelism, speaking and responding to the needs and hurts of individuals.[36]

All systems & structures

---

[33]Gombis, 'Racial Reconciiation and the Christian Gospel', 126.

[34]Gen. 12:1-3, Col. 3:11, Rev. 22:1-2.

[35]Boff, *Passion*, 125.

[36]Wright, *The New Testament and the People of God*, 449. For more on this line of thought, I recommend *Surprised by Hope: Rethinking Heaven, the Resurrection, and the Mission of the Church* (New York: HarperOne, 2008).

This would be the place to incorporate an ethic of atonement, were the scope of the work to allow for such a project. I commend the work of Linda Radzik and Miroslav Volf as great places to start in this regard. Radzik, *Making Amends*; Miroslav Volf, *Exclusion and Embrace: A Theological Exploration of Identity, Otherness, and Reconciliation* (Nashville: Abingdon Press, 1996).

To balance our treatment of the social aspects of the atonement, we turn to a focus much more limited in scope: the human body.[37] Scripture consistently refers to God and Jesus as Healer. God 'heals the brokenhearted and binds up their wounds' (Ps. 147:3), identifying himself as such: 'I am the Lord, your healer' (Ex. 15:26).[38] Isaiah connects this theme with the work of the Suffering Servant, by whose 'stripes we are healed' (Isa. 53:5),[39] and the Gospels are replete with Jesus' healings. Significantly, Jesus heals directly rather than by interceding to the Father, showing thereby 'his continuity with the divine healer of the Old Testament'.[40] James exhorts the Church to continue this ministry of healing (5:16), while 1 Peter connects the work of Jesus with that of the Suffering Servant, giving us all the more reason to consider the precise relationship between healing and the work of Christ, for 'by his wounds [we] have been healed' (1 Pet. 2:24).

One possibility is to develop wounds and sickness as a consequence of the Fall, such that Christ's saving work, by means of addressing the sin in our lives, also addresses its consequences.[41] And just as we still suffer from sin and its effects until the second coming of our Lord, so we also suffer the ailments of our bodies until that time, though not without witnesses to the power of Christ over the afflictions of the body in the form of miraculous healings witnessed today and throughout the history of the Church. Another approach explores sin not only as a consequence of sin, but also as sin itself. Sin, we might say, is the condition of human passibility, mutability and corruption resulting from our separation from God. This corruption is both spiritual and physical, and consists of the decay,

---

[37]Modern theology posited what was known as the 'Physical theory' of the atonement, working with Irenaeus, and emphasizing humankind's metaphysical status as it was changed through the incarnation of Christ. Cf. Hart, 'Irenaeus, Recapitulation and Physical Redemption', 154.

[38]As John DeGruchy notes, '[T]he New Testament regards Jesus' and the early Christian community's healing ministry as integral to the proclamation of the kingdom of God, a sign of the salvific purposes of God.' John de Gruchy, 'Salvation as Healing and Hominization', ibid., 34.

[39]In this context (writing on Isa. 53:3), Luther writes that Christ being the 'man of sorrows' means that he had many 'sicknesses and griefs'. *LW* 17, 220.

[40]Bruce R. Reichenbach, 'Healing View', in *The Nature of the Atonement: Four Views*, ed. James K. Beilby and Paul R. Eddy (Downers Grove, IL: IVP Academic, 2006), 130.

[41]Ibid.

not just to share - but to heal!

Christ came

sickness and disease that necessarily occur in those rebelling against the living God in whom is no decay or corruption. How does the work of Christ relate to bodily corruption and illness?

For such an approach, we do well to dwell on the suffering and wounds of Christ as portrayed, for instance, in Matthias Grünewald's famous *Isenheim Altarpiece*.[42] Commissioned for the chapel of a monastery caring for lepers, this piece graphically portrays the suffering of Christ with severely wounded flesh, distorted limbs, and hands contorted in agony. The impassible God became man that he might become passible, might suffer, taking upon himself our plight, our sickness unto death. Though he did not contract every illness or suffer from every bodily ailment, he nonetheless entered our condition, suffering in the flesh.[43] As such, he 'kn[ew] what it is to bear infirmity' (*AH*, 506). And with this reality, so powerfully depicted by Grünewald, the most sorely afflicted and desperately wounded can relate, for God has related to us, entering our pain, making it his own.[44]

But this is merely the prelude to the Gospel, and not the thing itself, for God did not come merely to share our pains, but to heal them. And as we open the wings of altarpiece, we are confronted with the annunciation, birth and resurrection of Christ, reminding us of the sweeping story into which Christ brings us, culminating in the restoration of full, abundant bodily life, where all wounds and pains are healed. The impassible God becomes man that he might share in the full reality of our fallen condition, but he does so in such a way as to share with us the full reality of the divine life inasmuch as the creaturely reality he has given us will endure such a blessing. And in the context of our suffering and sickness, in Christ he shares with us life, health and well-being of such an abundant and complete nature that it will have no end. The Healer

---

[42]Another approach would be that taken by Julian of Norwich in her mystical contemplation of the wounds of Christ. Norwich, *Showings*.

[43]There are, of course, many aspects of the human condition Christ did not make his own. He was, after all, a man, and did not experience those realities unique to the experience of women – a fact called powerfully to our attention by the beautifully provocative crucifixion by Edwina Sandys, *Christa*. The logic of the incarnation is not that Christ took upon himself every aspect of the human condition or experience, but that, in his unique individuality as an Israelite man, he took upon himself the core or essence of the human condition.

[44]On the pain of God, cf. Kitamori, *Theology of the Pain of God*.

not only heals us: he shares with us the wholeness and immutability proper to his own life, leaving us forever immune to any sickness or decay.

What are we to make of the suffering and pain remaining within the Church prior to the second coming? We live in the time between the times: a time where the power of the risen Christ is operative among us and where we can and should pray and expect to see God's healing power operative in the Church, but simultaneously a time where the power of God is veiled and not yet fully manifest (Heb. 2:8).[45] It is therefore a time where the Church has the calling and vocation to ease the burden of the sick and suffering, ministering to those suffering from diseases and disabilities, simultaneously working to alleviate those causes of suffering that lie within our power.

We serve a Lord to whom healing is so proper that he calls himself Healer. He became man so as to become weak enough to bear in himself our sickness, frailty and death, rising again that in him we might be impervious to death and its many servants: sickness, disease and bodily corruption. And as we wait for the full manifestation of this reality in the revelation of the sons of God (Rom. 8:18-21) at Christ's second coming, we, as his people, are to be a healing Church through both miracle and medicine.[46]

God became man for the animals

Paul Fryer's provocative sculpture 'Privilege of Dominion' portrays a crucified gorilla – intended to heighten awareness of the plight of western lowland gorillas. The eternal Son became incarnate as a man from the line of David, rather than a gorilla or lion, but does that preclude the possibility that his death might in certain ways have been for our animal brethren, just as it was for us? Given

---

[45] Gordon D. Fee, *Paul, the Spirit, and the People of God* (Peadbody, MA: Hendrickson, 1996), 52.

[46] Returning to our initial focus on the social/political dimension of the atonement, J. R. R. Tolkien, in the *Lord of the Rings*, develops the notion that one of the signs of a true king is that he is a healer. From the point when Strider first wins Sam Gamgee over by tending Frodo's wound, to old leech's recognition of Strider as the rightful king of Gondor through his hands of healing, Tolkien may provide some resources for developing an even stronger connection between the two halves of this section: politics and the suffering of the body.

our thesis that Christ redeems everything in accordance with the capacity of things to be saved, in what ways, if any, is the death and resurrection of Christ of significance for animals – dogs, elephants and the like? Is there some sense in which the Son 'willed to live and die' not only as a 'man for all men', but more generally 'as a creature for all creatures' (CD III/1, 381)?

Biblical and theological balance and symmetry would seem to demand it. At a surface level, given the prominence of animals at creation (Gen. 1-3) and in the eschaton (Rev. 5:13-14), their absence would be conspicuous in the story of Christ and his passion. More significantly, the idea of atonement as re-creation and the bold claim of Colossians 1:20 that God was pleased to reconcile all things to himself through the blood of the cross, whether on earth or in heaven, demands that we seek to develop 'a doctrine of the atonement that follows the doctrine of the incarnation in encompassing all creatures'.[47]

Wesley asks: 'If the Creator and Father of every living thing is rich in mercy towards all; if he does not overlook or despise any of the works of his own hands; if he wills even the meanest of them to be happy, according to their degree; how comes it to pass, that such a complication of evils oppresses, yea, overwhelms them?'[48] The key here is the passive role of the animals, who are oppressed and overwhelmed – for the dominant category seems to be that of a passive subjection to futility (Rom. 8:20), or to death and 'its train of preparatory evils'.[49] Creation suffers and longs for the time of its freedom and glory – not because of its own sin, but because its fate is bound up with that of the children of God. Implicit within this understanding is a definite order, in which humankind is the key to creation and its well-being.[50] Just as the narratives in Genesis 1–2 build towards the creation of humankind to tend and keep the garden, so it is the restoration of humankind that will result in the ultimate flourishing of that garden, for the fate of the two are

---

[47]David Clough, On Animals: Volume 1: Systematic Theology (London: T & T Clark, 2012), 105. Cf. Rom. 8:18-25; Eph. 1:7-10, 20-23; Heb. 1:2-3; 2 Pet. 3:13; Rev. 21:1-5.
[48]Sermon 60, General Deliverance, Rom. 8:19-20, Preface 2.
[49]Sermon 60, General Deliverance, Rom. 8:19-20, II.5. Cf. the similar line of thought in Nicola Hoggard Creegan, 'The Salvation of Creatures', in God of Salvation, ed. Ivor J. Davidson and Murray A. Rae (Burlington, VT: Ashgate, 2011).
[50]Cf. Stephen H. Webb, On God and Dogs: A Christian Theology of Compassion for Animals (New York: Oxford University Press, 1998), 175–8.

bound together. Though we are created in the image of God, and we alone receive the covenants,

> In all these things the beast will be a constant companion. Everything which will take place between God and himself is to be significantly accompanied by what takes place, by life and death, in the animal kingdom. . . Man's salvation and perdition, his joy and sorrow, will be reflected in the weal and woe of this animal environment and company. (CD III/1, 178)

In the meantime, animals suffer under the consequence of human sin, both directly and indirectly. God 'knoweth their pain, and is bringing them nearer and nearer to the birth, which shall be accomplished in its season',[51] but it is a real pain nonetheless. And while the pain and suffering may not be the result of the sin of animals, who are not generally held to be moral agents,[52] it is nonetheless a concern to God, and one to be remedied by Christ's death and resurrection, with emphasis on the latter.[53] Christ's atoning work includes, though it is not limited to, redemption, and in this case it seems that 'victims of sin need redemption rather than reconciliation: their victimhood does not separate them from God in a way that requires the work of Christ to overcome'.[54] That is to say, the victims of sin need rescuing from these circumstances, inasmuch as they are not part of an intentional conflict calling for reconciliation.

To put it simply, Christ's death and resurrection affects the animal kingdom similarly to the way that it redeems our bodies from the plight of sin – by means of bearing the full consequences of evil, and then restoring creation in the resurrection, through which

---

[51] Sermon 60, General Deliverance, Rom. 8:19-20, III.1.

[52] Sermon 60, General Deliverance, Rom. 8:19-20, III.9.

[53] As Webb notes, the 'key to this restoration is not so much the crucified Christ', for animals do not seem to have a personal burden of sin for which to atone, 'but the exalted Christ', for what they need is the restoration of order and justice achieved by the resurrection and exaltation of Christ, and the cosmic effects these bring. Webb, On God and Dogs, 167.

[54] Clough, Animals, 120. This is a common move by theologians working on this topic. Cf. Denis Edwards, who uses 'the word redemption, like the word salvation, in the wide sense of transformation in Christ, rather than in the limited sense of forgiveness of human guilt'. Denis Edwards, 'The Redemption of Animals in an Incarnational Theology', in Creaturely Theology: On God, Humans and Other Animals, ed. Celia Deane-Drummond and David Clough (London: SCM Press, 2009), 81.

all creation - NEW

God makes all things new. Until that time, Romans suggests (8:18-25), creation must continue to wait in its pains of childbirth – a waiting that includes ignorance as to the manner or extent of the resurrection of individual creatures.[55] Julian of Norwich ties this joint suffering to the work of Christ, suggesting:

> All creatures able to suffer pain suffered with him. And for those that did not know him, their pain was that all creation, sun and moon, ceased to serve men, and so they were all abandoned in sorrow at that time. So those who loved him suffered pain for their love, and those who did not love him suffered pain because of the comfort of all creation failed them.[56]

All creation suffers with Christ, but the suffering of Christ is different from that of his creation for it is vicarious and specifically human. The Creator takes the form of a creature, that in himself he might bear the suffering and plight of creation, restoring creation to its proper glory and flourishing in his resurrection.

To push the limits of this line of inquiry just a little further, there is some reason to think (contra Wesley) that certain animals may in fact be moral agents, and thus have a more complex relationship with sin and atonement, calling for both redemption *and* reconciliation. The Old Testament sometimes punishes animals as moral agents (Ex. 21.28-36). The Church has sometimes treated animals as moral agents as well. Taking the great commission of Mark with utmost seriousness,[57] St Francis preached to a wolf that had been terrorizing a region.[58] On the more scientific side of things, Clough recounts work by Jane Goodall, in which a chimpanzee demonstrates what we

---

[55]Petroc and Eldred Willey suggest that there are two ways animals could participate in the redemption of Christ: in a representative manner, in which the animal kingdom is risen from the dead generically in Christ's animal flesh, and non-representatively, where animals are redeemed individually. Petroc and Eldred Willey, 'Will Animals Be Redeemed?', in *Animals on the Agenda: Questions About Animals for Theology and Ethics*, ed. Andrew Linzey and Dorothy Yamamoto (Urbana, IL: University of Illinois Press, 1998), 191–3.

[56]Norwich, *Showings*, 143.

[57]'Go into all the world and proclaim the gospel to the whole creation' (Mk 16:15).

[58]Francis of Assisi, *The Little Flowers of Saint Francis*, trans. Raphael Brown (New York: Doubleday, 1958), 89.

could consider to be moral disgust, accompanied by attempts of the chimp to clean itself, which in the context could well be explained in terms of atoning purity.[59] It is possible that some animals participate in the sin of creation in more complex ways than mere suffering – that they are perpetrators of sin. If that is the case, how might the atoning work of Christ be relevant to them? There are a variety of possibilities, each extending us well beyond the scope of the present argument, bringing in tow a series of considerations including the nature of animal souls,[60] whether they continue in some form of existence after death, and the nature of Christ's incarnation as a human animal (and therefore in a general sense connected with all animals).[61] My tentative suggestion would be that inasmuch as certain kinds of animals are moral agents, the work of Christ applies to them as such, but material for developing such work would be scant and worrisomely speculative. Nevertheless, it may be a worthy field of limited study, in that it provides an unusual route for exploring Christology as well as asking questions about the nature and identity of our animal brethren (as St Francis would call them). Moreover, such an inquiry helps us attend to the fact that the work of Christ is no mere matter of the individual soul and its God,[62] but a cosmic event of determinative significance for every creature.

One last benefit of this consideration is that it awakens us to the modest but significant role of creatures (human and otherwise) witnessing to the reality of Christ's work by bringing about the partial effects of atonement in our midst. Just as we are co-participants in the redemptive work of our Lord, bringing reconciliation to conflicting parties, deliverance to captives, forgiveness to the guilty and so on, in a more modest way the animals around us play a similar role. For example, dogs, horses and other animals have been shown to be of powerful assistance in bringing about health, restoration and well-being to humans in great need and suffering.[63] In this way, creaturely

---

[59] Clough, *Animals*, 113.

[60] Others have noted this difficulty. '*That* animals will be redeemed is certain. . . . *How* that redemption is to be conceived . . . turns on [the] question of the nature of the animal itself. This is a matter on which scripture and tradition give us no *definitive* answer.' Willey, 'Will Animals Be Redeemed?', 198.

[61] Cf. Edwards, 'Redemption of Animals', 92; Webb, *On God and Dogs*, 168–72.

[62] Harnack, *What Is Christianity*, 56.

[63] Examples of this would be 4 Paws for Ability, which provides service dogs to children suffering from such things as autism and seizures.

witnesses to the reality of Christ's atoning work may make us all the more appreciative of the animals surrounding us, and some of the ways in which our conditions mutually inform each other.

God became man for creation itself

Salvation is not a matter 'of "going to heaven", of a salvation that is essentially *away from* this world'; rather, the 'Christian hope is for God's new creation, for "new heavens and new earth"', a hope that 'has already come to life in Jesus of Nazareth'.[64] It is our hope for 'the eighth day . . . on which Jesus . . . rose from the dead', the Sabbath on which, 'after [he] has set everything at rest, [he] will create the beginning of an eighth day, which is the beginning of another world'.[65] But if our hope is for life in a new earth, and that hope has already come to life in Jesus, what do the atonement and new earth have to do with each other? Is Jesus' death and resurrection relevant for creation as such? Caspar Friedrich's painting 'Morning in the Riesengebirge' depicts the crucifixion overlooking a vista of mountains and valleys, devoid of anything human apart from the crucified Christ. Did Jesus die for this scene, and countless others like it?

The short answer is 'yes', and the key lies in understanding that the resurrection of Jesus is the new creation.

> The resurrection of Jesus offers itself . . . not as an odd event within the world as it is but as the utterly characteristic, prototypical, and foundational event within the world as it has begun to be. . . . Jesus of Nazareth ushers in not simply a new religious possibility, not simply a new ethic or a new way of salvation, but a new creation.[66]

And this foundational event was the beginning, for 'God [will] do for the whole cosmos what he had done for Jesus at Easter'; the resurrection of Jesus 'resonates out, in ways that we can't fully see or understand, into the vast recesses of the universe'.[67] Given such

---

[64]Wright, *Surprised by Hope.*
[65]Barnabas, 'The Epistle of Barnabas', in *The Apostolic Fathers in English,* ed. Michael William Holmes (Grand Rapids, MI: Baker Academic, 2006), XV.8–9.
[66]Wright, *Surprised by Hope,* 67.
[67]Ibid., 93, 97.

an all-encompassing vision, how does the atoning work of Christ relate to such things as the earth itself: trees, mountains and lakes? Can we bring these too within the scope of our vision of the work of Christ? To draw on the thesis for this chapter, how might we apply the claim that God, through the work of Christ, redeems everything in accordance with the capacity of things to be saved?

Paul provides valuable insight into this area of inquiry:

> Creation was subjected to futility, not willingly, but because of him who subjected it, in hope that the creation itself will be set free from its bondage to corruption and obtain the freedom of the glory of the children of God. For we know that the whole creation has been groaning together in the pains of childbirth until now. And not only the creation, but we ourselves, who have the firstfruits of the Spirit, groan inwardly as we wait eagerly for adoption as sons, the redemption of our bodies. (Rom. 8:20-23)

The first thing we note from this passage is the utter passivity of creation. Just as it was (unwillingly) subjected, so it will be (passively) set free from its bondage to corruption. While animals, as we have seen, may fill some middle ground between humankind and inanimate creation, there is a creaturely reality which plays an utterly passive role in the drama of salvation, groaning and waiting until it will be set free. Second, the nature of its freedom is the 'freedom of the glory of the children of God', and its pains are not generic, but the pains of childbirth, as it awaits our adoption and redemption. Just as God's creative work built towards humankind in the creation narratives of Genesis, so humankind is once more the focus in God's re-creating work. Creation generally, in its origin, fall and salvation, plays its distinctive role in specific relation to God's primary interest: relationship with humankind.[68] Third, we see the difference between the groaning of humankind and that of creation generally – for we groan *with* the first fruits of the Spirit. Though the atoning work of Christ is real and effective in us through the Spirit, our experience of Christ's salvation is incomplete, in that our bodies have not yet been transformed. While the atoning work

---

[68]As Barth would put it, creation has the glory of being the external basis of the covenant – a glory that is fulfilled, rather than diminished, in the work of Christ.

of Christ is real and effective for creation generally, its experience is simply that of our bodies – it is passively awaiting the reality of the resurrection, witnessing simultaneously to the reality of sin and death which he has overcome, awaiting his second coming.

'The present cosmos [will be] renewed from top to bottom,' which will be a 'great act of healing and rescue'.[69] The pollution, disease, suffering and death which afflict creation are best understood, I suggest, in terms of those same realities within the human body; to be more precise – within the human body of Jesus Christ. The plight of Christ's body, culminating in his death upon the cross, was done away with in the resurrection. Likewise, our own bodily suffering is done away with, in and through the resurrection of Jesus – a reality which is presently hidden from us, but which we long to see (Heb. 2:8). The plight of the body of Christ, our own bodies and of creation generally is the same plight, on a different scale. Inasmuch as we are in Christ, his resurrection is our resurrection, and we long, therefore, for this reality to be made manifest. At the same time, the perfection of Christ's creaturely body is the perfection of creation generally – a perfection awaiting full manifestation when, in keeping with the order of creation, the sons of God are revealed in their glory.

What then will happen to the mountains levelled by volcanic activity, rivers made toxic by pollution, or seas made barren by human irresponsibility?[70] The same thing that happened to Jesus' body – they will be renewed, made new, or resurrected, just as he was brought to life in a new and perfected state. We know little about what this will mean, for we know little about the resurrected body of our Lord, which was in some ways continuous and in some ways remarkably different from the body he had prior to his resurrection (1 Cor. 15). The important thing is not what this means precisely in terms of every continent, canyon or cactus. The important thing is that in Christ all things are made new – a reality which will come to completion in the second coming of Christ, and to which we must now bear witness, in part (though not exclusively) in a theologically informed environmentalism.[71]

---

[69] Wright, *Surprised by Hope*, 80, 202.

[70] A provocative piece for considering this line of thought is Roger Wagner's painting, 'Menorah'.

[71] Wright offers a delightful exploration of the implications of such a vision for the life of the Church and its members. Cf. Wright, *Surprised by Hope*, 46, 56, 197.

God became man for the demons

Due in part to the great influence of Gustaf Aulén's *Christus victor*, treatments of the atonement in the last century have had a relatively heightened awareness of Christ's victory over Satan. The biblical witness incorporates the demonic realm into the overall cosmology and storyline of salvation,[72] but for our present purposes it suffices to note that Christ came to disempower and triumph over the prince of this world and the powers and principalities (Jn 12:31; Col. 2:25), destroying his/their works (I Jn 3:8; Heb. 2:14-15). Theologians throughout the history of the Church have sought to formulate this material into different theories of the atonement. Irenaeus, for instance, offers a comprehensive vision of God's economy of salvation, in which the serpent, which had beguiled the first Adam and his wife, would be bound and despoiled of his goods by the second Adam.

> For at the first Adam became a vessel in his (Satan's) possession, whom he did also hold under his power, that is, by bringing sin on him iniquitously, and under colour of immortality entailing death upon him. For while promising that they should be as gods, which was in no way possible for him to be, he wrought death in them: wherefore he who had led man captive, was justly captured in his turn by God.[73]

Irenaeus does not tell us precisely how Satan was 'bound' or 'captured' by Christ, partly because he is so intent on affirming the fulfilment of God's plan, and the giving of incorruptible life to humankind. Athanasius likewise refers to the role of Satan's deceit in our fall, without developing a full explanation of how Christ defeats him through the death and resurrection (*De inc*, 63).[74] We find a much more developed account in that of Gregory of Nyssa, who argues that God took the more circuitous route of

---

[72] Gregory A. Boyd, *God at War: The Bible and Spiritual Conflict* (Downers Grove, IL: InterVarsity, 1997); 'Christus Victor View', in *The Nature of the Atonement: Four Views*, ed. James K. Beilby and Paul R. Eddy (Downers Grove, IL: IVP Academic, 2006).
[73] *AH*, III.23, p. 456.
[74] At the most, Athanasius correlates the salvation of man with the defeat of Satan, without attending directly to the defeat of Satan as an end in itself (*De inc*, 69–71).

saving humankind (via incarnation rather than sovereign power) in order to deal justly with Satan, leaving him without 'a just cause of complaint'.[75] Namely, in Christ, Satan found a bargain of such worth as to be sufficient to exchange for all those held in his power. Just as with a 'greedy fish', he 'swallow[ed] the Godhead like a fishhook along with the flesh, which was the bait. Thus, when life came to dwell with death and light shone upon darkness, their contraries might vanish away'.[76] In this way Gregory secures both the justice of God towards Satan, and an explanation of precisely how Jesus deprived Satan of his power over us.

Aulén encourages us to think of this as the classic theory of the atonement, largely abandoned after the first four centuries of the Church, but this is a grave historical mistake.[77] Anselm, for instance, develops his theory of satisfaction as a form of ransom theory – one in which the honour of God, rather than the rights of Satan, dictates the way in which Christ accomplishes this defeat. Though it is 'not the case that God needed to come down from heaven to conquer the devil', for the devil had no rights or power demanding such a course of action on God's part, God nevertheless 'demanded it of man that he should defeat the devil' (CDH, 354, cf. 308) – an action only the incarnate God could properly fulfil through a work of satisfaction.[78] Thomas likewise devotes considerable attention to Christ's defeat of Satan (ST, 3.49.2), developing a threefold account of the way in which Christ freed us from the power of Satan: (1) freeing us from our sin, (2) reconciling us to God and (3) allowing Satan to overreach his power. This trajectory extends into the Reformation and beyond and still thrives today.

This line of thought is ongoing, as reflection on Christ's defeat of Satan currently boasts some of the most interesting developments in the doctrine of the atonement today. Denny Weaver, Kathleen Darby Ray and Mark Heim have become standard names in these

---

[75]Nyssa, 'An Address on Religious Instruction', 299. Cf. the claim in the Epistle to Diognetus that 'When he sent him, he did so as one who saves by persuasion, not compulsion, for compulsion is no attribute of God.' 'The Epistle to Diognetus', in *The Apostolic Fathers in English*, ed. Michael William Holmes (Grand Rapids, MI: Baker Academic, 2006), VII.4.

[76]'An Address on Religious Instruction', 301.

[77]Aulén, *Christus Victor*.

[78]Anselm's argument with 'ransom' theories of the atonement is therefore best construed as an intramural one.

discussions, each building in some fashion upon Christ's defeat
of Satan.[79] Pre-eminent among these theologians is René Girard,
who combines his theory of mimetic violence with a scapegoat
mechanism, developing an account of Satan's power (and its defeat)
in an exceptionally creative manner.[80] A thorough account of this
movement (including but not limited to the work of Girard) is
beyond the scope of the present work, and at present I will merely
voice a commendation and approbation. It is beneficial to the
Church that these theologians are exploring and developing new
insights into the work of Christ and how it counteracts the power
of Satan. Among these benefits is the increasing awareness of the
systemic nature of evil which liberation theology has also helped us
to see.[81] I am concerned, however, that current work in this area is
building upon a loose or generic account of 'victory' and 'evil', and
an equally loose account of the biblical material on Satan.[82] This
would partly explain why it is the locus for such creative work –
the flexibility and ambiguity of the thematic foundation provides
ample room for innovative exploration. Our response should be to

root such reflection more deeply in biblical foundations, an effort
that will either chasten or strengthen this line of thought, to the
benefit of the Church either way.

But what are we to make of this historical material, and how
ought we to constructively appropriate it into a full account of
Christ's saving work? Because of the biblical witness, which includes
a good deal of material pertaining to the limited though real reign
and power of Satan, and the fact that Christ's work freed us from
his power in some sense, we are bound to incorporate this into our
account of Christ's work. But what is the best way to do so? What
follows are several points contributing to a way forward.

First, it is mistaken to refer to the *'Christus victor'* or 'ransom
theory' of the atonement, for at best these are a family of theories,
each offering a different explanation of how Christ's death defeated

---

[79]Weaver, *The Nonviolent Atonement*; Darby Kathleen Ray, *Deceiving the Devil:
Atonement, Abuse, and Ransom* (Cleveland: Pilgrim Press, 1998); S. Mark Heim,
Saved from Sacrifice: A Theology of the Cross (Grand Rapids, MI: Eerdmans, 2006).
[80]Girard, *I See Satan*, 189. Cf. Johnson, *God's Being*, 158–63.
[81]Trelstad, 'Cross Examinations', 14–15.
[82]Cf. Ray's demythologized view of Satan in: Ray, *Deceiving the Devil: Atonement,
Abuse, and Ransom*, vii, 130–1.

Satan and rescued humankind from his power or influence. Lumping these theories together simply due to their shared interest in Satan obscures their distinct insights while overlooking the disagreements between the proponents of these views.

Second, we do better to locate our treatment of Satan within our account of the scope of the atonement, and more specifically within the list of characters with significant roles in the drama, rather than as a discrete theory of the atonement. Reducing theories to an account of how Christ's death and resurrection affects specific parts of God's creation cultivates an unnecessarily myopic approach, though such questions clearly have a place. The problem is a matter of emphasis. Specific questions of this sort are best considered within the broader framework of an account properly built around the life and character of God which he seeks to share with the whole of his creation through Christ's atoning work, for such an account provides far more conceptual resources, and theological proportion, within which such inquiries can fruitfully take place. Furthermore, emphasizing Satan as a significant character rather than the focus of a single theory encourages each theory of the atonement to consider its implications for the demonic realm. *Christus victor*, in other words, should be a constitutive element of every theory of the atonement, variously construed depending on the particular insight or vantage point in question.

The third implication following from this history is that *Christus victor* accounts of the atonement help us understand the work of Christ by opening our eyes to the ways in which sin functions at both individual and social/systemic levels, by means of reflection on the different ways in which Satan exercises the power he has over creation. Such a move pushes us outside of an individualistic and pietistic account to the Christian life, opening our eyes to a more expansive vision of the nature of our sins of omission and commission.

Thus far, however, we have focused on how Satan ought to be included in accounts of the atonement, without asking the central question of this chapter: what are the ways in which we can speak of Christ's atoning work being *for* the various aspects of God's creation, including Satan and the demonic realm? One possibility is that Christ's work brings order to the cosmos, and in so doing offers some elements of salvation to the demons, which are no longer able to do harm. Gregory of Nyssa tentatively suggests that Christ benefited not only the one who had perished, but also the very one who had brought us to ruin. For when death came into contact with life ... the worse of these things disappeared into a state of nonexistence, to the profit of him who was freed from these evils. ... Not even the adversary himself can question that what occurred was just and salutary – if, that is, he comes to recognize its benefit.[83]

Boethius provides us with resources to build the first half of this concept, bypassing the question of whether Satan will ultimately recognize this benefit. 'It may be incredible to some,' he writes, 'but it must be the case that the wicked are less happy if they achieve their desires than if they are unable to do what they want. For, if desiring something wicked brings misery, greater misery is brought by having had the power to do it, without which the unhappy desire would go unfulfilled.'[84] In other words, the victory of Christ and the plundering of the city of Dis benefits the demons, preventing their suffering the fulfilment of their wicked desires.

Through Christ's work, as we see in Bramantino's painting, *Crucifixion*, the demonic realm kneels before Christ in subjection, while the angelic realm bows in adoration. Traditionally, this submission is thought to be involuntary, awaiting the final judgement to come. Boethius helps us see that this judgement would be saving for the demons in the sense that it would put an end to their acts of evil. God's love for beings wholly given over to sin is such that he will do the one thing left for them: give them the happiness of being unable to do that which they desire. In this sense, the subjection portrayed by Bramantino becomes not merely the powerful act of a tyrant,[85] but the only appropriate act of a compassionate Lord.

A second way that Christ's atonement is significant for the demonic realm has to do with knowledge: God's desire to promulgate his self-justification, it would seem, extends beyond humankind to the angels, for God sought, through the Church, to make known the 'manifold wisdom of God' to 'the rulers and authorities in the heavenly places' (Eph. 3:10) – which includes precisely

---

[83]Nyssa, 'An Address on Religious Instruction', 303–4.
[84]Boethius, *The Consolation of Philosophy*, trans. V. E. Watts (New York: Penguin, 1969), 127.
[85]Boethius is aware of this possibility: '[I]t would hardly seem a happy government if it were like a yoke imposed upon unwilling necks instead of a willing acceptance of salvation.' Ibid., 111.

those spiritual forces of evil, those rulers and authorities against whom Paul claims we struggled in Ephesians 6:10ff. In this way the atonement is *for* the demonic realms in revealing the wisdom and goodness of God to them, and as we have seen, revelation is an aspect of salvation.

A third possibility, though an admittedly dangerous and thinly attested one in Scripture and history of theology, is that Christ atoned for demons in such a way that they will in fact be saved.[86] Origen, for instance, leaves it to the reader to approve of whether 'any of those orders who act under the government of the devil, and obey his wicked commands, will in a future world be converted to righteousness because of their possessing the faculty of freedom of the will, or whether persistent and inveterate wickedness may be changed by the power of habit into nature'.[87] The question is whether the free will of the demons has cemented into nature, for if so, there is no longer hope of salvation (which occurs in Christ according to the capacity of the nature for salvation).[88] Gregory of Nyssa suggests that through Christ God 'healed the very author of evil himself', giving little elaboration of how this might be the case.[89] To be sure, this idea received little traction within the history of the Church, which tended to emphasize with Irenaeus that hell was the place originally prepared for demons (*AH*, 456), where 'their worm does not die and the fire is not quenched' (Mk 9:48), and with Augustine, who (gently) affirmed the condemnation of Origen in this regard.[90] It would seem that if it would have been better for Judas had he not been born (Mk 14:21), the same would be true of Lucifer and his followers. Should this be the case, Christ's atonement is ultimately for the demons only inasmuch as an act can be beneficial for those who ultimately resist it.[91]

---

[86]Cf. C. A. Patrides, 'The Salvation of Satan', *Journal of the History of Ideas* 28, no. 4 (1967): 467–78.

[87]Origen, 'De Principiis', 261.

[88]Recall the quotes from Pseudo-Dionysius and John Wesley at the beginning of the chapter, exploring the idea that things participate in the salvation of Christ in accordance with their nature's capacity to do so.

[89]Nyssa, 'An Address on Religious Instruction', 304.

[90]Augustine, *City of God*, 1077. Cf. *CDH*, 354–5.

[91]The same would be true for humankind. Cf. Burgess' sketch of the idea that 'God's judgment *when it brings death and not life* [is] itself *also* the judgment of Grace'. Andrew Burgess, 'Salvation as Judgement and Grace', in *God of Salvation*, ed. Ivor J. Davidson and Murray A. Rae (Burlington, VT: Ashgate, 2011), 57–8.

Cosmic reconciliation

Why should we develop the implications or the 'for-ness' of Christ's saving work for angels and demons, trees and horses, and for God's own self? Simply put: because the Bible does, and the history of theological reflection built upon it. While spending too much time on these matters could lead to an imbalance in which the anthropological significance of Christ's work in keeping with the canonical emphasis would be minimized, overemphasizing the anthropological impact of the atonement is equally detrimental, ultimately eroding or compromising precisely that which it sought to secure. That is to say, anthropological overemphasis compromises our understanding of the salvation of human life because we are intrinsically connected with these other aspects of the created whole which God has brought into existence. Knowing and worshipping God like the angels (Lk. 20:36; Heb. 12:22), fallen like the demons and under their influence (Eph. 2:2), made of earth we walk on (Gen. 2:7) and groaning with it in its cursedness and its pains of childbirth (Gen. 3:16-17; Rom. 8:22), needing sustenance like our animal brethren (Gen. 1:29-30), and made in the image of God himself (Gen. 1:26-7; 2 Cor. 4:4), our existence and nature is bound up with the cosmos and its Creator. To be saved in Christ is part of a cosmic reality, the dimension of which we share with creation and its elements.

Though we are obviously a distinct element of God's creation, we are nonetheless an element of God's creation – a part of a whole which is discrete and independent precisely as a member of this whole. An anthropocentric account of Christ's work does more than ignore a significant amount of biblical material: it ultimately erodes a full understanding of what it means to be human. Inasmuch as our doctrine of the atonement ignores the impact of Christ's work upon God himself, it ignores the covenantal nature of both divine and human life. Insofar as we ignore the implications of Christ's death and resurrection on the angels, we are inclined to ignore the way that our understanding, worship and order are built on Christ's salvation. The more we overlook the ways which Christ effects our animal brethren, the more we are tempted to overlook the essential role of the body in our salvation, reducing the Gospel to a matter of the soul or conscience (with similar consequences for our view of heaven). The same goes for the earth – the more we ignore the role of the body in salvation, the more we ignore both the plight and the hope of the planet upon which we walk. And the more we ignore the relevance of the atonement for the demons, the less inclined we are to acknowledge the ultimate possibility of rejecting that which Christ has done for us.

The result is a Gospel with very little traction in whole spheres of human and creaturely existence, or a faith that considers these spheres, but in a manner unrelated to or disconnected from the Gospel that it proclaims. The danger of the former is a Gospel unable to speak to human sexuality, ecological concerns, the life of the mind, or social welfare. The danger of the latter is that we will in fact speak about these issues, but will do so in such a way that neither builds upon nor returns to a full understanding of the work of Christ, so that our speaking and action do not ultimately stem from or lead others to a proper appreciation of the work of Christ. Coincident with this is a simultaneous over-reading and under-reading of Scripture, in which we overlook the interconnections in Scripture making it a whole, while simultaneously overdeveloping discrete pieces of Scripture in our attempt to find ways to relate the Bible to different contemporary needs and questions.

This chapter has sketched a properly cosmic account of Christ's saving work, cutting off these problems from the start. Such a move pushes us towards a fuller and more integrated account of the death and resurrection of Jesus Christ, which connects the various aspects of the created order with the structure of the doctrine of the atonement. The result is a more expansive view of the work of Christ, and, ironically, a properly anthropological one, for these interconnections simultaneously transcend and properly situate a full account of human nature and its salvation within a cosmic scope.

7

Conclusion

Perhaps more than usual, this book begs for a clear and helpful summary. While the point has been to offer an expansive and vision-casting project resistant to overly simplistic summary, the proclamation of Christ's saving work is too central to the mission of the Church to leave any ambiguity in this matter. Understanding and embracing the riches we have in Christ will nourish the Church and its members, as long as we articulate those riches, or the diversity proper to the doctrine, with a clear and concise summary of the doctrine. A thorough appreciation of the complexity of the atonement funds our delight and worship, while equipping the Church to relate Christ's work meaningfully to a host of other areas. An equally strong grasp of the simplicity of the doctrine yields a sense of the overall shape and structure of the doctrine, offering meaning and direction to our inquiries within its many elements. Just as in the doctrines of the Trinity and divine attributes (in fact, precisely because of them), the interplay between unity and diversity, simplicity and complexity, plays a vital role here as well.

Summary I

The best summary statements about Christ's atoning work in Scripture are the following two (closely related) verses:

> In Christ God was reconciling the world to himself. (2 Cor. 5:19)

> In [Christ] all the fullness of God was pleased to dwell, and through him to reconcile to himself all things. (Col. 1:19-20)[1]

In short:

> *God was in Christ, reconciling all things to himself.*

The beauty of this short statement is fourfold. First, the emphasis is first and foremost upon God, which is absolutely vital for the doctrine. The atonement is the work of God bringing God's creation back to God. God is the origin, means and end of this act, and the role of theology proper is singularly and absolutely determinative for the shape of the doctrine and the coherence of our account of the atonement. Second, this is the work of God as man, as Jesus. That is to say, it is an entirely human work, the work of God as one of us, one of our kind living out his life under the same realities and circumstances as we do. It is a work from within our life and experience, in which God makes our situation his own, rather than a work from the outside. Third, this is a work of reconciliation. One could say that *God was in Christ, atoning (at-one-ing) all things to himself in Christ*, though this does not communicate as readily in contemporary English. In principle, one could substitute 'reconciling' for any of a number of soteriological synonyms, including 'saving', 'redeeming', 'ransoming' or 'sanctifying'. 'Reconciliation' is preferable, however, for its positive (indicating salvation *for* just as much or more than it does salvation *from*) and comprehensive nature.[2] In other words, it isn't as readily reducible to merely marshal, judicial or commercial concerns as some of its peers.

The final reason which makes this summary the best single statement in Scripture concerning the work of Christ is its comprehensive scope: *all things*! Of course this must be unpacked, but such a comprehensive and indeed cosmic affirmation runs no

---

[1]In context, the 2 Corinthians passage has a much more anthropological focus than does Colossians. Though Barth prefers 2 Corinthians 5:19 (along with Jn 3:16) to sum up the doctrine of the atonement, I prefer the Colossians passage for its similar content and more expansive vision (*CD* IV/1, 70–8).

[2]Marshall, *Aspects*, 98–137. The same holds true within the sphere of human ethics. Cf. Radzik, *Making Amends*, 80.

risk whatsoever of leaving anything out.[3] All things are involved
and bound up in the death and resurrection of Christ. This is no
mere matter of meeting some particular need or void in our lives –
the death and resurrection of Christ are of much bigger scope than
that. They gather up the identity, condition and fate of all of God's
creation, for in Christ all things are taken up and reconciled to the
Father. Regardless of whether we recognize this to be the case, there
is nothing in life that is not reconciled to God through the work of
Christ (Col. 1:20).

In short, for a single statement that grasps the foundation of the
doctrine of the atonement in the being and act of God, the means
of the atonement in the man Jesus Christ, the positive and life-
giving nature of atonement as a work of reconciliation, a restoring
of relationships, and the scope of the atonement, which brings *all
things* into their proper relationship and fellowship with God, there
is no better statement than Paul's claim that *God was in Christ
reconciling all things to himself.*

Summary II: Expanding the statement

The purpose of a summary statement is to bring clarity by highlighting the basic elements or structure of that which it summarizes.
Accordingly, summary always plays its role as one part of the
task of understanding its object, which is to say, summaries play a
role within the dynamic movement necessary for understanding a
complex reality, moving between a vision of the overall structure and
interacting with the smaller parts of which the whole is composed.
To honour this dynamic movement, we will briefly unpack the
above summary, offering a slightly more complex rendition of the
same basic statement:

> The triune God, Father, Son and Holy Spirit, in the fullness of
> the divine perfections, was in Jesus Christ, the Messiah of Israel,
> bringing all created things in heaven and earth to the fulfilment
> of their God-given purposes through reconciliation with God.

---

[3]The risk it is most susceptible to is that of missing emphases and priorities. Proper attention to the foundation of Christ's work within the doctrine of God on the one hand, and
to the biblical witness on the other, should go a great distance towards minimizing this risk.

To affirm that God was in Christ, that this was the work of God and his presence in this act is what makes it what it is, what gives it its defining features, characteristics and significance, is to affirm first and foremost that this is the work of Father, Son and Holy Spirit – the triune God. The life, death and resurrection of Jesus are what they are because they are events in the life of God, willed by the Father, executed by the Son, in the fellowship and power of the Holy Spirit. It is only because the atonement is the work of the triune God, bringing our humanity and sin into the relational dynamics of Father, incarnate Son and Holy Spirit, that this work is what it is. And it is because God does this work through his own life, that it simultaneously involves the fullness of the divine character. In this event, God enacts his love, wisdom, mercy, righteousness, holiness and presence, the fullness of the divine attributes, in his overcoming of sin and evil, and restoration of all things according to his purposes for them.

To affirm that Jesus was a man is to embrace the fact that he was not any man, but an Israelite: born of the line of David, realizing in himself the covenants, prophecies and laws of the Old Testament as the Messiah, the prophet, priest and king, the one who in himself was the faithful Israelite.[4] As such, he is, of course, a human being just as we are, but one with a specific history, and with that history a specific identity and role. Salvation is from the Jews (Jn 4:22), and more concretely, from the Jew, Jesus, the son of Mary. And his work was a work of reconciliation, of atonement – of making one through restored relation to God and through him to all things. Relationally, he made things one by bringing about reconciliation or the restoration of fellowship. Cosmically, he made creation one by removing evil, conflict and decay. Judicially, he made us one by doing away with the crime, guilt and punishment. His work was a work of creating and sharing oneness according to the many forms it takes in different contexts and relationships, bearing in himself and thereby doing away with all sin, evil and discord.

---

[4] I have refrained from employing the threefold office of Christ as a framework for exploring the diversity of Christ's work for the limitations I perceive in this approach. Cf. Adam Johnson, 'The Servant Lord: A Word of Caution Regarding the *Munus Triplex* in Karl Barth's Theology and the Church Today', *Scottish Journal of Theology* 65, no. 2 (2012). Robert Sherman, on the other hand, takes the opposite approach. Sherman, *King, Priest and Prophet*. I much prefer a recapitulatory approach to the Old Testament, such as one finds in Irenaeus, which can appropriate the insights of the *munus triplex*, without being limited thereby.

And his work, as we have seen, touches on all things: angels and demons, Jews and Gentiles, dogs and cats, mountains and graveyards. And because the centre of God's election in Christ was for a people, for a relationship with humankind, his work relates to middle management and racial relations, body and soul, emotions and habits, families and friendships. Extending far beyond the guilty conscience, God became man in Jesus Christ to bring every aspect of creation, and every aspect of our human existence, under the Lordship of Jesus Christ, with all the flourishing and mutual exaltation that this entails for every aspect of our being (physical, spiritual, social, sexual, economic and otherwise) and that of the creation of which we are a part.

This more expansive summary is but a springboard to fuller reflection on each of these areas – a reflection we have made in more depth over the course of this book. But for the sake of clarity and definition, it is helpful that we be able to pull back from detailed exploration of the sub-points of the doctrine, and also be able to affirm with brevity and understanding that:

> The triune God, Father, Son and Holy Spirit, in the fullness of the divine perfections, was in Jesus Christ, the Messiah of Israel, bringing all created things in heaven and earth to the fulfillment of their God-given purposes through reconciliation with God.

Or even more briefly, that:

> *God was in Christ, reconciling all things to himself.*

Biblical and historical implications

What then do we do with this simple yet vast account of the work of Christ? A temptation is to emphasize simplicity, subtly twisting it into oneness or monotony: selecting one or a handful of favourite aspects of the work of Christ as the sum, heart or whole of the doctrine. My argument to this point has consistently fought such a move, so I will not repeat an argument against it here. The alternative is much more aggressive, challenging and exciting. We must continue to develop and understand the work of Christ and all that it entails.

Biblically, this means that we must approach Scripture with a hermeneutic which reads Scripture in dialogue with the death and resurrection of Jesus as the central event giving the whole its meaning: reading Scripture knowing nothing except Jesus Christ and him crucified (and risen) (1 Cor. 2:2).[5] To do this well, we must keep firmly in mind the synthetic nature of the doctrine of the atonement, comprised as it is of the doctrines of the Trinity, divine attributes, Christology, hamartiology and eschatology (especially the doctrine of heaven/salvation). Relatively few passages of Scripture offer a developed account of precisely *how* Christ's work is saving. But much of Scripture in some way speaks to one or more of the factors that together comprise the doctrine of the atonement. Our challenge is to read Scripture in such a way as to keep in mind the Paschal focus of the canon, while allowing the parts and pieces of Scripture to play their role in shaping our understanding of the larger synthetic picture of which they are a part.

A brief example may be helpful at this point. We may be tempted to gloss over much of the law in the Pentateuch. Leviticus 16 and a handful of other passages are clearly relevant to the atonement, but much of the material might seem to be largely irrelevant (bewilderingly so). But this may have more to do with the categories we bring to the table than anything else. When we think of law we think in judicial categories. And while these do have a place in the Pentateuch, the Law of Moses is far more interested in becoming and staying clean than it does in anything else. Guilt and punishment prove to be 'thin' categories for interpreting these matters, but cleanness proves much richer, as we see it developed in individual, social, physical, moral and theological ways throughout the law. And when we come to Hebrews (among other places), we find this emphasis on cleanness developed and brought to bear upon the work of Christ:

> For if the blood of goats and bulls, and the sprinkling of defiled persons with the ashes of a heifer, sanctify for the purification of the flesh, how much more will the blood of Christ, who through the eternal Spirit offered himself without blemish to God, purify our conscience from dead works to serve the living God. (Heb. 9:13-14)

---

[5] John Behr, 'The Paschal Foundation of Christian Theology', *St Vladimir's Theological Quarterly* 45, no. 2 (2001): 120.

Working back from this emphasis on defiling, cleansing and sanctifying, we come to the holiness of God, the source and ground of all these concepts, and a vision of the Christian life (and afterlife) as a life of sanctified holiness as the holy people of God (Lev. 20:26; 1 Pet. 1:16).

While the Mosaic law may seem to have relatively little to offer us by way of a doctrine of the atonement, this is in fact far from the case, for its development of the nature of holiness (and its perversions) falls within a canonical development of the holiness of God, his will for his holy people and the cleansing and sanctifying work of Christ and his Spirit, all of which develops a line of thought as foreign to Western theology as the sacrificial system or the worship of idols. If we expect detailed theology of the atonement in discrete passages of Scripture, we will find it thinly attested. However, if we embrace Scripture's development of the different elements that together constitute the synthetic doctrine of the atonement, we will find ourselves continually nourished and challenged by passages and books rarely if ever mentioned in treatments of the work of Christ.

Building on the synthetic nature of the Christian doctrine, we can move from an account of sin to the character of God which it perverts, and from there to an account of eternal life as a creaturely inhabiting of that aspect of God's character. On this basis, we can mine Scripture and theology for ways in which Christ bore in himself the reality and consequences of that dimension of sin, restoring us to life in fellowship with God through participating in the corresponding dimension of the divine life through the resurrection and ascension. In sum, because the atonement is both a synthetic doctrine, and is comprised of mutually related doctrines, it is a fluid and natural process to build an account of the work of Christ by starting with any of the constituent elements of a theory, facilitating faithful and creative work on the atonement through reading of Scripture.

Much the same is true with the history of doctrine. Whether we are reading Tertullian, Chrysostom, Melanchthon, Theresa of Avila or Ritschl, some of their works speak directly of the atoning work of Christ. In this case, our privilege is to interpret their works carefully, honouring them in the historical context, seeking to learn from the history of Christian interpretation of Scripture and theology, eager to embrace new and helpful categories, arguments and insights regarding the work of Christ. More often, we come across elements of the doctrine of the atonement not formulated as such, affording us the same opportunities delineated above concerning the reading of Scripture.

Quite often, however, we come across material that we cannot fully embrace, whether that is (perceived) sins of theological omission or commission. By means of the synthetic nature of the doctrine rooted in the divine life and act, we can move beyond careful and charitable interpretation to a more constructive project, taking the work of the theologian in question and breaking the various elements of their account into distinct components. That being the case, we are in a position to offer a more precise account of what we find to be their mistakes, while simultaneously freeing us to appreciate and appropriate the strengths of their account.[6]

That is to say, simply because a theologian's Christology is inadequate doesn't mean that their hamartiology is contaminated. This may well be the case, for theology, as it gives witness to the God who is one, ought likewise to be one, such that commitments in one doctrine will shape commitments in other doctrines. However, there are several reasons why this may not be the case. First, theologians, myself included, rarely live up to the task we have embraced, and are often inconsistent – sometimes for the better, and often for the worse. Second, the materials with which we work are so varied and complex, we may inadvertently develop lines of thought the connections of which we do not fully appreciate. Finally, just as the Holy Spirit is at work in the Church, so he is at work in its theologians, even those who more or less frequently err and even sin in their theological writing.

We need not therefore offer a wholesale rejection or affirmation of the work of any theologian (or school of thought). Assuming careful historical interpretation, breaking up the doctrine of the atonement into its many parts, we are free to appropriate and develop the work of these theologians in new and better directions. No matter the heterodoxy or danger attributed to the work in question, the possibility always exists that we might find therein doctrines or elements thereof that we can and should appropriate into a fuller account of the work of Christ.

---

[6]I sought to give a brief example of this kind of work with the thought of René Girard in: Johnson, *God's Being*, 158–63.

Ironically, this makes theological works with which we disagree one of the most promising avenues for further theological development, for such works are far more likely to take up lines of thought we minimize or fail to see altogether. Though our conclusions regarding these works may remain the same, the resources they contain for theological development have more promise than those with whom we are theologically more sympathetic. We should make every effort, therefore, to complement household theological staples with a combination of historical classics (including Irenaeus, Athanasius and many of those used throughout this book) and theological outcasts, whoever those may be.[7] We must be nurtured on classics, and test our mettle in constructive (though sometimes critical) interaction with those outside our own traditions and comfort zones.[8]

In short, this book provides some of the essential resources for a charitable and creative re-appropriation of resources within the history of the Church, as well as some of the key tools for a theological interpretation of Scripture focused on the atonement. Towards this end we have explored both the sum and gist of the doctrine, and a more in-depth exploration of its basic elements. All of this, however, is intended to energize further study more than to finalize or complete our faith seeking understanding of this doctrine.

Cultural implications

I conclude this book with an outward look: a gesture towards theological integration with culture. Theology is a task worth doing for its own sake. Employing the intellect in knowing God and his works needs no additional justification, as 'God is the only beatitude; for every one is blessed from this sole fact, that he understands God, in accordance with the saying of Augustine (*Conf.* v.4): *Blessed is he who knoweth Thee, though he know nought else*' (*ST*, I.26.3).

---

[7]What I am proposing fits firmly in line with a theology of retrieval, as outlined in: John B. Webster, 'Theologies of Retrieval', in *The Oxford Handbook of Systematic Theology*, edited by John B. Webster, Kathryn Tanner and Iain Torrance (New York: Oxford, 2007).

[8]Cf. C. S. Lewis' argument for reading old books in: Lewis, C. S. preface to *On the Incarnatio* by Athanasius. Translated by John Behr (Yonkers, NY: St. Vladimir's Seminary Press, 2011).

But that does not mean that there are no further benefits to the task; in fact, there are many. One of the chief of these is the way that theology provides us with resources for interacting constructively with culture.

Inasmuch as we think of the atonement in concrete terms through a specific theory or metaphor, we are limited in our ability to relate that theory to the culture around us. That is to say, inasmuch as we are limited to such concepts as bearing punishment vicariously, rescue from slavery, or the like, our opportunities for integration are both limited and wooden. But as we unpack the doctrine, and emphasize its synthetic nature, we have far more resources for interaction. Just as with the argument above concerning biblical interpretation, so with culture: while a given trend or artefact may have little or nothing to say about resurrection or the character of God, it may have a profound understanding of some aspect of human sin, or a vision of the *eschaton* and what such heavenly life looks like. We are then free to bring this understanding into dialogue with our synthetic vision of the atonement rooted in the divine life, expanding the cultural artefact to incorporate other necessary components of a full theory of the atonement.[9]

For instance, it seems that American culture is growing in its awareness of the reality of shame.[10] Films and TV shows are incorporating the word into their titles, and more importantly, into their content. So what might it look like, to bring the atonement into this cultural discussion? First, we must simply listen, seeking to understand, in its own terms and on its own premises, the American understanding of shame as found in specific artefacts. Second, we can bring the biblical material into the discussion, allowing the cultural material to heighten our awareness of material we overlook, or teach us material undeveloped in Scripture, while allowing Scripture to critique culture where it must do so. So far so good, but

---

[9]The dialogue, as I understand it, does not presuppose or support natural theology. Scripture remains the sole authority for the proclamation and teaching of the Church. Culture can contribute to our understanding in many ways, or awaken us to the realities in Scripture which we overlook, but should never be authoritative in the way that the Bible is.

[10]Much to the pleasure of Baker and Green, I am sure. Baker and Green, *Recovering*, 153–70.

the real challenge is to move the discussion more explicitly into the world of Christ's atoning work by asking: How might we develop an account of the atonement which would take as its understanding of sin this cultural understanding of shame (as chastened, critiqued and filled out by Scripture)? The film or show itself may have little to say on the matter, but that need not stop us from employing our theological resources to build a theory of the atonement around this vision of shame, that could speak richly and meaningfully to our culture.

We stand to gain theologically and culturally through this exercise. Theologically, we are blind to so much that the Bible and Church have to teach us. Sin and over-familiarity breed bad reading and thinking. If culture can awaken or teach us to better readings of Scripture, we stand to benefit. And on the other hand, culture stands to gain much if the value of the theological task is but a fraction of what the Church claims it to be. Our culture is working through the meaning of shame, freedom, law, individuality and a host of important issues – and we could bring the death and resurrection of Christ into these discussions in a manner that simultaneously presents the Gospel and relates powerfully to culture. This is reason enough for embarking on the project.

The key to doing this successfully is the synthetic nature of the doctrine. First, we must break the doctrine into its constituent parts, asking how the cultural trend or artefact in question relates to any and all of them. Does it contain an implicit or explicit understanding of God? How does it develop the plight or sin of humankind? Does it contain a vision of heaven, or of life as it was meant to be? Does it offer some way of understanding how our sin is overcome? Such questions begin our theological interaction with culture. Once we have answered the questions, we have the opportunity to bring them into the theological discussion, honouring and critiquing and expanding as need be. From there, we can fill out a theory of the atonement around culture's (modified) contribution. This last step is the most exciting of all, for ultimately, it is the vantage point from which we can meaningfully speak the death and resurrection of Christ back into precisely those cultural discussions from which we started, offering constructive and culture-building/affirming insight in a mode designed to speak to culture in its own categories and with its own values redeemed as much as this is possible.

Returning to the idea of shame, assume for the moment that while it is a pervasive theme in Scripture, it is thinly developed. We have the opportunity, therefore, to learn from culture, both from scholarly (psychological, sociological and philosophical studies) and popular sources (movies and TV shows). We need not take this testimony to the nature and effects of shame as definitively authoritative, but we can and should listen carefully and attentively, allowing what Scripture does say about shame to inform our listening. The result of such interaction will be a cultural vision chastened and qualified by Scripture, or a biblical vision enriched by culture. But shame has its meaning and place within the prior reality of divine honour and glory, for all things have their meaning and purpose in relation to the divine character and will. Filling out this aspect of the character of God, we are well on our way towards developing an account of the atonement as the work of the God who in himself is and has honour and glory, but in Christ makes our shame his own, that he might restore us in glory and honour. With this fuller understanding of shame by locating it within the shape of the Gospel, we have the constructive and life-giving side of the vision, the part that culture has a much harder time grasping. With our vision of Christ as the one who bears shame in order to share honour and glory, we have a vocation, vision and message that will not only communicate to those suffering from shame, but can also deeply shape how we interact (in thought, word and deed) with the shame around and in us.

The atonement is too big of a reality to relegate exclusively to theological discourse. It is the decisive reality for all creative beings, and it is our joy and privilege to honour it as such. But to do so, we must have a sufficiently rich understanding of the doctrine, and a care for the world around us that is deep and genuine enough both to listen to it carefully, and to find ways to communicate the work of Jesus Christ and its implications back to that world in ways that it can understand. But to be clear – this is not mere 'translation' or 'contextualization' of metaphors or anything of the like. Rather, it is a delving into the reality of both culture and atonement, to explore the many ways in which Christ has taken upon himself the plight of his creation, so as to reconcile all things to the Father in himself. This is no mere translation or application – this is an act of rejoicing in and worshipping God for what he has in fact done in Jesus Christ.

Conclusion

Christ's atonement is the lifeblood of the Church. It is the definitive re-creative act of God to bring his creation to its fulfilment. But it is an act that cannot be transcended, for while it is the means by which God accomplishes his purposes, it is simultaneously the end for which he acted. The life and work of Christ, in other words, is precisely the way that God brings us into the life and work of Christ. We cannot ignore, transcend or move beyond the life and work of Christ for it is our destiny, and perfection as those made in his image.

That being the case, the Church needs a vision for the doctrine of the atonement sufficiently expansive to fund ongoing study and preaching. It needs a doctrine that creates the conceptual, theological, historical and biblical room for an ongoing explorative and formative task. There is plenty of room for contemporary questions and concerns within such a vision, as well as levels at which binding and final claims can and should be made. But just as important as these is the sense of space, adventure and an ongoing task and responsibility, as the Church continues to inhabit, in thought, word and deed, the reality by which and into which it has been saved. My hope is that this book has offered precisely this, a vision of Christ's atoning work that invites us to:

Consider where and what is the strength of thy salvation, occupy thyself in meditating thereon, delight thyself in the contemplation thereof; put away thy daintiness, force thyself, give thy mind thereto; taste of the goodness of thy Redeemer, kindle within thyself the love of the Saviour.[11]

---

[11] Anselm, 'The Devotions of Saint Anselm', 105.

APPENDIX – LIST
OF RECOMMENDED
SOURCES ON THE
DOCTRINE OF THE
ATONEMENT

Classic sources

Anselm. 'Why God Became Man'. In *The Major Works*, edited by Brian Davies and G. R. Evans. New York: Oxford University Press, 1998.

Athanasius. *On the Incarnation*. Translated by John Behr. Yonkers, NY: St. Vladimir's Seminary Press, 2011.

Balthasar, Hans Urs von. *Mysterium Paschale: The Mystery of Easter*. Translated by Aidan Nichols. San Francisco: Ignatius Press, 1990.

Barth, Karl. *Church Dogmatics IV: The Doctrine of Reconciliation*. Edinburgh: T & T Clark, 1988.

Calvin, John. *Institutes of the Christian Religion. The Library of Christian Classics*. Vol. 20–21. Philadelphia: Westminster Press, 1960.

Campbell, John McLeod. *The Nature of the Atonement and Its Relation to Remission of Sins and Eternal Life*. London: Macmillan, 1869.

Edwards, Jonathan. 'The Wisdom of God Displayed in the Way of Salvation'. In *The Works of Jonathan Edwards*, edited by Henry Rogers, Sereno Edwards Dwight and Edward Hickman. Peabody, MA: Hendrickson, 1998, 141–57.

Irenaeus. *On the Apostolic Preaching*. Translated by John Behr. Crestwood: St. Vladimir's Seminary Press, 1997.

Thomas. *Summa Theologiae: The Passion of Christ (3a. 46-52)*. Translated by Dominican Order. Vol. 54. New York: Blackfriars, 1964.

Contemporary sources

Baker, Mark D. and Joel B. Green. *Recovering the Scandal of the Cross: Atonement in New Testament and Contemporary Contexts*. Downers Grove, IL: InterVarsity Press, 2003.

Boersma, Hans. *Violence, Hospitality, and the Cross: Reappropriating the Atonement Tradition*. Grand Rapids, MI: Baker Academic, 2004.

Davidson, Ivor J. and Murray A. Rae, eds. *God of Salvation*. Burlington, VT: Ashgate, 2011.

Girard, René. *I See Satan Fall Like Lightning*. Maryknoll, NY: Orbis, 2001.

Grensted, Laurence W. *A Short History of the Doctrine of the Atonement*. London: Longmans, Green & co., 1920.

Gunton, Colin E. *The Actuality of Atonement: A Study of Metaphor, Rationality, and the Christian Tradition*. Grand Rapids, MI: Eerdmans, 1989.

Kotsko, Adam. *The Politics of Redemption: The Social Logic of Salvation*. New York: T&T Clark, 2010.

McKnight, Scot. *A Community Called Atonement*. Nashville, TN: Abingdon Press, 2007.

Tanner, Kathryn. *Christ the Key*. Current Issues in Theology. Cambridge: Cambridge University Press, 2010.

BIBLIOGRAPHY

Alison, James. 'God's Self-Substitution and Sacrificial Inversion'.
In *Stricken by God? Nonviolent Identification and the Victory of Christ*, edited by Brad Jersak and Michael Hardin. Grand Rapids, MI: Eerdmans, 2007.

Anselm. 'The Devotions of Saint Anselm', edited by Clement C. J. Webb. London: Methuen & Co, 1903.

—. 'Why God Became Man'. In *The Major Works*, edited by Brian Davies and G. R. Evans. New York: Oxford University Press, 1998.

Assissi, Francis of. *The Little Flowers of Saint Francis*. Translated by Raphael Brown. New York: Doubleday, 1958.

Athanasius. *On the Incarnation*. Translated by John Behr Yonkers. New York: St Vladimir's Seminary Press, 2011.

Augustine. *The Augustine Catechism: The Enchiridion on Faith, Hope, and Love*. Translated by Bruce Harbert. Hyde Park: New City Press, 1999.

—. *The City of God against the Pagans*. Translated by R. W. Dyson. New York: Cambridge University Press, 1998.

—. *Confessions*. Translated by Henry Chadwick. Oxford: Oxford University Press, 1991.

—. *The Trinity*. Translated by Edmund Hill. Brooklyn, NY: New City Press, 1991.

Aulén, Gustaf. *Christus Victor: An Historical Study of the Three Main Types of the Idea of Atonement*. Translated by A. G. Hebert. New York: Macmillan, 1951.

Baker, Mark D. and Joel B. Green. *Recovering the Scandal of the Cross: Atonement in New Testament and Contemporary Contexts*. Downers Grove, IL: InterVarsity Press, 2003.

Balthasar, Hans Urs von. *Mysterium Paschale: The Mystery of Easter*. Translated by Aidan Nichols. San Francisco: Ignatius Press, 1990.

—. *Theo-Drama: Theological Dramatic Theory*. Translated by Graham Harrison. Vol. 4: The Action. San Francisco: Ignatius, 1988.

Barnabas. 'The Epistle of Barnabas'. Translated by J. B. Lightfoot. In *The Apostolic Fathers in English*, edited by Michael William Holmes. Grand Rapids, MI: Baker Academic, 2006.

Barth, Karl. *Christ and Adam: Man and Humanity in Romans 5*. Translated by Thomas Allan Smail. New York: Harper & Brothers, 1956.

—. *Church Dogmatics*. Translated by G. W. Bromiley. Edinburgh: T & T Clark, 1936–77.

—. *Community, State, and Church: Three Essays*. Translated by H. M. Hall, G. Ronald Howe and Ronald Gregor Smith. Garden City: Doubleday, 1960.

—. *Dogmatics in Outline*. Translated by G. T. Thompson. New York: Harper, 1959.

—. *Evangelical Theology: An Introduction*. Translated by Grover Foley. London: Weidenfeld and Nicolson, 1963.

Baur, Ferdinand Christian. *Die Christliche Lehre Von Der Versöhnung in Ihrer Geschichtlichen Entwicklung Von Der Ältesten Zeit Bis Auf Die Neueste*. Tübingen: C.F. Osiander, 1838.

Behr, John. 'The Paschal Foundation of Christian Theology'. *St Vladimir's Theological Quarterly* 45, no. 2 (2001): 115–36.

Beilby, James K. and Paul R. Eddy, eds. *The Nature of the Atonement: Four Views*. Downers Grove, IL: IVP Academic, 2006.

Belousek, Darrin W. Snyder. *Atonement, Justice, and Peace: The Message of the Cross and the Mission of the Church*. Grand Rapids, MI: William B. Eerdmans, 2012.

Benedict XVI. *Jesus of Nazareth: Holy Week*. San Francisco: Ignatius, 2011.

Bird, Michael F. *Jesus Is the Christ: The Messianic Testimony of the Gospels*. Downers Grove, IL: InterVarsity Press, 2012.

Blocher, Henri. 'Biblical Metaphors and the Doctrine of the Atonement'. *Journal of the Evangelical Theological Society* 47, no. 4 (2004): 629–45.

Boersma, Hans. *Violence, Hospitality, and the Cross: Reappropriating the Atonement Tradition*. Grand Rapids, MI: Baker Academic, 2004.

Boethius. *The Consolation of Philosophy*. Translated by V. E. Watts. New York: Penguin, 1969.

Boff, Leonardo. *Passion of Christ, Passion of the World: The Facts, Their Interpretation, and Their Meaning Yesterday and Today*. Maryknoll, NY: Orbis, 1987.

Borg, Marcus. 'Executed by Rome, Vindicated by God'. In *Stricken by God? Nonviolent Identification and the Victory of Christ*, edited by Brad Jersak and Michael Hardin. Grand Rapids, MI: Eerdmans, 2007.

Boyd, Gregory A. 'Christus Victor View'. In *The Nature of the Atonement: Four Views*, edited by James K. Beilby and Paul R. Eddy. Downers Grove, IL: IVP Academic, 2006.

—. *God at War: The Bible and Spiritual Conflict*. Downers Grove, IL: InterVarsity, 1997.

Brock, Rita Nakashima and Rebecca Ann Parker. *Proverbs of Ashes: Violence, Redemptive Suffering, and the Search for What Saves Us*. Boston: Beacon Press, 2001.

Brown, Raymond Edward. *The Death of the Messiah: From Gethsemane to the Grave*. New York: Doubleday, 1994.

Burgess, Andrew R. *The Ascension in Karl Barth*. Burlington, VT: Ashgate, 2004.

—. 'Salvation as Judgement and Grace'. In *God of Salvation*, edited by Ivor J. Davidson and Murray A. Rae. Burlington, VT: Ashgate, 2011.

Calvin, John. *Institutes of the Christian Religion*. Philadelphia: Westminster Press, 1960.

—. *The Epistle of Paul the Apostle to the Galatians, Ephesians, Philippians Colossians, Thessalonians, Timothy, Titus and Philemon*. Translated by William Pringle. Grand Rapids: Baker, 1979.

Campbell, John McLeod. *The Nature of the Atonement and Its Relation to Remission of Sins and Eternal Life*. London: Macmillan, 1869.

Carson, Donald A. 'Atonement in Romans 3:21-26'. In *The Glory of the Atonement: Biblical, Historical & Practical Perspectives: Essays in Honor of Roger R. Nicole*, edited by Charles E. Hill and Frank A. James. Downers Grove, IL: InterVarsity Press, 2004.

Catechism of the Catholic Church. Mahwah: Paulist Press, 1994.

Christensen, Michael J. and Jeffery A. Wittung. *Partakers of the Divine Nature: The History and Development of Deificiation in the Christian Traditions*. Grand Rapids, MI: Baker Academic, 2007.

Clough, David. *On Animals: Volume 1: Systematic Theology*. London: T & T Clark, 2012.

Cole, Graham A. *God the Peacemaker*. Downers Grove, IL: InterVarsity Press, 2009.

Cousar, Charles B. *A Theology of the Cross: The Death of Jesus in the Pauline Letters*. Minneapolis: Fortress Press, 1990.

Creegan, Nicola Hoggard. 'The Salvation of Creatures'. In *God of Salvation*, edited by Ivor J. Davidson and Murray A. Rae. Burlington, VT: Ashgate, 2011.

Crisp, Oliver. 'Original Sin and Atonement'. In *The Oxford Handbook of Philosophical Theology*, edited by Thomas P. Flint and Michael C. Rea. New York: Oxford University Press, 2009.

—. 'Penal Non-Substitution'. In *A Reader in Contemporary Philosophical Theology*, edited by Oliver Crisp. New York: T & T Clark, 2009.

Cross, John of the. 'The Spiritual Canticle'. Translated by Kieran Kavanaugh and Otilio Rodriguez. In *The Collected Works of St. John of the Cross*. Washington, DC: Institute of Carmelite Studies, 1979.

Cyril. *On the Unity of Christ*. Translated by John Anthony McGuckin. Crestwood, NY: St. Vladimir's Seminary Press, 1995.

Davidson, Ivor J. 'Introduction: God of Salvation'. In *God of Salvation*, edited by Ivor J. Davidson and Murray A. Rae. Burlington, VT: Ashgate, 2011.

—. 'Salvation's Destiny: Heirs of God'. In *God of Salvation*, edited by Ivor J. Davidson and Murray A. Rae. Burlington, VT: Ashgate, 2011.

de Gruchy, John. 'Salvation as Healing and Hominization'. In *Christ in Our Place: The Humanity of God in Christ for the Reconciliation of the World*, edited by Trevor A. Hart and Daniel P. Thimell. Allison Park, PA: Pickwick Publications, 1989.

Dillistone, F. W. *Jesus Christ and His Cross: Studies on the Saving Work of Christ*. Philadelphia: Westminster Press, 1953.

Donne, John. *The Sermons of John Donne*. Vol. 4. Los Angeles: University of California Press, 1959.

Dumas, Alexandre. *The Count of Monte Cristo*. Translated by Robin Buss. New York: Penguin, 2003.

Edwards, Denis. 'The Redemption of Animals in an Incarnational Theology'. In *Creaturely Theology: On God, Humans and Other Animals*, edited by Celia Deane-Drummond and David Clough. London: SCM Press, 2009.

Edwards, John. 'Lily-Crucifixions in the Oxford District'. *Oxford Art Journal* 2 (April 1979): 43–5.

Edwards, Jonathan. 'Concerning the Necessity and Reasonableness of the Christian Doctrine of Satisfaction for Sin'. In *The Works of Jonathan Edwards*, edited by Henry Rogers, Sereno Edwards Dwight and Edward Hickman. Peabody, MA: Hendrickson, 1998.

—. 'Dissertation on the End for Which God Created the World'. In *The Works of Jonathan Edwards*, edited by Henry Rogers, Sereno Edwards Dwight and Edward Hickman. Peabody, MA: Hendrickson, 1998.

—. 'The Wisdom of God Displayed in the Way of Salvation'. In *The Works of Jonathan Edwards*, edited by Henry Rogers, Sereno Edwards Dwight and Edward Hickman. Peabody, MA: Hendrickson, 1998.

—. *The Works of Jonathan Edwards*. Peabody, MA: Hendrickson, 1998.

'The Epistle to Diognetus'. Translated by J. B. Lightfoot. In *The Apostolic Fathers in English*, edited by Michael William Holmes. Grand Rapids, MI: Baker Academic, 2006.

Farrow, Douglas. *Ascension Theology*. London: T & T Clark, 2011.

Fee, Gordon D. *Paul, the Spirit, and the People of God*. Peadbody, MA: Hendrickson, 1996.

Feuerbach, Ludwig. *The Essence of Christianity*. Translated by George Eliot. Amherst, NY: Prometheus Books, 1989.

Finlan, Stephen. *Problems with Atonement: The Origins of, and Controversy About, the Atonement Doctrine*. Collegeville, MN: Liturgical Press, 2005.

Finlan, Stephen and Vladimir Kharlamov. *Theōsis: Deification in Christian Theology*. Eugene, OR: Pickwick, 2006.

Girard, René. *I See Satan Fall Like Lightning*. Maryknoll, NY: Orbis, 2001.

Godet, Frédéric Louis. *The Atonement in Modern Religious Thought, a Theological Symposium*. New York: Thomas Whittaker, 1901.

Godsey, John D. 'Reminiscences of Karl Barth'. *The Princeton Seminary Bulletin* (2002): 313–24.

Gombis, Timothy G. 'Racial Reconciiation and the Christian Gospel'. *ACT 3 Review* 15, no. 3 (2006): 117–28.

Grensted, Laurence W. *A Short History of the Doctrine of the Atonement*. London: Longmans, Green & co., 1920.

Gunton, Colin E. *The Actuality of Atonement: A Study of Metaphor, Rationality, and the Christian Tradition*. Grand Rapids, MI: Eerdmans, 1989.

Guðmundsdóttir, Arnfríður. *Meeting God on the Cross: Christ, the Cross, and the Feminist Critique*. Oxford: Oxford University Press, 2010.

Harnack, Adolf von. *What Is Christianity?* New York: Harper, 1957.

Hart, Trevor A. 'Irenaeus, Recapitulation and Physical Redemption'. In *Christ in Our Place: The Humanity of God in Christ for the Reconciliation of the World*, edited by Trevor A. Hart and Daniel P. Thimell. Allison Park, PA: Pickwick Publications, 1989.

Hector, Kevin W. 'Immutability, Necessity, and Triunity: Towards a Resolution of the Trinity and Election Controversy'. *Scottish Journal of Theology* 65, no. 01 (2009): 64–81.

Hegel, G. W. F. *Lectures on the Philosophy of Religion: The Lectures of 1827*. Translated by Peter Crafts Hodgson and Robert F. Brown. New York: Clarendon Press, 2006.

Heim, S. Mark. *Saved from Sacrifice: A Theology of the Cross*. Grand Rapids, MI: Eerdmans, 2006.

Hengel, Martin. *Crucifixion in the Ancient World and the Folly of the Message of the Cross*. Translated by John Bowden. Philadelphia: Fortress, 1977.

Herbert, George. *The Complete English Poems*. New York: Penguin, 1991.

Hill, Charles E. and Frank A. James, eds. *The Glory of the Atonement: Biblical, Historical and Practical Perspectives*. Downers Grove, IL: InterVarsity Press, 2004.

Hodgson, Peter C. 'Alienation and Reconciliation in Hegelian and Post-Hegelian Perspective'. *Modern Theology* 2, no. 1 (1985): 42–63.

Holmes, Stephen R. 'Ransomed, Healed, Restored, Forgiven: Evangelical Accounts of the Atonement'. In *The Atonement Debate: Papers from the London Symposium on the Theology of Atonement*, edited by Derek Tidball, David Hilborn and Justin Thacker. Grand Rapids, MI: Zondervan, 2008.

—. 'A Simple Salvation? Soteriology and the Perfections of God'. In *God of Salvation*, edited by Ivor J. Davidson and Murray A. Rae. Burlington, VT: Ashgate, 2011.

—. *The Wondrous Cross: Atonement and Penal Substitution in the Bible and History*. London: Paternoster, 2007.

Horton, Michael. *The Christian Faith: A Systematic Theology for Pilgrims on the Way*. Grand Rapids, MI: Zondervan, 2011.

Irenaeus. 'Against Heresies'. In *The Ante-Nicene Fathers*, edited by Alexander Roberts and James Donaldson. Peabody, MA: Hendrickson Publishers, 2004.

—. *On the Apostolic Preaching*. Translated by John Behr. Crestwood: St. Vladimir's Seminary Press, 1997.

Jenson, Matt. *Gravity of Sin: Augustine, Luther and Barth on 'Homo Incurvatus in Se'*. New York: T & T Clark, 2006.

Jenson, Robert. 'On the Doctrine of the Atonement'. *The Princeton Seminary Bulletin* 27, no. 2 (2006): 100–8.

Jersak, Brad and Michael Hardin, eds. *Stricken by God? Nonviolent Identification and the Victory of Christ*. Grand Rapids, MI: Eerdmans, 2007.

John of Damascus. *Exposition of the Orthodox Faith*. Translated by S. D. F. Salmond. Grand Rapids: Eerdmans, 1983.

Johnson, Adam. 'The Crucified Bridegroom: Christ's Atoning Death in St. John of the Cross and Spiritual Formation Today'. *Pro Ecclesia* XXI, no. 4 (2012).

—. 'A Fuller Account: The Role of "Fittingness" in Thomas Aquinas' Development of the Doctrine of the Atonement'. *International Journal of Systematic Theology* 12, no. 3 (2010): 302–18.

—. *God's Being in Reconciliation: The Theological Basis of the Unity and Diversity of the Atonement in the Theology of Karl Barth*. New York: T & T Clark, 2012.

—. 'The Servant Lord: A Word of Caution Regarding the *Munus Triplex* in Karl Barth's Theology and the Church Today'. *Scottish Journal of Theology* 65, no. 2 (2012).

—. "A Temple Framework of the Atonement." *JETS* 54, no. 2 (2011): 225–37.

—. "Where Demons Fear to Tread: Venturing into an Obscure Corner of the Doctrine of the Atonement Concerning the Un-Fallen Angels." *Journal of Reformed Theology* (Forthcoming).

Keating, James, and Thomas Joseph White. *Divine Impassibility and the Mystery of Human Suffering*. Grand Rapids, MI: Eerdmans, 2009.

Kerr, Nathan R. 'St. Anselm: *Theoria* and the Doctrinal Logic of Perfection'. In *Partakers of the Divine Nature: The History and Development of Deificiation in the Christian Traditions*, edited by Michael J. Christensen and Jeffery Wittung. Madison: Fairleigh Dickinson University Press, 2007.

Kharlamov, Vladimir. *Theōsis: Deification in Christian Theology*. Vol. 2. Eugene, OR: Pickwick Publications, 2011.

Kierkegaard, Sören. *Fear and Trembling: Dialectical Lyric by Johannes De Silentio*. Translated by Alastair Hannay. London: Penguin, 1985.

Kitamori, Kazo. *Theology of the Pain of God*. Richmond: John Knox Press, 1965.

Klager, Andrew P. 'Retaining and Reclaiming the Divine: Identification and the Recapitulation of Peace in St. Irenaeus of Lyons' Atonement Narrative'. In *Stricken by God? Nonviolent Identification and the Victory of Christ*, edited by Brad Jersak and Michael Hardin. Grand Rapids, MI: Eerdmans, 2007.

Kotsko, Adam. *The Politics of Redemption: The Social Logic of Salvation*. New York: T&T Clark, 2010.

Lane, Tony. 'Bernard of Clairvaux: Theologian of the Cross'. In *The Atonement Debate: Papers from the London Symposium on the Theology of Atonement*, edited by Derek Tidball, David Hilborn and Justin Thacker. Grand Rapids: Zondervan, 2008.

—. 'The Wrath of God as an Aspect of the Love of God'. In *Nothing Greater, Nothing Better: Theological Essays on the Love of God*, edited by Kevin J. Vanhoozer. Grand Rapids, MI: Eerdmans, 2001.

Lauber, David. *Barth on the Descent into Hell: God, Atonement and the Christian Life*. Burlington, VT: Ashgate, 2004.

Lewis, Alan E. *Between Cross and Resurrection: A Theology of Holy Saturday*. Grand Rapids, MI: Eerdmans, 2001.

Lewis, C. S. 'Meditation in a Toolshed'. In *God in the Dock: Essays on Theology and Ethics*. Grand Rapids: Eerdmans, 1970.

Louth, Andrew. 'The Place of *Theosis* in Orthodox Theology'. In *Partakers of the Divine Nature: The History and Development of Deificiation in the Christian Traditions*, edited by Michael J. Christensen and Jeffery A. Wittung. Grand Rapids, MI: Baker Academic, 2007.

Love, Gregory Anderson. 'In Search of a Non-Violent Atonement Theory: Are Abelard and Girard a Help or a Problem?'. In *Theology as Conversation: The Significance of Dialogue in Historical and Contemporary Theology*, edited by Bruce L. McCormack and Kimlyn J. Bender, Grand Rapids, MI: Eerdmans, 2009.

Marshall, I. Howard. *Aspects of the Atonement: Cross and Resurrection in the Reconciling of God and Humanity*. Colorado Springs: Paternoster, 2007.

—. 'The Theology of the Atonement'. In *The Atonement Debate: Papers from the London Symposium on the Theology of Atonement*, edited by Derek Tidball, David Hilborn and Justin Thacker. Grand Rapids, MI: Zondervan, 2008.

Maximus the Confessor. *On the Cosmic Mystery of Jesus Christ: Selected Writings from St. Maximus the Confessor*. Translated by Paul M. Blowers and Robert Louis Wilken. Crestwood, NY: St. Vladimir's Seminary Press, 2003.

McCall, Thomas H. *Forsaken: The Trinity and the Cross, and Why It Matters*. Downers Grove, IL: IVP Academic, 2012.

McCormack, Bruce L. 'The Ontological Presuppositions of Barth's Doctrine of the Atonement'. In *The Glory of the Atonement: Biblical, Historical and Practical Perspectives*, edited by Roger R. Nicole, Charles E. Hill and Frank A. James. Downers Grove, IL: InterVarsity Press, 2004.

McGrath, Alister E. 'The Moral Theory of the Atonement: An Historical and Theological Critique'. *Scottish Journal of Theology* 38, no. 2 (1985): 205–20.

McGuckin, J. A. 'The Strategic Adaptation of Deification in the Cappadocians'. In *Partakers of the Divine Nature: The History and Development of Deificiation in the Christian Traditions*, edited by Michael J. Christensen and Jeffery A. Wittung. Grand Rapids: Baker Academic, 2007.

McIntyre, John. *The Shape of Soteriology: Studies in the Doctrine of the Death of Christ*. Edinburgh: T & T Clark, 1992.

McKnight, Scot. *A Community Called Atonement*. Nashville, TN: Abingdon Press, 2007.

Macleod, Donald. 'The Atonement of the Death of Christ: In Faith, Revelation, and History'. *Scottish Journal of Theology* 41, no. 4 (1988): 535.

Migliore, Daniel L. *Faith Seeking Understanding: An Introduction to Christian Theology*. Grand Rapids, MI: Eerdmans, 2004.

Milton, John. 'Paradise Regained'. In *John Milton: The Major Works*. New York: Oxford, 2008.

Moffitt, David M. *Atonement and the Logic of Resurrection in the Epistle to the Hebrews*. Boston: Brill, 2011.

Molnar, Paul D. *Divine Freedom and the Doctrine of the Immanent Trinity: In Dialogue with Karl Barth and Contemporary Theology*. New York: T & T Clark, 2005.

Moltmann, Jürgen. *The Crucified God: The Cross of Christ as the Foundation and Criticism of Christian Theology*. Minneapolis: Fortress, 1993.

—. 'The Motherly Father: Is Trinitarian Patripassianism Replacing Theological Patriarchalism?' In *God as Father*, edited by Johannes-Baptist Metz, Edward Schillebeeckx and Marcus Lefébvre. New York: Seabury, 1981.

Morris, Leon. *The Cross in the New Testament*. Grand Rapids, MI: Eerdmans, 1965.

Muller, Richard A. *Dictionary of Latin and Greek Theological Terms: Drawn Principally from Protestant Scholastic Theology*. Grand Rapids, MI: Baker Academic, 2006.

Murray, Stephen B. *Reclaiming Divine Wrath: A History of a Christian Doctrine and Its Interpretation*. New York: Peter Lang, 2011.

Nazianzus, Gregory of. *On God and Christ*. Translated by Frederick
    Williams and Lionel Wickham. Crestwood, NY: St. Vladimir's
    Seminary Press, 2002.
Nelson, Susan L. 'Imagining the Cross: Through the Eyes of Marian
    Kolodziej'. In *Cross Examinations: Readings on the Meaning of the
    Cross Today*, edited by Marit Trelstad. Minneapolis: Fortress, 2006.
Norwich, Julian of. *Showings*. Translated by Edmund Colledge and
    James Walsh. New York: Paulist Press, 1978.
Nyssa, Gregory of. 'An Address on Religious Instruction'. In *Christology
    of the Later Fathers*, edited by Edward R. Hardy. Philadelphia:
    Westminster Press, 1954.
Oakes, Edward T. 'The Internal Logic of Holy Saturday in the Theology
    of Hans Urs von Balthasar'. *International Journal of Systematic
    Theology* 9, no. 2 (2007): 184–99.
Origen. 'De Principiis'. In *Ante Nicene Fathers of the Christian Church*,
    edited by Alexander Roberts and James Donaldson. Peabody:
    Hendrickson Publishers, 2004.
Osborn, Lawrence. 'Entertaining Angels: Their Place in Contemporary
    Theology'. *Tyndale Bulletin* 45, no. 2 (1994): 273–96.
Owen, John. *The Works of John Owen*. London: Banner of Truth Trust,
    1965.
Oxenham, Henry Nutcombe. *The Catholic Doctrine of the Atonement*.
    London: W. H. Allen, 1881.
Packer, James I. 'What Did the Cross Achieve: The Logic of Penal
    Substitution'. *Tyndale Bulletin* 25 (1974): 3–45.
Pascal, Blaise. *Pensées and Other Writings*. Translated by Honor Levi.
    New York: Oxford University Press, 1995.
Patrides, C. A. 'The Salvation of Satan'. *Journal of the History of Ideas*
    28, no. 4 (1967): 467–78.
Peterson, Robert A. *Calvin and the Atonement*. Fearne, Scotland:
    Christian Focus Publications, 2008.
Peterson, Ryan S. 'Genesis 1'. In *Theological Commentary: Evangelical
    Perspectives*, edited by R. Michael Allen. New York: T & T Clark,
    2011.
Pitstick, Alyssa Lyra. *Light in Darkness: Hans Urs von Balthasar and the
    Catholic Doctrine of Christ's Descent into Hell*. Grand Rapids, MI:
    W. B. Eerdmans, 2007.
Potiers, Hilary of. *On the Trinity*. Translated by S. D. F. Salmond. Grand
    Rapids: Eerdmans, 1983.
Pseudo-Dionysius. *Pseudo-Dionysius: The Complete Works*. Translated by
    Colm Luibheid. New York: Paulist Press, 1987.
Radzik, Linda. *Making Amends: Atonement in Morality, Law, and
    Politics*. New York: Oxford University Press, 2009.

Ratzinger, Joseph. *Jesus of Nazareth. Part Two, Holy Week: From the Entrance into Jerusalem to the Resurrection*. San Francisco: Ignatius, 2011.

Ray, Darby Kathleen. *Deceiving the Devil: Atonement, Abuse, and Ransom*. Cleveland: Pilgrim Press, 1998.

Reichenbach, Bruce R. 'Healing View'. In *The Nature of the Atonement: Four Views*, edited by James K. Beilby and Paul R. Eddy. Downers Grove, IL: IVP Academic, 2006.

Rudisill, Dorus Paul. *The Doctrine of the Atonement in Jonathan Edwards and His Successors*. New York: Poseidon Books, 1971.

Russell, Norman. *The Doctrine of Deification in the Greek Patristic Tradition*. Oxford: Oxford University Press, 2004.

Sabatier, Auguste. *The Doctrine of the Atonement and Its Historical Evolution; and, Religion and Modern Culture*. London: Williams & Norgate, 1904.

Sanders, Fred. *The Deep Things of God: How the Trinity Changes Everything*. Wheaton: Crossway, 2010.

Schleiermacher, Friedrich. *The Christian Faith*. Edinburgh: T & T Clark, 1968.

Schmiechen, Peter. *Saving Power: Theories of Atonement and Forms of the Church*. Grand Rapids, MI: Eerdmans, 2005.

Schweig, Graham M. 'Imagery of Divine Love: The Crucifix Drawing of St. John of the Cross'. In *John of the Cross: Conferences and Essays by Members of the Institute of Carmelite Studies and Others*, edited by Steven Payne. Carmelite Studies, Washington, DC: ICS Publications, Institute of Carmelite Studies, 1992.

Sherman, Robert. *King, Priest and Prophet: A Trinitarian Theology of Atonement*. Edinburgh: T & T Clark, 2004.

Sölle, Dorothee. *Christ the Representative: An Essay in Theology after the 'Death of God'*. London: SCM Press, 1967.

Sonderegger, Katherine. 'Anselm, Defensor Fidei'. *International Journal of Systematic Theology* 9, no. 3 (2007): 342–59.

Soskice, Janet Martin. *Metaphor and Religious Language*. Oxford: Oxford, 1985.

Southern, R. W. *Saint Anselm: A Portrait in a Landscape*. Cambridge: Cambridge University Press, 1990.

Stott, John R. W. *The Cross of Christ*. Downers Grove, IL: Inter-Varsity Press, 1986.

Sykes, Stephen. *The Story of Atonement*. London: Darton, Longman and Todd, 1997.

Tanner, Kathryn. *Christ the Key*. Cambridge: Cambridge University Press, 2010.

Terrell, JoAnne Marie. 'Our Mothers' Gardens: Rethinking Sacrifice'. In *Cross Examinations: Readings on the Meaning of the Cross Today*, edited by Marit Trelstad. Minneapolis: Fortress, 2006.

Thomas, Summa. *Theologica*. Translated by Fathers of the English Dominican Province. Westminster: Christian Classics, 1981.

Tidball, Derek, David Hilborn and Justin Thacker, eds. *The Atonement Debate: Papers from the London Symposium on the Theology of Atonement*. Grand Rapids, MI: Zondervan, 2008.

Torrance, Thomas F. *Atonement: The Person and Work of Christ*. Downers Grove, IL: InterVarsity Press, 2009.

—. *God and Rationality*. London: Oxford University Press, 1971.

—. 'John Mcleod Campbell (1800-1872)'. In *Scottish Theology: From John Knox to John Mcleod Campbell*. Edinburgh: T & T Clark, 1996.

—. *The Mediation of Christ*. Colorado Springs, CO: Helmers & Howard, 1992.

—. *Space, Time, and Resurrection*. Grand Rapids, MI: Eerdmans, 1976.

Treat, Jeremy R. *The Crucified King: Atonement and Kingdom in Biblical and Systematic Theology*. Grand Rapids: Zondervan, 2014.

Trelstad, Marit. *Cross Examinations: Readings on the Meaning of the Cross Today*. Minneapolis: Fortress, 2006.

—. 'Introduction: The Cross in Context'. In *Cross Examinations: Readings on the Meaning of the Cross Today*, edited by Marit Trelstad. Minneapolis: Fortress, 2006.

—. 'Lavish Love: A Covenantal Ontology'. In *Cross Examinations: Readings on the Meaning of the Cross Today*, edited by Marit Trelstad. Minneapolis: Fortress, 2006.

Troeltsch, Ernst. *The Christian Faith: Based on Lectures Delivered at the University of Heidelberg in 1912 and 1913*. Translated by Garrett E. Paul. Minneapolis: Fortress, 1991.

Turner, Henry Ernest William. *The Patristic Doctrine of Redemption: A Study of the Development of Doctrine During the First Five Centuries*. New York: Mowbray, 1952.

Turretin, Francis. *Institutes of Elenctic Theology*. Vol. 2. Phillipsburg: P & R Publishing, 1992.

Vanhoozer, Kevin J. 'Atonement'. In *Mapping Modern Theology: A Thematic and Historical Introduction*, edited by Kelly M. Kapic and Bruce L. McCormack. Grand Rapids: Baker Academic, 2012.

—. 'Atonement in Postmodernity: Guilt, Goats and Gifts'. In *The Glory of the Atonement: Biblical, Historical and Practical Perspectives*, edited by Charles E. Hill and Frank A. James. Downers Grove, IL: InterVarsity Press, 2004.

—. *The Drama of Doctrine: A Canonical-Linguistic Approach to Christian Theology*. Louisville, KY: WJK, 2005.

—. 'Ezekiel 14: "I, the Lord, Have Deceived That Prophet": Divine
    Deception, Inception, and Communicative Action'. In *Theological
    Commentary: Evangelical Perspectives*, edited by R. Michael Allen.
    New York: T & T Clark, 2011.
—. *First Theology: God, Scripture and Hermeneutics*. Downers Grove,
    IL: InterVarsity Press, 2002.
—. *Is There a Meaning in This Text? The Bible, the Reader, and the
    Morality of Literary Knowledge*. Grand Rapids, MI: Zondervan, 1998.
Volf, Miroslav. *Exclusion and Embrace: A Theological Exploration of
    Identity, Otherness, and Reconciliation*. Nashville: Abingdon Press, 1996.
Weaver, J. Denny. *The Nonviolent Atonement*. Grand Rapids: Eerdmans,
    2001.
Webb, Stephen H. *On God and Dogs: A Christian Theology of
    Compassion for Animals*. New York: Oxford University Press, 1998.
Webster, John B. *Holy Scripture: A Dogmatic Sketch*. New York:
    Cambridge University Press, 2003.
—. '"It Was the Will of the Lord to Bruise Him": Soteriology and the
    Doctrine of God'. In *God of Salvation*, edited by Ivor J. Davidson and
    Murray A. Rae. Burlington, VT: Ashgate, 2011.
—. 'Theologies of Retrieval'. In *The Oxford Handbook of Systematic
    Theology*, edited by John B. Webster, Kathryn Tanner and Iain
    Torrance. New York: Oxford, 2007.
Weingart, Richard E. *The Logic of Divine Love: A Critical Analysis of the
    Soteriology of Peter Abailard*. London: Clarendon, 1970.
Willard, Dallas. *Spirit of the Disciplines*. New York: Harper Collins, 1991.
Willey, Petroc and Eldred. 'Will Animals Be Redeemed?' In *Animals on
    the Agenda: Questions About Animals for Theology and Ethics*, edited
    by Andrew Linzey and Dorothy Yamamoto. Urbana, IL: University of
    Illinois Press, 1998.
Williams, Delores S. 'Black Women's Surrogacy Experience and the
    Christian Notion of Redemption'. In *Cross Examinations: Readings
    on the Meaning of the Cross Today*, edited by Marit Trelstad.
    Minneapolis: Fortress, 2006.
Williams, Thomas. 'Sin, Grace, and Redemption'. In *The Cambridge
    Companion to Abelard*, edited by Jeffrey E. Brower and Kevin Guilfoy.
    New York: Cambridge University Press, 2004.
Wright, N. T. *Jesus and the Victory of God*. Minneapolis: Fortress, 1996.
—. *The New Testament and the People of God*. London: Fortress, 1992.
—. *The Resurrection of the Son of God*. Minneapolis, MN: Fortress, 2003.
—. *Surprised by Hope: Rethinking Heaven, the Resurrection, and the
    Mission of the Church*. New York: HarperOne, 2008.
Wynne, Jeremy J. *Wrath among the Perfections of God's Life*. New York:
    T & T Clark, 2010.

AUTHOR INDEX

SUBJECT INDEX

SCRIPTURE INDEX

Made in the USA
Las Vegas, NV
02 July 2021